Extraordinary Dr

Extraordinary Dreams

*Visions, Announcements
and Premonitions
Across Time and Place*

KIMBERLY R. MASCARO

McFarland & Company, Inc., Publishers
Jefferson, North Carolina

Library of Congress Cataloguing-in-Publication Data

Names: Mascaro, Kimberly R., 1973– author.
Title: Extraordinary dreams : visions, announcements and
   premonitions across time and place / Kimberly R. Mascaro.
Description: Jefferson, North Carolina : McFarland & Company, Inc.,
   Publishers, 2018. | Includes bibliographical references and index.
Identifiers: LCCN 2017053278 | ISBN 9781476668826 (softcover :
   acid free paper) ∞
Subjects: LCSH: Dreams.
Classification: LCC BF1078 .M345 2018 | DDC 154.6/3—dc23
LC record available at https://lccn.loc.gov/2017053278

British Library cataloguing data are available

ISBN 978-1-4766-6882-6 (print)
ISBN 978-1-4766-3045-8 (ebook)

Front cover images © 2018 iStock

Printed in the United States of America

*McFarland & Company, Inc., Publishers
   Box 611, Jefferson, North Carolina 28640
   www.mcfarlandpub.com*

From cheetahs to ducks and from relatives deceased
to those yet-to-be born, this book is dedicated
to all those lovely members of my family who have,
over extensive periods of time, trusted enough to share
their dreams with me. You and I know exactly who you are,
and I thank you so very much. Each of you also offered
support in so many ways, so this book is for you
and is truly from the heart.

Acknowledgments

This all would not have been possible without the support and assistance of so many wonderful others. The list of names is incredibly long, so, in short, I say to you, my family, close friends, dear colleagues, those who were of ongoing inspiration, and all of my mentors and advisors past and present: *thank you from the depths of my heart.* In addition, I am honored and full of gratitude for every man and woman who trusted me by sharing personal stories, dreams, cultural and spiritual knowledge, and who participated in lengthy interviews—this book is possible because of each and every one of you! Last but not least, I would like to give special thanks to my mother for the time she dedicated to my request for grammar corrections; to Dr. Kristin Sorensen for her assistance in the final versions of editing; to my father for his continuous support and dream discussions; to my sister for her encouragement; and to Dr. Stanley Krippner, who time and time again kindly made himself available for consultation, inspiration, and direction with regard to traditional wisdom, dreams and dreaming.

Table of Contents

Introduction

Humanity's interest in the world of dreams and visions has been documented for centuries. From this extensive record, it can be concluded that dreaming held a privileged position within pre-literate, oral, storytelling peoples and cultures. Evidence of recorded dreams from ancient Greece, Egypt, China and India can be found as far back as the seventh century BCE, and possibly as early as 3000 BCE. One of the world's oldest dream journals was created in the early third century by Perpetua, a Christian martyr who was put to death in Carthage (Koet, 2012). For some individuals, dreams and visions have always been an integral part of life, ever since childhood. For other individuals, these subjective realities are neither recalled nor viewed as significant, let alone seen as direct channels for communication with the spirit world. Hence, various communities hold diverse attitudes and beliefs about dreams, visions, and dreaming. Depending on the cultural group, sometimes these occurrences include what Western scholars refer to as the out-of-body experience (OBE), which others refer to as "soul flight" (Jones & Krippner, 2012, p. 216; Krippner, 2002, p. 966). Flexible consideration is needed since such states are not well understood. Clare Johnson (2016), the first person to complete a doctoral dissertation on lucid dreaming and the creative writing process, explains:

> The OBE is a state in which self-perception (perceived sensory input, self-location and self-identification) seems external to and independent from the physical body; a state which may be entered spontaneously, involuntarily and abruptly from diverse waking and sleeping states of consciousness. In terms of onset, the out of body experience (OBE) differs from lucid dreams in that an OBE might arise from the waking state, trauma, meditation, fainting, or in the midst of great physical danger. However, the OBE can also arise from sleep states such as hypnagogia, sleep paralysis, non-lucid dreaming, and lucid dreaming [pp. 130–131].

As we will see in later chapters, both OBEs and lucid dreams can be found in the reports of pregnant women.

The scholarly literature on dreams and dreaming is vast and has a fairly extensive history (Van de Castle, 1975; Yu, 2012). Some reports come from the ancient Eastern (Botz-Bornstein, 2007; Gracie, 2012) and Western worlds in pre–Biblical times (Edelstein & Edelstein, 1945), dating as far back as the fifteenth century BCE (Pettis, 2006). Very early, and lengthy, examples can be found in the Bible in Genesis (37, 40 & 41). The King James version of the Bible states Genesis 37:3–11 as follows:

> Now Israel loved Joseph more than all his children, because he was the son of his old age: and he made him a coat of many colors.
>
> And when his brethren saw that their father loved him more than all his brethren, they hated him, and could not speak peaceably unto him.
>
> And Joseph dreamed a dream, and he told it his brethren: and they hated him yet the more.
>
> And he said unto them, hear, I pray you, this dream which I have dreamed:
>
> For, behold, we were binding sheaves in the field, and, lo, my sheaf arose, and also stood upright; and, behold, your sheaves stood round about, and made obeisance to my sheaf.
>
> And his brethren said to him, Shalt thou indeed reign over us? or shalt thou indeed have dominion over us? And they hated him yet the more for his dreams, and for his words.
>
> And he dreamed yet another dream, and told it his brethren, and said, Behold, I have dreamed a dream more; and, behold, the sun and the moon and the eleven stars made obeisance to me.
>
> And he told it to his father, and to his brethren: and his father rebuked him, and said unto him, What is this dream that thou hast dreamed? Shall I and thy mother and thy brethren indeed come to bow down ourselves to thee to the earth?
>
> And his brethren envied him; but his father observed the saying.

Across time and place, dream reports have ranged from the ordinary to the extraordinary. Mundane dreams may be forgotten upon awakening and reflect a muddle of day-to-day events. Waking up to recall a disorganized shopping trip and the accompanying frustration that the toilet paper was left in the cart or casual conversations with dry co-workers are examples. Yet these seemingly meaningless dreams serve a purpose, such as functions related to memory. Extraordinary dreams, in contrast, are often remembered for significant periods of time, such as months or even several years after the initial experience. Some extraordinary dream reports may include various nonlocal forms of perception commonly known as clairvoyance, telepathy and precognition (premonitions or warnings), in addition to heightened lucidity and communication with the deceased. Extraordinary dreams may be much more vivid than mundane dreams and may even occur while one is dreaming lucidly, that is, dreaming with the awareness that one is dreaming.

Because being asleep and being awake are not always precise, extraordinary experiences may take place in hypnagogic and hypnopompic states. Hypnagogia is the state we sometimes experience as we are falling asleep, sometimes filled with unusual images as brain waves slow down, moving into alpha and theta waves. Later, we enter several episodes of rapid-eye-movement (REM) sleep when dreams are the most vivid. As we are waking up, we often find ourselves in a hypnopompic state. Since we can still perceive visual, auditory, tactile and sensory stimuli, many people report images, sounds and sensations as they are falling asleep or waking up. Visions, which may occur when one is asleep, awake, or somewhere in between, are often reported to occur within these states and during other states. A visionary episode may leave a person impacted just as much as he or she would be from a dream, if not more. Furthermore, as is the case of many non-ordinary states of consciousness, including extraordinary dreams, some people prefer not to reveal their experiences. Consequently, having a vision may be deemed as odd or unusual in some cultures and may even be judged negatively. Yet, like dreams, written reports of visions exist as far back as when the Bible was written, and even much earlier. An early example comes from the Bible's King James version: "After these things the word of the Lord came unto Abram in a vision, saying, Fear not, Abram: I am thy shield, and thy exceeding great reward" (Genesis 15:1).

In addition, some groups distinguish between visions that take place during dreams and waking-state visions, as well as visions of prophets (Corbin, 1966). For others, such as some Native American groups, sharp distinctions are irrelevant because these phenomena are their own reality. It can become difficult to dissect such human experiences with precision; therefore, an open mind and an open heart are always advisable.

OBEs have been referred to by other terms outside of Western scholarly literature. Examples of these terms are mystic voyage, ecstatic journeying, soul flight, lucid projection, unfolding, astral travel, soul-journeying or simply a lived experience. While these episodes are included, I will primarily discuss dreams that most often fit into particular categories of the extraordinary realm. Specifically, dreams that announce a child-to-be, as well as a person soon-to-depart, will be given a greater amount of attention than other types of dreams.

Chapter Summary

Chapter One, The Phenomenon of Dreaming, examines dreaming through the lens of various religious and spiritual traditions, including

Islam, Judaism and Christianity. Situated alongside those traditions is the community wisdom of the Quechua of the Andean Mountians, as well as contemporary Western perspectives of dreaming. Dreams that include images of animals and insects are also discussed. A distinction is made between monophasic and polyphasic cultures, generalizing the value each gives to dreaming. Explanations for why humans dream is given attention, followed by some established dream theories and research. Dream incubation is also introduced. Ways that humanity benefits from some exciting, major discoveries by way of dreaming are presented. Before the chapter comes to a close, dreams that have encouraged peace or provoked violence are discussed.

Chapter Two, Extraordinary Dreams, addresses the concept of extraordinary dreaming and its acknowledgment in ancient times. Extraordinary dreaming is understood through descriptive stories told across time and place. This includes dream incubation and dreams as omens. Next, the Inquisition, the colonial witch hunts, and cultural views of dreaming, spirit and soul are explored. Through anthropological reports and anecdotes, those in the West see how dreaming is understood differently from what those in the West have come to know. "Big" dreams are separated into common categories to gain an understanding of them. Extraordinary dream perception, such as precognition and telepathy precede discussion of lucid dreaming and out-of-body experiences. The chapter concludes by highlighting dreamwork among traditional religious and spiritual practitioners.

Chapter Three, Dreams During Pregnancy, addresses dreams during a major life transition: the time of pregnancy. Pregnancy dream accounts include fetal sex prediction and popular folklore. Pregnancy dreams may be in service to the individual as well as the family, and these benefits are discussed. Across cultures and beyond couvade syndrome, expectant fathers' experiences hold meaning as well. Fathers' individual dreams are discussed, followed by the dreams of pregnant couples.

Chapter Four, Dreams That Announce an Arrival, introduces a particular phenomenon for pregnant or expectant dreamers—the announcing dream. Announcing dreams are defined and discussed throughout history, alongside fertility and conception dreams. This chapter is packed with the announcing dream episodes of pregnant women; however, fathers' experiences are also given attention here. Contemporary reports are included among those from many different parts of the world.

Chapter Five, The Announcing Dream Study, introduces the research focus of my doctoral study—one of the first of its kind—which highlighted announcing dreams and their impact on the pregnant women having them. A look at the participant demographics and dream narratives is the focus of this chapter. Each participant is introduced; however, identities have been disguised. The dream reports are grouped into age categories—the four clusters are prior-to-birth, newborn or infant, toddler and school-aged children. The chapter closes with a summary of fetal sex as indicated in the dream and the gestational age in which the dream took place.

Chapter Six, The Announcing Dream Study Continues, discusses the significance and particular experiential impact of the announcing dreams collected from the doctoral study in the previous chapter. The emergent themes are explained and defined with examples in each category. The chapter concludes with a summary of some of the more noteworthy effects.

Chapter Seven, Dreams of Departure, takes a sharp turn due its focus on death-related dreams. As people age and approach their own death, significant dreams may emerge. These dreams are contrasted with dreams of deceased loved ones, a phenomenon experienced by the bereaved of all ages and of various cultures. Deceased loved ones appear in dreams to instruct or teach. They may also appear in dreams to forewarn or prepare the living for what is to come. Demands may be placed, as well, thus extending the dream message beyond comfort and guidance. This chapter also includes reports by dreamers who claim to have been attacked by the dead.

In Chapter Eight, A Dual-Directional Announcing Dream Discussion, an announcing dream and death dream discussion unfolds. This chapter enlivens the study by discussing common elements found in announcing dreams. We will also take a look at how these dreams differ from the more usual pregnancy dreams. Decision-making after an announcing dream is given attention in order to recognize the important role dreams can play in the lives of expectant families. Unresolved conflicts, particularly whether the pregnancy was planned, are given particular attention. Prominent dream theories are revisited in the context of announcing dreams. The first part of the chapter concludes by engaging the reader as to the influence and impact announcing dreams have for families. The second part discusses death and consciousness from the perspective of various cultural beliefs. The death dream discussion also includes the experiences of hospice clients and nursing home residents.

Chapter Nine, Tips and Techniques for Extraordinary Dreaming, offers tips and techniques for enhancing dream recall, as well as how one can increase awareness in dreams and in daily life. The modern-day application of dream incubation is discussed along with potential motivations for the dreamer. A general relaxation script is also included.

Provocative questions are asked within Chapter Ten, Coming Full Circle, a brief concluding chapter. By weaving together such extraordinary dream experiences, we come full-circle. Non-Western notions of death are discussed. The benefit of integrating dreams into one's life is also explored. Weaving these ideas together may prompt one to delve further into the dream landscape, so additional resources for those wanting to go deeper are provided.

Every man and woman who shared dreams with me or had stories described in this book have been given pseudonyms (fake names) and have had aspects of their identity changed or hidden in order to protect anonymity.

CHAPTER ONE

The Phenomenon
of Dreaming

Across time and place, among various religions and cultures of the world, the dream has been regarded as both mundane and significant. Dreams and visions that hold significance have been reported by shamans, traditional practitioners and indigenous healers worldwide (Eliade, 1966; Kremer, 2006). Among them are diverse groups such as the Achuar of the Ecuadorian Amazon, the Quechua of Peru, the indigenous people of Siberia, as well as cultures throughout the Western Pacific Islands and many others. While using caves for vision quests and fasting, the Northern Paiute of the California and Nevada regions sought power and connection to the spirit world through a dream or vision. These dreams and visions assist the traditional healer, sometimes referred to as shaman, in many ways, one of which is to make predictions regarding important events (Patterson, 1989). For the Diné (Navajo), the approach to dreams is quite complex. The Diné consider dreaming to be very personal and, similar to other groups, feel that dreams are not to be ignored for they hold a predictive element (Dadosky, 1999). Dreams provide instruction and inform decision-making for Mapuche shaman-healers (*machi*) of Chile, offering wisdom such as how to perform a particular ceremony or who should become a *yegulfe*, a ritual helper (Bacigalupo, 1999).

Various Religious and Spiritual Perspectives

Significant dreams and visions are recorded in the contemporary, traditional and mystic writings of Judaism, Christianity and Islam (Csordas, 1994; Fahd, 1966). Dreams are also recorded in the pre–Christian Mediterranean religious traditions, Hinduism, Buddhism, Jainism, Taoism (Lee, 2007; Struve, 2007), the Baha'i faith (Edgar, 1995), many

7

Native American religions (Hallowell, 1966), the traditional religion of the Yolngu of Aboriginal Australia's Northern Territory (Petchkovsky & Cawte, 1986), the traditional religion of the Asabano of Papua New Guinea (Lohmann, 2000), and in the religions of African origin (Shango of Trinidad, Lucumi/Santeria, Voudon, Candomble), to name a few. Given the vastness of meaningful dream reports, how is it that the West today continues to be dismissive of this tradition by holding dreams and visions in such low regard?

ISLAM AND SUFISM

The lack of interest in dreams by contemporary western cultures stands in contrast to what can be found in other times and places. In many of the world's religious and spiritual traditions, dreaming is believed to open a communicative and interactive channel with another reality or another world. Dream tradition seems to be valued across most branches of Islam, for example. Three dream reports are found in the Qur'an, but many more "true" dreams appear in the Hadith literature. The Hadiths are narratives or reports documenting the traditions and sayings of the Prophet Muhammad. The Hadiths offer moral guidance and are an important source of Islamic guidance. In the mystical Muslim tradition, it is believed that dreams may act as transports to the divine. Edgar (2007) writes, "Islam is probably the largest night dream culture in the world today" (p. 59), and "the tri-partite schematization of dreams ... is part of the worldview of the majority of Muslims" (p. 61). These three types of dreams are true dreams that come from God (*ruya*); dreams that come from the Devil; and *nafs*, dreams of the "earthly spirit that dwells in the dreamer's body" (p. 60). Kreinath (2014) calls attention to the dream-vision ambiguity in Islamic tradition, noting that these experiences are identified by the same term. Kreinath (2014) states, "Deriving from the same Semitic word (Arab: *ru'ya*; Turk: *rüya*), dreams and visions are closely related and associated with one another in the Arabic and Turkish languages. The reference to the term *ru'ya* (or *rüya*) ranges between deep and light sleep, and coincides in elements extending from nocturnal dream to prophetic vision" (p. 44).

The inner mystical dimension of Islam is known as Sufism (*Tasawwuf*). Sufis seek to be close to and obtain a direct personal experience of God. As a primarily psych-spiritual aspect of Islam, Sufism focuses on understanding the truth of divine love. Abandoning typical worldly pursuits and cleaning the heart bring Sufis closer to God. The following verse from the Qur'an relates to their purpose in life: "And I (Allah) have only created jinns' and men, that they may woship (and serve) me" (51:56).

Among members of the Ghzawa tribe in the Western Rif mountain villages of Morocco (Morocco's Chefchaouen and Ouezzane Provinces), where Sufism holds great strength even today, dreaming is the means through which the living may interact with saints as well as the dead (Gonzalez-Vazquez, 2014). As noted from Crapanzano's fieldwork in the 1960s and 1970s, this is similar to the beliefs of the Hamadsha, a religious brotherhood of Moroccan Arabs living in Meknes, a city in northern central Morocco. The Hamadsha regard saints (known as *siyyid, salih,* or *wali*) as "intermediaries to Allah [who] are reputed for the blessing, or *baraka,* which they confer on those who venerate them" (Crapanzano, 1975, p. 146). This blessing, said to take place after a pilgrimage has been made to the saint's tomb, is associated with the appearance of a saint in a dream or vision. Additionally, in contemporary Pakistan's Chishti Sabiri Sufi Order, "dreams mirror the interior states and stations of the Sufi journey to God (*suluk*)" (Rozehnal, 2014, p. 69). The words of the well-known fourteenth century scholar and historian, Ibn Khaldun are relevant:

> God, therefore created man in such a way that the veil of the senses could be lifted through sleep, which is a natural function of man. When the veil is lifted, the soul is ready to learn the things it desires to know in the world of Truth. At times, it catches a glimpse of what it seeks. (1967:81)

JUDAISM AND CHRISTIANITY

In addition to the abundance of Islamic writings that reference dreams, Judaism contains works that acknowledge one's status with regard to dreaming. In the Talmud (recorded between the third and fifth centuries.), it was noted that dreams are one-sixtieth part prophecy (Covitz, 1990). In the Jewish tradition, a relationship between dreaming frequency and being worthy of divine inspiration is brought forth, whereas a lack of dreaming denotes that one is unworthy of divine inspiration (Covitz, 1990). Every great story of the Jewish people begins with a dream, according to Bonnie Buckner, who developed a Kabbalistic approach to working with dreams.

Within Zionist and Pentecostal churches in several African countries, dreams and visions hold special status in these regions as well. As a researcher from one independent African church wrote, "The local branch among immigrants in western Uganda of a Kenyan church [is] similar to the African Israel Church Nineveh" (Charsley, 1973, p. 245). He added that dream telling was a regular part of services within these churches. Among that population at the time, dreams were most often viewed as messages from God. In contrast, "the extraordinary, impossible kind of dream" may have come from Satan. Furthermore, dreaming was not thought of as a "special spiritual gift," but "the ability to interpret dreams was [a gift]" (p. 248).

Dream researcher and scholar Kelly (1995) writes about how the vast majority of the world's religious and cultural traditions not only gain spiritual insight from dreams, but dreams have guided, instructed, informed, and inspired people in many ways. Within the African Independent Churches, for example, a dream could provide the inspiration for becoming a charismatic leader (Bulkeley, 2008).

ASIAN RELIGION AND SPIRITUALITY

In China, during the eleventh century BCE, the Duke of Zhou helped found the Zhou Dynasty. Highly regarded by many, including Confucius himself, the Duke of Zhou has been referred to as the "God of Dreams." The Duke of Zhou is said to have alerted people through a dream that something significant was going to take place in that person's life (Gracie, 2012).

A report reflecting important information in a dream is found in Firth's writings. In *The Meaning of Dreams in Tikopia,* Firth (1934) reported that (as noted in Lohmann, 2003, p. 2) Polynesia's Tikopia Islanders, as did many other groups, understood dreams to be the movements of the wandering soul, which after death could also appear in the dreams of others. Firth (2001:17) (as noted in Lohmann, 2003, p. 2) described a man who dreamed of his son, who was working on another island; because of his dream, the man became convinced that his son had died. Two days later, word arrived that the young man had indeed passed away. In this case, the dream image was interpreted as the result of a journey of the dream alter, traversing the sea to take leave of his father.

Research across cultures reveals the tendency of people to believe that dreams, even when implicit, are meaningful and can be used to inform one's judgment and actions (Mischel & Mischell, 1958; Qureshi, 2010). Hence, dreams hold greater significance in some cultures than in others.

NAVAHO TRADITIONAL RELIGION

For the Diné, the "significance ascribed to dreams is intricately woven into the matrix of their society as a whole," but "dreams during ritualized activity are especially significant." (Dadosky, 1999, p. 17). Either way, the topic of dreaming itself is given respect and typically considered personal for the Diné. They do not often speak of dreams, although this can vary to some degree from person to person. In general, however, sharing a dream with a relative can be one way of gaining support.

Alternatively, for other cultures, sharing the nature and content of one's dreams among group members is a social process, even though what is revealed can have an effect on that person's social status and networks (Ewing, 1994). Ewing (1994) highlights that "one may also be expected to take certain specific actions as a result of having experienced a particular dream" (p. 572). In contrast, certain cultures advise against the sharing of dreams with just anyone. It is inadvisable to share a dream with non-virtuous people, especially in a careless manner. Doing so is ill advised because dreams may contain spiritual content or messages from God.

I found this to be the case when I was studying and practicing with an esoteric group. During the nearly five years I spent participating in the free courses and activities geared toward lucid dreaming and out-of-body experiences (OBE), it was commonplace to keep OBEs and dream imagery private; one could, however, reveal specific components to the instructors if guidance was needed. The reason given was that dreams, whether lucid or not, and OBEs were meant for the dreamer and the dreamer only. Furthermore, revealing material publicly was believed by some to lead to a significant reduction in the experiences' future occurrence for some people, especially if the knowledge gained was used in an egotistical way. For example, a dreamer who has fallen ill may learn of a medicine needed to heal the ailment. According to some, this would be considered personal help from the divine. Telling others about the medicine could be viewed as bragging. In addition, the medicine might only be meant for the dreamer and no one else.

Thus, dreaming may be considered to be much more than simply internally generated imagery or a reflection of the dreamer's inner subjective world. The *imaginal* world "exists outside of the conventional world of space, time, and matter" (Jones & Krippner, 2012, p. 29). This term should not be confused with one's imagination, as 'imaginal' implies something beyond the ordinary cosmos, yet just as real. Western culture rejects the notion of an "imaginal world," but this concept's existence is taken for granted by many indigenous people.

The Contemporary West

Dutch psychiatrist Frederick van Eeden (1913) coined the term "lucid dreams" and described his experiences with lucid dreams in his 1913 publication titled *A Study of Dreams*. He wrote, "In a lucid dream the sensation of having a body, having eyes, hands, a mouth that speaks, and so on, is perfectly distinct; yet I know at the same time that the physical body is sleeping and has quite a different position" (p. 447). Van Eeden (1913) also told of a few of the experiments he performed in his lucid dreams and other interesting details from his ongoing experiences. In late December 1911, van Eeden noted a lucid dream in which he flew and floated:

> I felt wonderfully light and strong. I saw immense and beautiful prosepects,—first a town, then country-landscapes, fantastic and brightly coloured. Then I saw my brother sitting—the same one who died in 1906—and I went up to him saying: "Now we are dreaming, both of us." He answered: "No, I am not!" And then I remembered that he was dead. We had a long conversation about the conditions of his existence after death, and I inquired especially after the aware-ness, the clear, bright insight. But that he could not answer; he seemed to lack it [p. 450].

At that point van Eeden's lucidity was interrupted and the dream took a shift. Between 1898 and 1912, van Eeden recorded three hundred and fifty two of his own lucid dreams. For him, this type of dream was worthy of attention and the most interesting type of dream.

Much earlier, however, long before the definition of lucid dreaming was established, Aristotle wrote about conscious perception in the sleep state. The first volume of *The Works of Aristotle* states that "when one is asleep, there is something in consciousness which declares that what then presents itself is but a dream. If, however, he is not aware of being asleep, there is nothing which will contradict the testimony of the bare presentation" (Aristotle, 1952, p. 706).

In my early personal experiences, I did not consider these states (e.g., OBEs, lucid dreaming) to be entirely distinct from one another. I thought of them instead as varying levels of awareness, or distinct places on a stream of consciousness, and I still do for the most part. While having read about the attributes that distinguish these experiences from each other, it still seems that these phenomena are very much related, or perhaps different parts on the same spectrum of heightened awareness. Whether that is the case, dreams, visions, and OBEs should be considered together, all encompassed within the imaginal world. Too much division, or compartmentalization, isn't always a good thing; however, some terminology is more comfortable for some people, so lucid dreaming has been used as the term to describe these related experiences within certain groups.

Quechua Notions of Dreaming

In December 2015, I met Professor Beatriz Pérez Galán for the first time, when she was vacationing in the United States with her family. Professor Galán, a social anthropologist at Universidad Nacional de Educación a Distancia (UNED), has worked with Peru's Quechua communities in the Andes since 1991, and so I had many questions for her. Initially, Professor Galán had studied indigenous political authority, and she quickly came to learn that all aspects of Quechua life and society are interwoven. Her attempt to understand one particular aspect of Quechua society in isolation was not possible; as in other societies these aspects are not compartmentalized, so it was necessary to use a holistic perspective to understand Quechua beliefs and social practices. I asked Professor Galán what she learned about that group's nocturnal activities and belief systems in relation to dreams and out-of-body experiences, explaining that these phenomena are somewhat dichotomized in Western literature. We had a brief, although insightful, conversation over coffee. Then, in the spring of 2016, I traveled to Spain and was invited to her home in Madrid where we continued the conversation. Professor Galán explained that, for indigenous peoples such as the Quechua, making such divisions was unheard of: it didn't really matter whether one was experiencing a vision, dream, or out-of-body travel because this was simply reality, a lived experience. I appreciated hearing this because I always felt that, whatever state one is in along the "awake" or "asleep" spectrum, what is experienced informs one's worldview and the way someone relates to family and community. Division and strict categorization of spiritual experiences has always been a bit uncomfortable for me. It seems that by doing so, something inherent is lost. It's as if the true essence of the occurrence is dissected and takes a back seat, becoming overridden by a rigid categorical system.

Due to geographical distance, Professor Galán and I continued dialoging through emails after those initial visits. In a personal conversation with me in May 2017, Professor Galán expanded upon her points (translated from Spanish to English):

> Ethnographic literature on indigenous peoples of the Americas illustrate, through numerous examples, how dreams are a substantial part of the everyday experience for these groups. Among the Quechua, the knowledge and skills necessary to convert into one of the ritual specialists of these communities, among whom are included musicians –*takiqkuna, tusuchiq*-, a hierarchy of shamans—*paqo, misayoq, altomisayoq*—and other traditional indigenous authorities, come from dreams and visions. The physical trigger that provokes this change frequently comes from an element of nature, which is often involuntary. In these communities this specifically regards lightning (*illapa*). If a local person is hit by *illapa* and resists its strike without dying, through dreams that person will acquire the knowledge and skills and will convert into a ritual specialist responsible for serving the community [B. P. Galán, personal communication, May 2017].

Professor Galán continued:

> [I]n many parts of the Amazon Region, shamans reach this state of consciousness through willfully ingesting hallucinogenic plants (or a combination of them) such as *ayahuasca* which is thought to provoke a connection with the spirit-world or afterworld (*inframundo*) and the knowledge necessary to heal, predict the future, cause an illness or change luck. From this perspective, we can say that among many indigenous peoples of the Americas the dreams and visions, produced in states of dreaming and wakefulness, voluntarily or involuntarily, constitute a social space in which they learn the skills and knowledge that differentiate them ethnically and culturally as groups [B. P. Galán, personal communication, May 2017].

Considering again the high regard and value placed upon dreaming among a vast array of peoples and places, such as the Hamadsha and Ghzawa, Diné, Tikopia Islanders, Quechua, and, as will be shown, many other groups, a question comes to mind: What is dreaming? While differences exist in the details, the Hamadsha of Morocco, for example, answer this question by echoing what is heard time and again among groups around the world across time: the act of dreaming is a result of the wandering of the soul during sleep. A unique contribution from this group is that daydreams are also considered to be the result of the soul leaving the body, although it stays close by or near the body of the daydreaming person. Nonetheless, "the dream gives access to a reality which, however different it may appear to be from ordinary waking reality, is real" (Crapanzano, 1975, p. 148). The soul is said to witness "real events that occur elsewhere in space and time" (Crapanzano, 1975, p. 150).

According to anthropologist Barbara Tedlock (2005), dreaming among indigenous people can take place whether one is asleep or awake. Visions, or waking dreams, occur in a wakeful state, while lucid dreams, prophetic dreams, and nightmares take place when one is asleep. Unlike shamans (who engage dreams and visions in a variety of ways, such as painting, drawing, poetry, song, and dance, and who appear to have an active working relationship with their inner worlds), contemporary Westerners typically disengage immediately upon waking up and claim to not remember many, if any, of their dreams. Tedlock (2005) reports that her grandmother assisted her in understanding the animals that appeared in her dreams as a child and how these animals related to her "spiritual development" (p. 104).

I wish I had had someone who could have helped me understand my childhood dreams of spiders. I recall several dreams from childhood that contained a variety of spider species appearing in large numbers, or swarms, as well as a single spider, standing alone. Sometimes the spiders would be in my bedroom and even on my bed, and other times they would be swarming my little sister in the dream. I don't recall seeing their webs, rather just the spiders themselves in those early dreams. Usually those dreams were scary, but not frightening enough to keep me from returning to sleep afterward. I recall that I slowly began to dislike spiders, yet this aversion might be typical for some people. However, when I was very young, like many children, I would hold a Daddy Long Legs or capture a big furry spider for observation in a container with breathing holes. (Remember those?)

Spider has made a strong appearance again in my adult years, but it wasn't until I was in my early forties that I began to pay attention to what they were teaching me and what I needed to learn. Now I admire spiders, although I must admit, the admiration is at a safe distance:, I do not want to handle them. I conducted an analysis of my dreams recorded from September 2008 until November 2016. Within that selection, I found a variety of nonhuman creatures. During this eight-year span, the following animals presented themselves: eagles, other birds (some tropical), spiders (including one tarantula), scorpions, a Great White shark, snakes (anacondas most often), cougars/mountain lions, puppies and a full grown dog, a baby fox, bears (a Grizzly and a baby brown bear), and a dragon as well as a chimera (mythological creatures). Each of these, except the chimera, has come in dreams in 2016 as well. Among all of these, snakes and spiders have been the most prevalent within this eight-year span, by far. Could these creatures have something in common when it comes to my own development? Tedlock's (2005) publication reminded me that, by consciously entering a dream state instead of unconsciously slipping into one, I can ask the dream myself: that's something I remember learning from my teachers in the mid–2000s. I often ask questions during an OBE, because that's when I seem to experience the highest grade of awareness, but there I go, splitting hairs. Using either process, there is the ability to ask, learn and develop.

As indicated, experiences of the psyche, defined as the essence of life, totality of mind, human soul or spirit, impact people across time and place; yet dreams, let alone OBEs and visions, do not appear to carry as much weight in the United States as in other countries today (Matsumoto & Juang, 2008). This may be because Western civilization has made a distinction between and has compartmentalized waking life and nocturnal life (Bastide, 1966), prioritizing rational thought process. The result is that dreams and nonordinary states of consciousness are devalued. Going a step further, we see that "the lack of Western indigenous systems of dream classification, and the cultural neglect of subjective experience led to a western ethnocentric bias against dreams" (Sered & Abramovitch, 1992, p. 1405). In other words, a lack of attention to one's inner world, coupled with little value placed upon dream research and literature, has resulted in dismissal and opposition in Western culture when it comes to dreams and altered states. After having done much comparative analysis of the dreams of the Native American Plains Indians, Irwin (1994) warned, "If we forget or do not attend to our dreams, to the images and activities that come to us unbidden, it is because our cultural environment does not support a means by which dreaming could transform and revitalize our awareness" (p. 9).

For some, dreams do hold religious meaning in modern Western culture (Bulkeley, 1994). Some people report much higher levels of dream recall than do others (Lackman, Lapkin, & Handelman, 1962). Punamäki and Joustie (1998) reported, "Research is scarce about how daily life experiences, cultural socialization, and personal issues incorporate in dream contents" (p. 322).

Monophasic and Polyphasic Sleep

Let's briefly overview the basic distinction between monophasia and polyphasia. In general, monophasic cultures (whose individuals typically sleep in one cycle, usually seven to eight hours per night) typically view dreaming as unreal, insignificant, and as something that just happens. Dreams are not given attention in the schools or in the home. The information obtained in dreams is often dismissed and given little relevance. Dream recall may be low. However, polyphasic cultures, whose members may engage in several short sleep periods throughout a twenty-four-hour cycle, thus aiding dream recall, view dreams as another dimension of reality, generally speaking. Hence, to polyphasic cultures, dream-life is more meaningful and such experiences are considered valuable. In short, dreams are real. Those living in "polyphasic cultures develop their sense of identity by incorporating memories of experiences had in dreams … as well as those in waking life" (Laughlin & Rock, 2014, p. 236). There is value in both living experiences. All conscious experience has worth.

A case in point is the Mehinaku, a small village of Arawakan-speaking individuals in Central Brazil, who are easily able to recall several dreams each night. They awaken periodically throughout the night to add logs to their fire for warmth: this typical sleep pattern aids in dream recall. Additionally, the concept of a soul (*iyeweku*) is at the heart of Mehinaku dream theory, and souls interacting with other souls (while the body sleeps) is a phenomenon taken at face value, or considered real (Gregor, 1981). From my experience, this perspective does not often sit comfortably with secular Westerners in particular. In addition, religious Westerners have historically viewed such phenomena as diabolical, but it wasn't always that way (see Breslaw, 2003; see Pansters, 2009). Very long ago, ancient Western documents, along with those of more recent saints, reveal that dreams were seen to be a gift from the divine (see Pansters, 2009).

As babies and children, we begin life sleeping in polyphasic cycles. However, by the time children enter elementary school in the United States, they are conditioned to become monophasic, as naps are eliminated from the day and a set schedule is built. This brings to mind my two nephews, both of whom are under the age of seven. When we have sleepovers (which entail me staying over at their parent's house), the first thing I say to them upon awakening is, "Tell me what you did when you were asleep," or, "What happened in your dreams?" Their responses are held fondly in my heart. Last month, the oldest boy, now entering the world of video games, shared his dream of playing a video game then deciding to jump into the television and become part of that game. Last year, he told me about how he rode a cheetah, how they communicated, and the relationship they had. A couple weeks after that, I drew him a colorful cheetah and we talked about *Cheetah* much more, although he said that he had forgotten a lot about that dream by then.

As my nephews go further along in school and their lives become increasingly routine-based, might they continue to engage their nocturnal experiences? Their relationship with their dream life may continue to develop, or it may fall to the wayside. Hearing the oldest one say on occasion, "it's just a dream," leads me to wonder.

The Power of Incubated Dreams

On his study tour in 2005, Edgar (2006) conducted dozens of interviews in Turkey and found that almost every interviewee "related purposefully to their dreams" (p. 265) regardless of their profession or social status. From interviews in Pakistan, Edgar (2006) found that people "fervently believed in the power of dreams" and reported that "dreams had changed their lives" (p. 266). Some believed that "dreams [were] a channel of divine wisdom and [could] be especially helpful in personal problem solving" (Covitz, 1990, p. 133). In the past, dream incubation was common. It was a part of day-to-day culture. This practice, at times, has been mediated through religious or spiritual leaders and even cunning folk or wise men and women. Dream incubation often prompts the dreamer into real-world action. The ritual of Islamic dream incubation (*Istikhara*) is thought to generate "true" dreams and has been used for requesting "divine guidance, or fortune/grace (*baraka*);" it is even used for making practical decisions and choices surrounding marriage, mating, business, politics and economic affairs (Edgar, 2006; Gonzalez-Vazquez, 2014). Islamic dream interpretation (*ta'bir*) translates "the imagery of dreams in order to forecast the future" (Rozehnal, 2014, p. 67). Even today, Arabic television channels feature programs on dream interpretation.

In India, dreamers who awaken from a dream of significance go to an expert, such as a *pir*, for interpretation. Kakar (1982) noted that "skilled *pirs* strive to elicit from the dreamer himself the source of tension that may have initiated the dream, often inquiring about his marital relations and family problems[;] ... there exists a great deal of culturally instilled confidence in the patient that the *pir* will understand his problems as communicated through the dream" (p. 49). Dream-visions play a guiding, and sometimes healing, role in the lives of contemporary Indians, Egyptians, and Moroccans, among other groups, who also incubate dreams and report dreams frequently (Hoffman, 1997). Because incubated dreaming is considered important to many groups (the Hamadsha brotherhood being just one example), practices such as visiting the tomb of a saint becomes ritualized.

The dreams of Christian saints, such as Francis of Assisi, have been pivotal in shaping the course of the lives of such highly religious people (see Pansters, 2009). Similar dynamics are present today, even among more secularized Western populations. For example, White and Taytroe (2003) conducted a study of one hundred undergraduate and graduate students. The researchers found that dreams recalled after the use of dream incubation techniques led to reported improvements in personal problems and moods.

Benefits to Society

Beyond individual gains, society as a whole has benefited from those who dream. Libraries are filled with publications highlighting inventions, discoveries, works of art, and more that were influenced by dreams and visions. For example, German composer and theorist Richard Wagner (1813–1883) felt that his inspirations and music came from his dreams and intuition. While not common knowledge, it is generally known that dreams inspired some major scientific and technical discoveries, such as Parkinson's computer-controlled antiaircraft gun, the M-9 and Horowitz's telescopes (Barrett, 2001). Other examples are Howe's invention of the sewing machine (Ullman, Krippner, & Vaughan, 2002); Mazur's mathematical proof of the Schoenflies Theorem (Barrett, 2001); Mendeleev's contribution of the Periodic Table of Elements (LaBerge, 2009); Huang's computer using optical circuits (Barrett, 2001); Ramanujan's mathematical discoveries, which still influence polymer chemistry and computer science (Barrett, 2001); Descartes' "philosophical and mathematical formulations that were to change the course of Western thought" (Ullman et al., 2002, p. 179); Profet's evolutionary theory of menstruation (Barrett, 2001); and Agassiz's classification of a particular fossilized fish (Barrett, 2001). A dream helped composer, violinist and theorist Giuseppe Tartini (1692–1770) come out of a creative block. His best-known piece of work (a sonata) was inspired by a dream.

Dreams have been particularly important to many writers. The works of fantasy and horror fiction writer Clive Barker have been influenced by his dreams. From dreaming, Barker discovers images, which develop into scenes, thus they become starting places for his stories (Epel, 1993). Also known for the same genre, Stephen King credits his dreams for several of his creative works. King uses his dreams in many ways—whether to advance a story, bring to life an odd dream situation, or disguise things symbolically—and he understands that weaving together writing and dreaming can lead to success (Epel, 1993). Writer Amy Tan knows the power of dreams. Her first novel, *The Joy Luck Club*, was a bestseller, and some portions of it were inspired through dreams. When Tan becomes lost as to a story's potential conclusion, she'll take the story to bed with her to see if guidance surfaces while dreaming. Tan claims to easily recall her dreams and has experienced lucid dreaming. She understands that her dream-life supports her work as a novelist, and that, any time she needs material to work with, a dream will be there for her (Epel, 1993). Thus dreams may have powerful effects on people, leading them to reconsider important decisions and even change the course of their lives, and ultimately the world (Edgar, 2006).

With this in mind, dreaming may be considered a gift to communities and nations alike. The same can be said for creative dreams that inspire art and propel other aspirations, such as athletics. For example, among professionals, dreams have been credited for completing key scenes in novels, entire musical pieces, and even athletic improvements among athletes (Barrett, 1993). For more information about such nocturnal productivity, I highly suggest reading Dr. Deidre Barrett's *The Committee of Sleep: How Artists, Scientists, and Athletes Use Dreams for Creative Problem-Solving* (2001). I never get tired of this exciting book! Later on, I'll touch on how pregnant women have made decisions and found solutions as a result of their dreams. Unfortunately, such impactful dreams, once revealed, can lead to accusations of dishonesty or outright dismissal. One's culture influences the origin of dreams and what one considers to be real. For those who actively engage dreams, or incubate them, the nightly assistance sometimes just keeps on coming, and it can be a source of ongoing guidance.

For some, dreams have also provoked activism in waking life. Dream groups exist with the purpose of coming together to dream with specific intention. Jean Campbell, founder of the World Dreams Peace Bridge, told me about this international group of dreamers, who primarily meet online for the purpose of dreaming about and for peace. Group members have used their dreams to propel actions and activities in both waking and dream states with the intention of bringing the world closer to peace. Whether it is refugee support and assistance, aid to those affected by war, healing for those with illness, or something else, World Dreams Peace Bridge members ask, "How can the dream facilitate peace?" Jean Campbell's third book, *Group Dreaming: Dreams to the Tenth Power*, dedicates several chapters to the World Dreams Peace Bridge.

I contacted Jeremy Seligson, whose Peace Train dream is included in Campbell's book. For the last thirty-eight years, Seligson has resided in South Korea. Seligson and I corresponded regarding his World Dreams Peace Bridge activities, and on October 9, 2016, he told me the following:

> Periodically, North Korea has threatened to destroy Seoul in "a Sea of Fire," including this year, 2016. Yet, when sending those threats and from the South's responses, I have never heard one word spoken on behalf of the children from either side. It's as if they don't exist. Yet they do, in the millions, of all ages from 0–17, and millions could be brutally maimed, slain or traumatized in the wake of an actual "Sea of Fire." The prospects of such a horrific, scorching, skin melting tragedy like Hiroshima and Nagasaki is why in 2002 I asked my students at Hankuk University of Foreign Studies, "Why should we study English Conversation today if tomorrow we are going to get burnt up in a 'Sea of Fire?'" Why should children be blown up and mutilated just because adults don't know how to sit down and make peace? Why don't you go out and ask children for their opinions? Shouldn't they have a

say, since they are ones who are going to die? Without them there would be no future for this country. Why don't you go out and ask them to talk about and then "draw or paint a picture of peace in your own life?" Unanimously, the students agreed to do so. Resourceful, the students found children in playgrounds, or friends who were teaching in kindergartens and primary schools, Sunday and art schools, who were willing and eager to participate. This is how the Children's Peace Train was born. It was called "Children's Peace Train" partly because former South Korean President Kim Dae-jung (b. 1924—d. 2009) had proposed building a "Peace and Prosperity Railroad" that would link up the two Koreas and continue on through China and Russia, all the way to Paris and London.

Dae-jung received a Nobel Prize for Peace in 2000.
     Seligson continued by sharing with me one of his own dreams:

Furthermore, in the summer of 2002, I dreamed a dream. In it, I was walking through barren land without hope when a young man came up and tapped me on the shoulder, saying "A train has come." I looked back and saw a long black locomotive waiting there. So I got on and rode through all the night. In the dining car I met the Israeli Peace activist Ada Aharoni, who told me, "You should work with us, since we already have an organization (IFLAC)." Years later, she helped me organize an Israeli-Arab Children's Peace Train in Israel. Our dream train continued on the steps of the U.S. Capitol Building in Washington D.C. The U.S. president (who was Al Gore!) and many senators were standing on the steps applauding. Walking toward them, I glanced back and saw around the smoke stack of the train, a large white paper sign with the words "PEACE TRAIN" around it in black. Overjoyed, I leaped in the air and floated down a grassy hill, landing on my feet. People were amazed.

Seligson further explained the significance of his dream to me:

The dream has come true. I have ridden on AMTRACK from Atlanta to D.C. for a Peace March against the war in Iraq in 2003. Also, the Children's Peace Train has participated in the 2007, 2011 and 2015 International Children's Art Festival in Washington, D.C., within sight of the Capitol Building and The White House.
     In Seoul, my students asked young children to draw or paste color paper wheels on their drawings or paintings, each making a carriage for a Children's Peace Train. Cooperating in groups, they cut out a colorful engine and caboose, and connected the carriages with hooks to link up each complete train. Children explained to each other the meaning of their drawings and stood in a circle with their Peace Train. They also sang a Children's Peace Train song, which I composed. Each child was presented with a signed certificate making him or her "A Conductor of the Children's Peace Train" to take home and hang on their wall. The beauty and imagination of many of their pictures is astonishing. Together, they tell a story of Peace in their own lives with family, friends, animals, flowers, et cetera, play and music, love and peace, especially directed at friendship and unification between the North and South. In the summer of 2016 the crisis continues to simmer with blustering saber-rattling and more powerful weaponry than in 2002 when the Children's Peace Train began.

As demonstrated above, dreams have led to loving waking-life actions in the service of humanity. Unfortunately, dreams have also prompted others to act in violent ways. Dreams have been linked with the killings of individuals, children and groups. On December 26, 2016, *People* magazine reported that a Texas man recently accused of the murder of his wife and infant son had a dream in which he decapitated his wife and her father. Less than two weeks after revealing this dream to one of his coworkers, he allegedly murdered his wife and their baby. Their bodies were found in the master bedroom with knife wounds to their necks (Harris, 2016). While a dream cannot force anyone into action, it can bring forth imagery associated with a wish or desire, no matter how terrible. When one can see a terrible act committed in the mind's eye, through dreaming, how might that experience alone affect a person? Some would be startled and describe a nightmare, but that might not be the case for everyone.

Dangerous Outcomes from Dreams

At the 33rd annual conference of the International Association for the Study of Dreams (2016), Iain Edgar of Durham University spoke about the dreams and decision-making processes of radical, militant or extremist individuals and group members. For example, the May 2015 Garland, Texas, attacker Elton Simpson posted his dreams online, which indicated that his martyrdom was near (Edgar, 2011, 2015). The 2016 Brussels Metro bomber had dreams prompting him to act. In addition, dreams of Al-Qaeda members and Taliban leaders have been reported, including some of the most well-known jihadist commanders (Edgar, 2007). Osama Bin Laden spoke about the dreams of his followers in one of the first videos released after 9/11. Bin Laden said, "Abu'l-Hassan al-Masri told me a year ago: 'I saw in a dream, we were playing a soccer game against the Americans. When our team showed up in the field, they were all pilots'" (Edgar, 2007; Kuper, 2002). Bin Laden continued, "He [Al-Masri] didn't know anything about the operation until he heard it on the radio. He said the game went on and we defeated them. That was a good omen for us" (Edgar, 2007).

"Dreams can facilitate conversions, either into Islam or into militant jihadism" (Edgar, 2007, p. 62), and dreams have confirmed and legitimized radical group membership and action. According to Edgar, "Dreams of heavenly spaces and the glorious reception of the martyrs are reported; dead friends appear with metaphysical information" (2007, p. 62). Many militant Islamists and Jihadis attach a considerable amount of significance to dreams, as they are an important part of their religious experience. Futhermore, Islamic State/Daesh sympathizers have discussed dreams on Twitter, and it is quite possible that dreams have impacted the decisions made by these group members. For more information, a section of Edgar's *The Dream in Islam: From Qur'anic Tradition to Jihadist Inspiration* gives attention to these topics. As an important note, Edgar (2015) reminds us that "not all Muslims who believe they have true dreams about jihad or martyrdom become militants. For some radicalized individuals, however, a dream or series of dreams can be a catalyst for taking up arms" (p. 74).

Contemporary Western Dream Theories

As we often experience, dreams consist of imagery that occurs during the sleep state (without external stimulation), which can seem very real— but is it real? It all depends who you ask. Rapid eye movement (REM) sleep, during which dreaming is most easily remembered, is "a biological state of cyclic regularity found in all humans and shared by animals" (Breger, 1967, p. 2) that involves primitive neural mechanisms. REM sleep is also known as paradoxical sleep because the level of arousal, as indicated by Electroencephalograph (EEG) patterns, is similar to that of the waking state (Rathus, 2009). During an EEG test, the brain's electrical activity is measured. Small metal disks, called electrodes, are attached to the scalp, which measure the electrical impulses of the brain. Brain cells constantly communicate through electrical impulses, even while we sleep. One's emotional life is often expressed in the dream state, although the experience may be considered unconscious (Kron & Brosh, 2003). Bonime (1962) states, "Two significant contemporary movements are to be noted in regard to our knowledge of dreams, one experimental, physiological, and concerned with the process of dreaming itself, the other psychological, theoretical, clinical, and concerned primarily with meaning" (p. vii).

Freud's 1900 publication of *The Interpretation of Dreams* laid the foundation for modern Western scholarly inquiry into the meaning of dreaming, claiming that dreams reveal hidden conflicts and serve as a form of wish fulfillment that stems from repressed desires or cravings. Psychologists have not reached consensus regarding the meaning, significance and impact that dreams have on individuals.

Carl Gustav Jung was a highly influential and controversial Swiss psychologist and psychiatrist. He was the founder of analytic psychology, also known as Jungian psychology. His complex theories changed the face of psychology and are of interest today. Jung in 1964 said that a "dream is a specific expression of the unconscious" (p. 18). Later, in 1974, Jung stated, "In the superstitions of all times and races the dream has been regarded as a truth-telling oracle" (p. 41). According to contemporary Jungian theorist Hall (1983), "The dream in Jungian psychology is seen as a natural, regulatory psychic process, analogous to compensatory mechanisms of bodily functioning" (p. 23). Hall (1989) adds that "dreams seem to be primarily in the service of the individuation process" (p. 83). In *The Clinical Use of Dreams*, Bonime (1962) provides the "first systematic and detailed clinical exposition of the analysis of dreams from a basically non–Freudian point of view" (p. vii). Bonime further writes, "Dream symbols arise out of the specific life history of each individual, and it is only from the individual's life history that we can derive the meaning of his dream symbols" (p. 32).

Other researchers have provided biological explanations for dreams, such as the activation-synthesis hypothesis (Hobson, Pace-Schott, & Stickgold, 2010), noting that dreams are simply by-products of the brain's electrical impulses (Ciccarelli & White, 2009; Rathus, 2009; Schönhammer, 2005). According to Morewedge and Norton (2009), "Although researchers still debate the function of dreams and dream content's meaning, laypeople around the world appear to believe that dreams serve an important func tion and have meaning, revealing hidden truths" (p. 253).

More recently, a relationship between dreaming and memory consolidation has been suggested (Llewellyn, 2013; Solomonova, Stenstrom, Paquette, & Nielsen, 2015). REM sleep appears to assist in emotional memory-consolidation, according to the latest research. (Corsi-Cabrera, Velasco, Del Rio-Portilla, Armony, Trejo-Martinez, Guevara, & Velasco, 2016). This is an area ripe for further investigation with exciting new discoveries to come.

Dreams often represent an internal aspect of the self and can impact one's behavior, sometimes resulting in a long-standing influence on the dreamer's life (Knudson & Minier, 1999). The dreamer's personal beliefs influence perception and interpretation, which, in turn, influence behavior (Knudson & Minier, 1999; Mischel & Mischel, 1958). Morewedge and Norton (2009) found that "dreamed events, even when unpleasant, are perceived to be meaningful sources of information, to be more meaningful than similar conscious thoughts, and can even be perceived to provide information as important as similar real-world events" (p. 254).

This appears to be the case for some children who report having special dreams, which offer them comfort, support and guidance, or which have helped to resolve current real-life conflicts (Adams, 2003; Adams & Hyde, 2008). One of the girls participating in Adam's research on Christian ten to twelve year-olds, credited a dream for easing her anxiety about an upcoming event in which she had to participate. Some of these children found reassurance from dreams that appeared to serve as coping mechanisms amid all of their busy, pressure-filled daily activities. Other children reported seeing a religious figure or felt the presence of one in these supportive or comforting dreams (Adams, 2003). Dreams touch the "immediate, lived world of everyday existence and perception" and enter "into both our individual and our collective history" (Irwin, 1994, p.9), merging past and present in the service toward greater awareness and new insight. Some experiences in the dream state result in long-lasting, profound personality structure changes, "an effect parallel to some religious conversions and to some peak experiences in waking life" (Hall, 1983, p. 21).

Before reviewing the two major dream theories below, consider the following dreams. Both of these dreams were told to me by a male family member with a history of dreams similar to the two here:

> Dream 1: I was dreaming I couldn't get my ducks to stand in a row. As soon as I got a couple of ducks to line up and move on, those ducks would not stay in a row with the others, so I had to go back and get them lined up again. Then the other ducks would be out of line. I spent all night going back and forth trying to get my ducks all in a row.
>
> Dream 2: I was smoothing concrete on a walkway and after completing the first section, I turned around to do the next section. When I looked back to admire my work, there were footprints in the first section, so I smoothed it out again. Again, turning around to admire my work, I found there were footprints in the next section. I spend all night going back and forth smoothing out the footprints. I never knew where the footprints came from.

While dreams hold significance for many who recall them, controversy exists with regard to how they are of service to the human psyche. In the West, two dominating yet competing theories emerge among those who study dreaming (King & DeCicco, 2007). Many people who recall their dreams may feel drawn to one or both of these dominant theories. Firstly, the complementary (or compensatory) theory posited by Jung (1964) regards dreaming as a function whose purpose is to restore psychological equilibrium. According to Jung, when one dreams, the material produced during that state re-establishes balance within the psyche, so that when the personality is deficient in some manner, a dream can compensate for that deficiency. According to Jung (1974), "Dreams, I maintain, are compensatory to the conscious situation of the moment" (p. 38); "The dream does in fact concern itself with both health and sickness, and since, by virtue of its source in the unconscious, it draws upon a wealth of subliminal perceptions, it can sometimes produce things that are very well worth knowing" (p. 68). In his book *Jungian Dream Interpretation*, Hall (1983), writes, "Dreams are compensatory in all states of psychological functioning—in ordinary life (where they compensate the individuation process), in psychosis (where they attempt to produce a stable ego), and in neurosis, where they are active in bringing the ego out of a neurotic byway or impasse and into the mainstream of individuation" (p. 101).

Secondly, rather than dreams compensating for waking life, they may be understood as a way of unifying waking and sleep states. Alfred Adler (1936), founder of individual psychology, regards the conscious and unconscious to "form a single unity" (p. 6), instead of existing in opposition to each other. Adler posits that both the conscious and unconscious may be understood as a unifying whole. Hall and Nordby (1972), responsible for formulating the continuity hypothesis, analyzed more than fifty thousand dreams from several countries. Hall and Nordby propose that dreams are a reflection of a person's life in the waking state: "Dreams are continuous with waking life; the world of dreaming and the world of waking are one" (1972, p. 104). In a similar fashion, American psychiatrist Aaron Beck, who developed cognitive therapy and ways to work with dreams, points to a dream's outward content instead of its symbolism. Beck focuses on the relationship between one's behavior and dream themes (Freeman & White, 2002). Hence, dreams may serve to highlight what one should attend to in the waking state.

In this regard, King and DeCicco (2007) conducted a correlational study among twenty-seven undergraduate students examining the relationships between dream content and physical health, mood and self-construal. King and DeCicco define self-construal as "the way in which one views him/herself in reference to other people and other things" (p. 129). The students in the study were all enrolled in a course on dreams and dreaming. Four dream reports were collected during class time as part of a course assignment before the participants filled out three surveys. Physical health, mood and self-construal were expected to significantly relate to dream content. Each volunteer completed the Medical Outcomes SF-36 Health Survey, the Profile of Mood States Scale and the Self-Construal Scale. Multiple significant correlations were found among the variables after analysis. King and DeCicco's (2007) findings "support continuity between dreams and waking life physical and mental functioning" (p. 127); however, a sampling bias existed in that only college students were available to volunteer for the study. This sample therefore consisted primarily of motivated, female, privileged youth; they were white, middle class, single, had access to a four-year college and had the time to volunteer. The authors note that this study's findings are not generalizable due to the demographics. Furthermore, a larger participant pool is suggested for further research (King & DeCicco, 2007).

Another view on sleep and dreaming that is related to the continuity hypothesis comes from an evolutionary perspective. This perspective highlights physiological processes, particularly those involving neurochemical and neurocognitive activation. Emotional memories are solidified during REM sleep. Research shows a relationship between sleep, social functioning and health status. McNamara, Pace-Schott, Johnson, Harris and Auerbach (2011) conducted a sleep laboratory study with sixty-four participants to test the hypothesis that "measures of REM sleep architecture and REM sleep-related mentation would be associated with attachment orientation" (p. 141). Ten minutes into REM sleep and ten minutes into a control NREM sleep period, the participants were awakened. At that moment, the participants were asked to report a dream. They were also asked to rate themselves and a significant other on a list of trait objectives. Securely-attached participants took longer to enter REM sleep than anxiously-attached participants. REM dreams with themes of aggression and self-denigration were more frequent among those with anxious-attachment orientations. The researchers suggest that "REM sleep plays a role in processing experiences and emotions related to attachment, and that certain features of sleep and dreaming reflect attachment orientations" (McNamara, et al., 2011, p. 141). From the above-described study and related dream-content studies, McNamara and colleagues (2010) concluded that "specific dream content variables (including number and variety of dream characters) may predict mood states during the following morning" (p. 81). These theories may be helpful in informing future investigations on announcing dreams and other types of extraordinary dream experiences. Further investigations on whether, and how, dreams illuminate, impact, balance, inform and give meaning to the dreamer's life could be discovered.

Considering the various possible functions of dreams and their adaptive roles, how might dreams serve those in challenging stages of life? Could dreams serve those in certain stages of substance abuse recovery? Some women have told me that, in dreams, they are in the presence of their drug of choice, yet they do not consume the substance. Sometime they are even handling the drug in the dream, but they do not ingest it.

Instead, they may just touch it briefly or simply stare at it. This may be considered progress in that the desire or impulse to "pick up and use" is absent in the dream. Upon awakening, the dream memory could act as a source of inner strength in these individuals' efforts to remain clean and sober. It is also possible that such a dream could serve as a warning to not get to close, or next time things could take a turn for the worse.

Another example can be found in the adaptive function of dreams when, for instance, soldiers living in dangerous war zones dream of being captured as a way of preparing or alerting them to the danger that lies ahead. These dreams may also keep soldiers from relaxing too much or sleeping too deeply, during which time their vulnerability would have risen. Another example of the adaptive function of dreams comes from the dreams of prisoners of war. A POW may have serene dreams that impart hope, helping him or her to carry on and not give up (Weiss, 1993).

CHAPTER TWO

Extraordinary Dreams

While most dreams are of the ordinary variety, many people report extraordinary dream experiences (see Bulkeley, 2006, 2009; Hermansen, 1997; Luke, Zychowicz, Richterova, Tjurina, & Polonnikova, 2012). Some reports of extraordinary dreams come from ancient and medieval times (Katz, 1997), while some come from the modern day. Extraordinary dreams are also sometimes referred to as exotic, big, impactful, significant, prophetic or memorable, among other names. These terms, therefore, will be used interchangeably throughout the remainder of this book. Perhaps you have had a dream like this—one that you recognized as different from the usual mundane activity of the night. Maybe you awoke sensing its importance, or reflected upon its vividness, or maybe you haven't been able to forget it all week.

Extraordinary Dreaming in Ancient Times

Before the common era, shortly after the Peloponnesian War began, Xenophon, a Greek historian, philosopher, soldier and prolific writer, was born. Dreams, including their nature and function, come up in many of Xenophon's writings. Even though critics existed, the general belief during Xenophon's time was that dreams came from the gods and were a type of omen, predicting what was to come (Hughes, 1987). As for extraordinary dreams, an early example is The Dream of Scipio, as recorded by Cicero. Oneiromancy, divination by means of dreams, was popular prior to and during late antiquity. Xenophon interpreted his own dreams, yet he noted that "many armies and states had official interpreters of dreams" (Hughes, 1987, p. 280). Today, this practice still occurs in certain cultures, as having a member assigned to dream interpretation is not all that uncommon.

Ages ago, a distinction was made between ordinary and extraordinary dreams. Born in 245 CE, Syrian philosopher Iamblichus believed that a predictive dream, which was caused by the gods, was not the same as a fantasy. Iamblichus encouraged dream incubation and oneiromancy (Athanassiadi, 1993). In the Mediterranean region, the practice of dream incubation, in some form, has existed since antiquity. The Berbers in northwest Africa, various groups in Morocco, the Romans, the ancient Greeks, the Egyptians, the Syrians and well beyond practiced incubation of dreams, in various forms. This practice was known by different terms: *Incubatio* in Latin; *egkoimesis* in Greek (*egkatakoimesis* in Greek refers to sleeping in a dormitory, as it was common to sleep in a mausoleum, shrine, temple, or other structure); and *istikhara* in Arabic (although this term has more than one meaning). For example, Asclepius was a hero in ancient Greece who later became the god of healing and medicine (Leadbetter,1997). For hundreds of years after his death, the Greco-Roman god Asclepius (also spelled Asklepios in Greek and Aesculapius in Latin) continued to heal the sick, maimed and blind through dreaming in his temples. Those who prayed, sacrificed, and slept in the temple reported that "the good physician would reveal to them how to be cured." (Hamilton, 1940, p. 281). Snakes, the sacred servants of Asclepius, played some part in the cure, and it was said that "thousands upon thousands of sick people through the centuries believed that he had freed them from their pain and restored them to health" (Hamilton, 1940, p. 281). The sanctuary, Asklepieion, can be found in the small Greek town of Epidaurus (Mark Cartwright, 2012 http://www.ancient.eu/epidaurus). To be healed or shown a cure in a dream is significant indeed; yet, as time went on, in Europe, the Mediterranean region, and the future colonies of the United States of America, such things were liable to get a person banished, imprisoned or executed, and there appeared to be little exception if that person was female.

Dreaming around the Time of the European Inquisition

The Inquisition, a period of institutionalized violence and persecution spanning about seven hundred years, began around 1231 with Pope Gregory IX.. The Vatican set out to persecute those who disputed its authority. The Spanish Inquisition, formally known as the Tribunal of the Holy Office of the Inquisition, took place from 1478 to 1834. The Spanish Inquisition was a tribunal, which began under Ferdinand II of Aragon and Isabella I of Castile, that has been referred to as an institution to maintain Catholic orthodoxy, to combat heresy throughout Spain, and to consolidate power in the monarchy of the newly unified Spanish Kingdom. The last execution related to the Spanish Inquisition was in 1826, long after other nations ceased such tribunals. In England the last such execution was 1684; in the colonies of the United States of America it was 1692; in Germany it was 1775 (Achterberg, 1991). In Italy, under the Vatican, the Inquisition was formally abolished in 1908.

Jeanne Achterberg was an American psychologist who produced groundbreaking work which wove together Western interdisciplinary history of women healers. Achterberg writes, "The witch-hunts had always been most severe in the regions ruled by Roman law and in the countries where Protestantism was most integrated into government" (Achterberg, 1991, p. 98). Historical records differ, yet it is likely that thousands of people were burned at the stake for various "convictions," some of which were for the crime of superstition and for craft (Henningsen, 2009). It was believed that by making a pact with the devil, a witch would in exchange gain supernatural powers for curing, problem-solving or causing harm. During one period, bewitched women were said to fly or travel through the air (at times in groups), sometimes after having already gone to bed and fallen asleep, thus traveling by means of the "soul." Provoked mutual dreaming or collective OBEs might have been taking place, but we'll never really know for certain. This "night-going" was only one component of so-called evil witch activity.

In Sicily and the south of Italy, it was a little different than the rest of Europe. Magical agents of southern Italy and Sicily included highly regarded "women who were thought to be able to transform themselves into animals, and to have the power of flying, curing, and divining," invisibility, and "the ability to penetrate buildings through locked doors" (Henningsen, 209, pp. 62, 70), thus serving their communities as fairy doctors, or intermediaries between human and fairy worlds. Spanish Inquisitors of Palermo obtained confessions and persecuted the fairy doctors (all women) in Sicily. One exclaimed that the confessed activities seemed to have taken place in dreams because, each time she awoke, she would find herself in bed (Henningsen, 209, p. 63). In addition, these women declared that they had not known that their behavior was considered bad or wrong until the Inquisitors told them it was. Accusations and criticisms across Europe and the Mediterranean, however, were far from over. For example, the *Index of Forbidden Books* (the *Index Librorum Prohibitorum* in Latin) lived on until 1966, with the first issue being published in 1557 by Pope

Paul IV. In addition, Scotland by the 1500s and England by the early 1600s had become a hotbed for witch hunting and witch trials. Mass arrests and executions continued well into the 1700s. The most famous manuscript promoting the execution of witches was the *Malleus Maleficarum* (Latin for "The Hammer of the Witches"). It was written in 1486 by two German Dominicans—zealous inquisitors employed by the Catholic Church—Heinrich Kramer and James Sprenger, and first published in Germany the following year. The *Malleus Maleficarum*, endorsed by Pope Innocent VIII, was the official witchcraft manual and has been attributed to the centuries of witch hysteria that spread across all regions and nations mentioned above. This infamous handbook for combatting witchcraft includes the case against its use (the notion that any disbelief in demonology is to be viewed as heresy), supposed witch activities such as transvection (supernatural flight) and metamorphosis (any change from one's original form), the promotion of securing confessions through the use of torture, legal witch trial procedures and much more. Witchcraft was blamed chiefly, but not always, on women—many were poor widows, midwives or cunning folk (simple country people who used herbs and magic to cure and heal community members). Some of the accused may have been viewed as burdens who had strong personalities, or who were unconventional or were disliked. It was fairly effortless to accuse a neighbor, and it was even easier to find "proof" of witchcraft. For example, any skin blemish such as a mole or birthmark discovered anywhere on the body could be used as "proof" because, after making a "pact with the devil" and consummating it by sex, such a mark was left. If this ridiculous practice wasn't enough, methods of torture such as sleep deprivation and a practice known as "swimming the witch" were applied to gain confessions. At the heart of all this, there appears to be a connection to sexuality, and only that of women. Men considered women to be much more susceptible to sexual temptations of demons. If Eve was not faithful to Adam, how could any woman be faithful to her husband?

At its core, the popular *Hammer of the Witches* is a publication of misogynist ideology for Catholics and Protestants alike, coupled with explicit torture endorsements. Hatred and fear of women course through its pages, and it was republished over and over again for some two hundred years. As just one example of the longstanding impact, fifteen women were convicted at one time and hung in a single day in England. It's not difficult to imagine the intense fear that must have run through a village or town during this chaotic time. Eventually, no hunts were necessary, as the residents of the town would just offer people up! Some confessors, whose witch hunting territory could have spanned several hundred miles, were paid large sums for every witch. These men profited handsomely from these Christian-sanctioned murders. Careers built in such a way are not given up.

In North America

Enforcing religious views through intimidation and violence also took place in the Americas during that time, spanning centuries. According to Breslaw (2003), "It was assumed that witches were bent on corrupting the particular church, whether of Protestant or Roman Catholic" (p. 45). In April 2016, I traveled to Salem, Massachusetts. Having never been there before, and being very interested in women's history, I was excited about what I would discover, although I knew the town had a dark history. I was especially curious about how dreams and visions may have played a role in the accusations of witchcraft that ultimately led to the deaths of several women. While wandering through the town, I stopped by The Witch House and the Salem Witch Museum, just like a good tourist would.

At one time, The Witch House on Essex Street was home to the wealthy merchant, civic leader, and magistrate Jonathan Corwin. In 1692, he was called upon to investigate and examine the activities and lives of those accused of practicing witchcraft. Some of the infamous witch "trials" took place in that house.

My next stop was the Salem Witch Museum in Washington Square. There, I attended the museum's short presentation and tour based on witch trial documents. While the various museum attendants and tour guides at these two establishments had little to say with regard to how dreams, visions or even out-of-body experiences may have played a role in the examinations and confessions, I did come across informational installations and exhibits, papers and wall plaques, as well as printed material for sale, that shed some light on my inquiry.

I learned that, although controversial, "spectral evidence" (evidence based on visions) was considered in cases tried, though only between the months of May and October of 1692. With the assistance of evil forces, and for malevolent purposes, it was believed that a person's spirit, or spectre, could travel or freely move about, independent of the body. Some claimed that they could "see" the spirit of the other when awake or in an ordinary state of consciousness, but some claimed to have visions or apparitions where they could "see" the spirit of someone moving about.

A person's presence was sensed even without her physical body present. These claims were considered in the examinations that took place during those five months.

Professor Elaine G. Breslaw touches on these ideas in her publications. Her 1997 article titled "Tituba's Confession: The Multicultural Dimensions of the 1692 Salem Witch-Hunt" was published in the journal *Ethnohistory*. Breslaw (1997) examines Tituba's controversial role in the 1692 "witch scare" (p. 535). As a Native American woman (although some claimed she was African), Tituba's cultural beliefs were in conflict with those of the Puritans (the people among whom she served and lived), as Puritans often feared Native Americans and associated them with evil spirits and demonic practices. For example, the belief that in the dream state one could travel with the soul to distant places while the body slept was associated with making a pact with the devil and other diabolical activities. Traveling in a dream state could be viewed, by some, as a magical practice, and such things related to folk magic were directly associated with evil and special powers that could only come from the devil, or Satan, according to Christian beliefs. Some rituals were considered an acceptable element of religious expression, so long as they took place in the church; however, similar rituals practiced outside of the church were considered appeals to the devil (Breslaw, 2003).

It was unclear in Tituba's testimony whether she traveled to Boston via her soul in dream time or whether her physical body had been there. Another time, Tituba spoke specifically about dream states—once about a tall man who visited her as she was falling asleep, and later about a dream in which "evil took the shape of a man" (p. 546). Such explanations, in part, appeared to have alluded to the presence of Satan in the community within the minds of important Puritan figures. Such a stir had devastating consequences.

While I left Salem with less concrete evidence than expected or hoped for, Breslaw's books, which were for sale in the Salem Witch Museum gift shop, were eye-opening. I left feeling motivated to read much more on the topic. Fortunately, even after centuries of repression, torture and executions, 'night-goers' and 'wise women' still exist today, in Europe, the Mediterranean region, throughout the Americas and in many other parts of the world. Unfortunately, the misguided notion connecting folkloric rituals or folk-magic, (and even dreamwork, I believe), with forces of evil "lingers on in the mythology of witchcraft" (Breslaw, 2003, p. 45).

In the final analysis, these terrorist, ruling-class campaigns were not spontaneous but were instead well organized and calculated—they were "initiated, financed and executed by church and state" (Ehrenreich & English, 1993, p. 9), and they were responsible for thousands of barbaric executions of which women of all ages made up eighty-five percent (Ehrenreich & English, 1993). The true history of these often poor, illiterate, peasant women is not recorded, and so what we can learn about their lives has been produced by an educated male elite class, some of which whom were the persecutors themselves (Ehrenreich & English, 1993).

Big Dreaming Elsewhere

Jung (1974) noted the difference between little or insignificant and big or significant dreams, claiming that some dreams were more important than others. This difference is seen across cultures. India's healing traditions regard dreams as valuable sources of information. Insight gained from a patient's dreams may point to a course of action for healing. The Pir (wise elder) of Patteshah's Dargah commonly began his interaction with his patients by asking, "What do you see in your dreams?" (Kakar, 1982). The Mehinaku of Brazil make a similar distinction with the terms "true dream (*jepuni yaja*)" and "everyday dreams (*jepuni he te*, literally "mere dreams")" (Gregor, 1981, p. 712). While true dreams are not as common as everyday dreams, true dreams may serve as a signal for those entering shamanism. Thus, they are significant for the community. A related example is reported in *Imagining the Course of Life: Self-transformation in a Shan Buddhist Community* by anthropologist Nancy Eberhardt. The village guardian spirit (*tsao moeng*) of Baan Kaung Mu, in Northwest Thailand, chose "Uncle Pon," an illiterate man struggling to overcome alcohol abuse, to become a traditional healer (*saraa*). Never having studied or having been taught traditional healing ways, Uncle Pon "had a dream in which the *tsao moeng* simply gave him the powerful verses, called *katha*, that are recited during a healing rite" (Eberhardt, 2006, p. 31) in order to cure community members from ailments and illnesses. Among many traditional Shan healers, curing power comes straight from the *tsao moeng* (Eberhardt, 2006).

Australia's indigenous people are referred to as Aborigines, which lumps together numerous different language groups and clans. Echoing the concepts above, Aborigine David Mowaljarlai explains (as cited in Hume, 1999, p. 5) that for Aborigines there are two kinds of dreams: *Yarri* and *burraal*. When one is soundly asleep and quiet, things descend or come down to the dreamer—this is *yarri*. The second kind of dream is known as *burraal*. *Burraal* is when the mind is not in a deep sleep, but instead awakens quickly with pressure changes, leaving the person feeling giddy, seeing things with the imagination, light headedness, and flying up and about.

Moving deeper into existences where dream and waking states have little-to-no separation, I have found this notion more common than expected. To Vodouisants, dreams are vital, and serve religious, spiritual and transformative functions. Adam McGee is a scholar of African Studies. He is also a male priest in Haitian Vodou tradition (*oungan*). According to McGee (2012), dreams act as "a site of intersection—between the dreamer and disembodied entities, and between our physical world and a broader field of spiritual action" (p. 85). Dreaming, he adds, is "an extension of normal action conducted in sleep" (p. 86); thus, the waking and dreaming divide does not exist. Dreaming serves as an important mechanism for receiving direct spiritual guidance. McGee (2012) concludes, "Vodou is ultimately a dreamed religion" (p. 89), thus highlighting aspects of life that are interwoven. This is quite distinct from the disintegrated views of contemporary Western society.

Similarly, inhabitants of the Timpaus Island (Indonesia) regard experiences during sleep and dreams (*mimpi*) to be as real as what happens in the waking state. Just as you or I can acquire important information during our day-to-day waking life, so too, can we acquire equally important information from spirits (*satan, hantu, jin*) during sleep, according to the Timpaus Islanders. Furthermore, these invisible thoughts (similar to soul, spirit, energy and mind), or "the non-corporeal self, may leave the body and travel to other places on its own power. Experiences from such journeys are remembered as dreams" (Broch, 2000, p. 10). While much more common in polyphasic cultures, such dreams, or dream-like experiences, would be considered 'big.'

In a region where Sufism is strong, the Ghzawa tribe of Morocco is inseparably intertwined with many aspects of oneiric and mantic practices, which include both men and women in dreaming, dream-sharing and dream-interpretation, although each group has a different purpose. A complex theory of space and soul exist in the Sufi tradition, which allows for communication between the living and dead in dreams, whether at night, or while napping during the day (Gonzalez-Vazquez, 2014). This can be explained as follows:

> [I]n dreams, the sleeper's soul (*ruh*) abandons the body (*jism*) and rests in the *alam al-mithal* ('imaginal world'). Thus, the sleepers' souls and the souls of the dead meet in the same 'place.' Dreams and visions form part of the Sufi's mystical expe-

riences, within which the boundaries between life and death and the places where the soul exist are fluid [Gonzalez-Vazquez, 2014, p. 98].

It is believed that the souls of the dead and the soul of the sleeping person can meet in this 'space' (known as *barzakh*) where these dead souls reside before joining God. There, in *barzakh,* connection and relationship can exist. To prolong interaction with the dead, whether they are saints or ancestors, Ghzawa women are known to induce lethargic, or prolonged, sleep at some point in their lives, which may last anywhere from an entire day to over a week's time. Lethargic sleep is characterized by slow breathing and lack of movement, and it can also prompt visionary dreams, even more so if the sleeper is at a saint's tomb. This relates to the mystic knowledge of Istikhara, connecting believer and God, or believer and saint (Gonzalez-Vazquez, 2014). According to Gonzalez-Vazquez (2014), "In Morocco, as in the whole of North Africa, *Istikhara* continues to be practiced" (p. 107).

Not all dreams, however, connect one with divinity, or even descendants of the Prophet. While not far away geographically, those of the Hamadsha brotherhood in Meknes distinguish good (or true) dreams from bad (or false) dreams, noting that false dreams are caused by Shitan, the devil, or demons, known as *jnun.* The characteristics and attributes of the *jnun* make them potentially dangerous, as their revenge for perceived infractions can bring physical and psychological problems to the living (Crapanzano, 1975). In addition, the beliefs surrounding *jnun* and their roles are quite complex, including the interactions and relationships that exist between humans and these spiritual beings. Their role in resolving conflict is just one example. While particular behaviors and rituals are performed to influence bringing on a good dream, neutral ones exist, but bad dreams happen, too, and can be troublesome for anyone. In these cases, the dreamer may consult a traditional teacher for help, or the dreamer may tell the bad dream to a rock in an attempt to neutralize the dream's effect upon the dreamer (Crapanzano, 1975).

Among Nahua in Huitzilan, Mexico, dreams have authority as well. Dreaming (*temicti*) is given "special status in Nahuat culture," as it is "a way of seeing the invisible world" (Taggart, 2012, p. 419). This non-ordinary way of seeing is of particular importance because it allows the dreamer to see beyond appearances, and, in particular, to perceive the envious dead, who may come after their living children and cause them to fall ill with "envy sickness" (p. 420).

These ideas sit well alongside the views of several other groups. For example, Indonesians such as the Toraja of the highlands of South Sulawesi assert that one's *bombo* (the soul or spirit one is born with) may on occasion temporarily detach from the body in dreams and completely detach at death. Upon completion of proper mortuary rites, people can then refer to that ancestral spirit as *nene'*. *Nene'* also refers those who have become grandparents or even great-grandparents. *Nene'* occasionally makes visits in dreams to deliver "blessings or misfortunes," as well as to "watch over their living descendants" (Hollan, 2014, p. 183). While the Toraja have extraordinary dream experiences, they are visited by the deceased, a topic of discussion in later chapters. As with other ethnic and cultural groups, there is a social relationship that continues even after one's body no longer exists.

Anthropologist Douglas Hollan (2014) writes that "many Toraja consider certain types of dreams to be prophetic" (p. 184). While Hollan spent time with the Toraja in the 1980s, a high-status elder in the community shared many prophetic-type dreams with him. The community elder attributed these dreams as foretelling his ability to survive approaching threats of various types. Further details will be discussed in chapter seven with dreams related to death.

The Asabano of the Papua New Guinea highlands at Duranmin in Sandaun Province are a small ethnolinguistic community. The semi-nomadic Asabano assert that dreams are real and highly regarded sources of information. For the Asabano, dreams offer so much. They may "represent the wanderings and adventures of one's disembodied soul" (Lohmann, 2000, p. 77), or they may be platforms for learning through interactions with various spirits, beings and the deceased. The conveyed information may come in words (auditory) or through images (visual). Roger Lohmann (2000), an anthropologist who spent about a year-and-a-half living with the Asabano before the time of the report, noted that "the use of dreams to communicate with powerful beings has not changed through the conversion to Baptist Christianity in the 1970s" (p. 77). Lohmann (2000) also noted that "dreams played a major role in the initial acceptance of Christianity" (p. 77). Such significant dreams, again, are commonplace. One community elder said God spoke to her and told how she flew to heaven in a dream. In the first dream, she saw fire, and it spoke to her about how "stubborn" people go to the fire. Then she saw an ocean, which told her that believers turn to birds, flying to heaven, while non-believers would drown when the ocean comes and covers the earth on "the last day" (p. 90). In a second dream, the elder noticed the changes to the earth and, while her impulse was to run, she instead "turned into a butterfly and flew up" (p. 90).

Comparable to Mowaljarlai's explanation of *yarri* and *burral*, the Asabano religious beliefs hold that every person has, in fact, not one, but two souls. There is a little soul, known as the *alomo kamalanedu*, and a big soul, known as the *alomo kamayadu*. Both big and little souls are important in life and death, so one is not valued above the other. In dreams, the big soul "goes around at night" while the little soul watches over the body. Dreams are what the big soul sees, and what the big soul sees will happen later.

The Mehinaku of Brazil stretch these concepts beyond a dyad, as their perspective incorporates three kinds of souls, which are referred to as the shadow soul, the sweat soul and the eye soul. Each soul has diverse properties and functions. The eye soul is most closely related to dreaming. One of its functions is to wander about while the community is asleep at night. A "dream is the individual's awareness of the nocturnal wanderings of his eye soul" (Gregor, 1981, p. 717). As highlighted earlier, during sleep, souls may interact with one another, even from other villages, and these events in the dream are regarded as true encounters. Equally noteworthy, the Mehinaku value dream recollections not only for their quality of foresight and predictive nature, but also because of their connection to community rituals, religious activities, health, well-being and fundamental way of life (Gregor, 1981).

These examples—the Ghzawa, the Toraja, the Asabano, and the Mehinaku—illustrate only a handful of realities belonging to the vast groups of people who live their lives without the dreaming-waking, asleep-awake dichotomy. While a distinction is made for dialogue, understanding, and researcher and investigator articulation, the predominantly Western view of "contrasting the *two* worlds" is not typically lived that way throughout much of the world.

Jung was introduced to the term "big vision" from the Elgonyi (Jung 1943/1966, p. 276) of Central-East Africa. These natives of the Elgon forests differentiated between the ordinary dreams and the big dreams experienced by the group's healers or leaders (Jung 1943/1966, p. 276). Arising from the collective unconscious, Jung believed that big, extraordinary or significant dreams "are often remembered for a lifetime" (1974, p. 76) and usually take place during critical phases of life (1948/1969, p. 555). For example, when someone has a disease, a healing shaman may seek "big" dream guidance to learn the cause and a cure (Laughlin & Rock, 2014). Along those lines, when a group or community is troubled with a great concern, or is in distress, significant dreams may offer direction. Thupten Ngodup's 1987 journey of becoming a medium (*kuten*) for Nechung and occupying the socio-political role of the State Oracle of Tibet was paved with portent dreams and visions. Some included dreams of the possessing diety and precognitive abilities at an early age, occurrences that have been common for a number of mediums (*kutens*). One time, Ngodup bled from the nose and mouth for two days, lost consciousness and had repeated visions of Nechung (Sidky, 2011). Big dreams can serve individuals, families and communities alike.

Beyond Five Senses

Extraordinary dreaming includes perceptions that occur outside of the five senses while asleep. Dreams in which one is clairvoyant, telepathic, precognitive, lucid, miraculously healed or shown details of a past life are some examples of extraordinary dreams. For clarification, it is necessary to define some of these terms. *Clairvoyance* is "receiving information from a distance, beyond the reach of the ordinary senses" (Radin, 1997, p.15). *Telepathy* can be understood as transmitting thoughts to another or knowing the thoughts of another (see Ullman, Krippner, & Vaughan, 2002), or "exchanging information between two minds" (Radin, 1997, p. 14). *Precognition* includes foreknowledge of an event and is sometimes called a premonition. *Lucidity* in a dream state takes place when "we are explicitly aware that we are dreaming" (LaBerge & Gackenbach, 2000). Extraordinary dreams may also be highly creative and the dreamer may be shown solutions to challenging problems (LaBerge, 2009). In contemporary Western societies, it is commonplace that, when one shares these types of dreams, they are not often believed or well received. After all, contemporary Westerners typically have been taught that these experiences are not real or rational, yet extraordinary dreams have been experienced across time and place. These episodes may startle or shake some people; however, extraordinary dream occurrences, especially precognitive (or premonition) dreams, have so much to offer humanity. They can prepare us for difficult times ahead and possibly prevent accidents, illnesses or disasters. For example, precognitive dreams about 9/11 and the Twin Tower attacks were shared; some reported these dreams to authorities, yet those dreamers were often laughed at. Instead of prompting action, they were dismissed. For those who want to understand more about premonitions, in general, *Premonitions in Daily Life* (2012) by Jeanne Van Bronkhorst is an entertaining, friendly read. Van Bronkhorst dedicates a section to learning to become more aware of premonitions in daily life, along with a section on techniques for "finding premonitions"—one of the four techniques is dreams.

Some precognitive or premonition dreams may repeat themselves, leaving the dreamer to ponder the meaning of the dream. I've known Rebecca, an adventurous Jewish woman in her forties, for a long time. She had such an experience and shared it a few times in our over two decades of friendship. With regard to her recurring dream, she told me the following:

> When I was seven or eight, I had a reoccurring dream. I do not remember much of the dream. I know that it was a little different each time, but the ending was always the same. I was in the middle of the desert sitting on cement steps with nothing else around but the desert. I was sitting on the steps and my leg was on the shoulder of a very large man.

It wasn't until Rebecca's adolescence that the dream made sense, while also leaving some big questions unanswered. She explained the dream's meaning:

> When I was sixteen, my parents sent me on a wilderness survival program, one of those tough love things for "bad kids." I was in Big Ben National Park in Texas, in the desert. I fell within my first few days there. They would not pull me out of the program to take me to see a doctor. I had to hike around for another couple weeks all day, every day. My ankles were the size of grapefruits. I was in a lot of pain. They told me I was a wimp and to quit whining. Finally after nearly three weeks, they brought me into base camp. It was just a trailer in the middle of the desert with some cement stairs leading up to the trailer door. There was nothing else around, just desert. There was not even a road. I sat on the cement steps with my leg on the shoulder of one of the workers while he wrapped my ankles in ace bandages. He was a very large man. This experience was just like my dream. The dream I had had about eight years prior. That really got me thinking. Here I was at a tough love wilderness program for bad kids at sixteen, I dreamt this around the age of eight…. Was I destined to be a bad kid?

To this day, Rebecca asks herself that question—was she destined to be sent away on that program … to be a bad kid? What might these types of dreams imply about destiny, self-determination, one's fate and Western concepts of time and space? Could this dream have helped to provide Rebecca a kind of mental and emotional preparation for what was to come? After all, this was a very difficult period of her life.

Stanley Krippner, Fariba Bogzaran, & André Percia de Carvahlo (2002) wrote a fascinating book titled *Extraordinary Dreams and How to Work with Them*. This little gem has been on my bookshelf for years and has become a valuable resource in much of my work. In this book, various types of extraordinary dreaming is categorized as it was experienced and reported across time and place. The authors remind us that we can work with our extraordinary dreams to further understand their meaning and integrate them into our lives.

Some of these particular types of extraordinary dreams obviously overlap, so they are not easily compartmentalized. In the Dream Laboratory of the Maimonides Medical Center in Brooklyn, years of experimental research into dream telepathy was conducted in the 1960s and 1970s. From those studies, certain telepathic dreams also appeared as precognitive (Ullman, Krippner, & Vaughan, 2002). A single dream may contain elements of telepathy, clairvoyance, or more. Bernard Gittelson reported a case by a woman on a farm in Oregon:

> At 3:40 a.m., the woman suddenly awoke by the sound of people screaming. The sound quickly vanished, but she felt a smoky, unpleasant taste in her mouth. She woke her husband, and together they scoured the farm but found nothing irregular. That evening on a television newscast, they heard about a plant explosion that started a huge chemical fire which killed six people. The explosion had occurred at 3:40 a.m. [as cited in Radin, 1997, p. 92].

While lucid dreaming may seem a little more straightforward, experienced lucid dreamer and author Robert Waggoner introduced me to the idea of levels of lucidity in his co-authored book with Caroline McCready, *Lucid Dreaming, Plain and Simple* (2015). I hadn't previously given the idea much thought, but reflecting on my own experiences, I agree that lucidity occurs on a kind of spectrum, if you will. Lucid dreaming is not a black-or-white, all-or-nothing affair. In the past, I had only labeled my dreams as lucid ones when I experienced a great amount of clarity. Now I look for varying grades of lucidity. For example, even if I am not lucid enough to control the dream, I may be lucid enough to recognize that some things are not as I would expect.

Not only can lucidity in dreams (and OBEs for that matter) be long- or short-lived, they can vary in clarity and awareness. In their book, Robert Waggoner and Caroline McCready highlight Ed Kellogg's Lucidity Continuum. Ed Kellogg has studied lucid dreaming for well over thirty years and is well published on the subject. Incredibly, he has recorded over 30,000 dreams. In short, Dr. Kellogg's lucidity continuum spans from pre-lucidity to a super lucid state. He explains more than six possibilities, some of which are pre-lucid, sub-lucid, semi-lucid, lucid, fully lucid and super-lucid. The full article can be found at www.improverse.com/ed-articles/kellogg. According to this scale, pre-lucidity is quite common when I am dreaming, as I often come across an unusual event or situation, yet find myself going right along with it. Without a consistent meditation practice and frequent *reality checks* (more on this in upcoming chapters), I find that fully lucid states to be rare. In my experience, achieving the mastery associated with ongoing fully lucid states requires a great amount of discipline in the waking state. Even with attention and skill development, the degree of lucidity can fluctuate in the same dream sequence. There is no guarantee that the level of lucidity at the start of a dream will maintain itself—lucidity can ascend or descend.

According to a Buddhist perspective, various levels and types of consciousness (gross and subtle) are acknowledged. The wholesome mental state of compassion, for example, can be cultivated during both waking and sleep states. By entering into "wholesome mental states prior to sleep and allow[ing] them to continue right into sleep without getting distracted, then sleep itself becomes wholesome" (Varela, 1997, p. 124).

Lucid dreaming can be applied in many ways and effect one's mood upon awakening. In a recent online study of lucid dreaming, Stumbrys and Erlacher (2016) found that out of their 528 respondents, 386 reported at least one lucid dream, and 263 of the participants had at least one lucid dream per month. These proportions highlighting the participant's lucid dreaming frequency are higher than what would be expected in the general population. In this study, which included a large quantity of experienced lucid dreamers, the most frequent application of lucid dreaming, especially from the younger participants was wish fulfillment; older participants (the more frequent/experienced of the lucid dreamers) applied lucid dream states to more serious applications, such as the inner work of solving waking-state problems, physical/mental healing and meditation (Stumbrys & Erlacher, 2016). Regardless of how one applied the lucid dream state, all participants had more positive or neutral moods upon waking. In general, lucid dreaming appears to be associated with a boost in positive mood for the dreamer.

During my time as a Faculty Associate at Arizona State University, I asked my students about whether they had lucid dreams. In classes of about forty to sixty students, there were typically a handful that claimed to dream with some degree of lucidity. Most students were in their twenties and used their lucidity in the dream state to fly, fight, race muscle cars, eat junk food or have sex with very attractive people. They appeared to be gleeful when sharing their experience to the class. No one shared a negative experience or negative impact as a result of lucid dreaming among those with whom I spoke. I asked the students if they had ever asked an important question in their dream, such as the meaning of life, their particular purpose in this lifetime, or if they had asked the dream to allow them to meet an important deceased figure. The students claimed to not consider such possibilities, but said they would consider a wider range of possibilities in the future.

Schmidt, Stumbrys, and Erlacher (2014) carried out a creative study in lucid dreams that highlighted dream characters. Participants in the study were asked to question a dream character they came across in the lucid dream and perform a number guessing experiment. In the end, it was concluded that some form of connection exists "between the dream ego and dream characters" (p. 148). Additionally, some lucid dreams may have precognitive elements. In *Man and his Symbols*, Jung (1964), wrote:

> Thus, dreams may sometimes announce certain situations long before they actually happen. This is not necessarily a miracle or a form of precognition. Many crises in our lives have a long unconscious history. We move toward them step-by-step, unaware of the dangers that are accumulating. But what we consciously fail to see is frequently perceived by our unconscious, which can pass the information on through our dreams [p. 36].

Illness and disease are often announced in dreams long before a physician's diagnosis. Dreamers who recall and pay attention to the messages by writing them down and interpreting them have reported catching signs and getting treatment early. Not only do dreams review the past, represent the present and predict the future, they also have the power to reflect important aspects of one's life situation during these times, according to many Alaskan Eskimo/Inuit shamans (Jones & Krippner, 2012, pp. 121–122).

The not-so-mysterious explanation above is just one of many possible explanations of what may be taking place in the psyche. Whether indicating good or bad fortune, the Navajo/Diné also believe that dreams hold a predictive element. As one's inner spirit travels during dreamtime, "messages from deities, deceased people, and animal spirits" are obtained (Jones & Krippner, 2012, p. 124). Animal symbols in dreams are given special consideration because they effect the interpretation of the dream (Dadosky, 1999). If dead livestock appear in a dream, the dream may be predictive of illness, while buzzards, hawks and snakes may warn of death (Jones & Krippner, 2012). Animal images may not only be considered significant but also healing. An animal can call to the dreamer and make itself known for spiritual purposes, or set the stage for what is to come. For Tedlock (2005) it was a turtle that presented itself. She later recognized it as a prophetic dream. For others, animals serve functions such as guidance in visions, dreams, and OBEs. Snakes, spiders, large felines and birds are also common for many people. In some cultures, animal images are more common in the dreams of children rather than those of adults. In

2016, *Dragon* began to make an appearance in my dreams. Animals that are currently extinct or "mythological" are reported in visions, dreams and OBEs.

Animal images in dreams may be considered for diagnostic purposes and in determining whether one has been possessed. For example, the snake or the monkey may be associated with *balas* (evil forces) that, according to some Muslim healers in India, suck blood from the patient (Kakar, 1982). To remove such forces from the patient's body and his dreams, special actions and rituals must be performed.

Societies across the globe vary in their interpretations, yet they hold similar beliefs in spirits, souls, life after death and anomalous capacities. Within the anthropological literature, analyses of anomalous perceptions, to include paranormal dreams, indicate that these episodes have transforming qualities (McClenon & Nooney, 2002). The same can be said for out-of-body dreams.

Out of Body?

Townsend (1997, as reported in Laughlin & Rock, 201, p. 246) wrote, "Dreaming and having visions are commonly conceived by polyphasic peoples as the separation of the 'soul' or spiritual body from the material body." While lucid dreams, out-of-body dreams and OBEs had, for me, appeared to be quite similar, in March of 2016 I had what would most likely be classified by some Western authors as an out-of-body *dream*. It was extraordinary, indeed, and a first for me. Prior to that, I was usually able to place my conscious nocturnal experiences in one of two categories: either a lucid dream or an OBE, although each of these states contained fluctuating levels of awareness/lucidity. This OBE dream experience brought me greater clarity and has helped me make distinctions between these experiences so I could more clearly voice the subtleties of the nocturnal experiences I have had over the past dozen years or so. Even with several experiences, categorization can be tricky. At the same time, in many of the world's cultures, these divisions are irrelevant and unproductive. No matter the category, these experiences impact the dreamer in one or more ways.

That night in March of 2016 began as most nights typically would for me. The difference that night was that I awoke in the middle of the dream from an extraordinary experience; one that, in the moment, had me frantically recording it in my dream journal, and, in the long-term, remembering that consciousness exists in all states. In my dream journal, I wrote:

> I dreamt that I went to try to sleep on the little rug on my hard kitchen floor to escape the noise or disturbance from the others. [It was as if my kitchen was connected to a bigger house, like my parents' home.] I recall my mother being there. As I prepared to get comfortable and snooze, I heard growling in my kitchen area, coming from under my sink. I realized at that point that I was dreaming and dreamt that I woke up (but I was still really dreaming). In the dream I realized I was dreaming so I was not scared and began to recall my waking life plans. It took a second or two, but then I recalled that I wanted to be taken to the sun and visit a person (but couldn't recall whom). At that moment in the dream I felt my body partially leave my body with some vibrations but was pulled back down, in my body. I dreamt that I awoke, but again was really still dreaming. I dreamt that I attempted an OBE and was immediately successful of *dreaming* an OBE. I noticed that things were dim and lacked clear sight and asked (a divine source) to take me to the sun, as this was the big goal. I moved upward toward the roof, but then woke up.

I was semi-lucid during the *out-of-body dream*, which is considered different from an OBE, according to some but not all authors and scholars. This experience impacted me by helping me to clarify distinctions and categories of phenomena that are in the literature on these subjects. Regardless of what one calls it, the OBE is an experience that is easily recalled, not only by me, but by many who share such reports.

In early 2016, I contacted the International Academy of Consciousness (IAC). Per my request, the IAC's associate office in California connected me with instructors and researchers at the IAC Research Campus in the peaceful and gorgeous Alentejo region of Portugal. Ever since I learned of this place, I had had a strong desire to visit and tour the site. A tour was eventually scheduled after some email communications, and by mid–June of that year, I traveled to Portugal for the planned tour and meeting. The IAC campus is a beautiful and very natural sixty-something-acre space with four laboratories; a large building for conferences and classes, which contained an impressive library collection; plus an additional smaller building that is suitable for housing visitors during their on-campus intensive courses and other self-study opportunities. Upon arrival, I was greeted by a woman named Angélica, with whom I had spoken extensively before the tour. We discussed our thoughts on the often-proposed distinction between projections or OBEs and dreaming. I mentioned earlier that while spectrums of lucidity have been presented by those that study and write about lucid dreaming, a similar scale appears in Luis Minero's 2012 book, *Demystifying the Out-of-Body Experience: A Practical Guide for Exploration and Personal Evolution*. Named the Extraphysical Lucidity Scale, a spectrum, from 0% lucidity to 100% lucidity, is broken up into six levels. To summarize this classification, 0% lucidity (Unconsciousness), is when one awakens and she has no recollection of dreaming. This "state" is quite common in contemporary Western society. For example, at least one, but maybe more, of my family members claims to never recall dreams. Moving forward, one might recall some of their dreams. By 20% lucidity (Semiconsciousness), one may dream in a way similar to what has been called lucid dreaming: "[t]his state is equivalent to having a lucid dream" (Minero, 2012, p. 100). By 40% lucidity (Doubt), however, the sleeping person may lack the clarity to figure out if she is dreaming or having a projection (aka an OBE). Visual images may appear cloudy or hazy, and determining whether we are having a projection or a dream may be difficult, as the experience may be a bit of both. At 60% lucidity (Certain), the sleeping person is sure that a lucid OBE, or projection, is taking place due to her "internal condition of lucidity" (p. 101). In this range of lucidity, one can "enjoy a decent level of rationality, association of ideas, comparison of intraphysical and extraphysical dimensions, and others" (p. 101). One is certain that an OBE is taking place, and the experience is not at all confused with the ordinary physical reality. When one obtains 80% lucidity (Self-consciousness), the level of awareness is so high that the person possesses "the same level of faculties and attributes" (Minero, 2012, p. 101) that she would during her typical day. This includes thinking, analyzing and decision making. At 100% lucidity (Superconsciousness), the mental capacities are beyond what one would normally experience: this is a special and distinct experience that is not covered in this book, so I will not pursue the superconscious experience. If you are interested in exploring this area further, concepts about "projections with the mentalsoma" can be found in Minero's book.

What is interesting about Minero's scale is that the lucid dream state is contained within it, at 20–39% lucidity. Instead of a separate experience, lucid dreaming is a particular level of awareness. Considering this scale superimposed over Kellogg's scale is quite interesting. Attempts to curiously pin-point a specific level or percentage, depending on the theorist, can be challenging. For example, in August 2016, I had the following dream that left me unable to specifically locate my experience on the spectrum:

> I'm at home and lying comfortably in my bed under my new white duvet. There is soft lighting in my bedroom so I assume it must be around sunrise. It's fairly quiet and peaceful, and I feel calm and relaxed. I hear somewhat muted tussling sounds on the side of my bed. So, I decide to learn the cause of this noise, and I roll over on my right side to take a look and see what is going on. I'm a little sur-

prised to discover a baby fox. Delighted, I pick up the baby fox and roll over with it onto my left side, still lying down. I'm happy to have this animal in my hands because I have always adored foxes. This baby fox seems comfortable in my presence. As I look at the baby fox and cuddle it, I have the realization that a fox would never be hanging out in my bedroom and with that realization I am fairly certain that I am dreaming. To confirm my suspicion, I conduct the usual "reality test"–I use my right hand to pull my left index finger. My finger stretches out and so I am now certain I am dreaming. At that moment, I consider what I want to do and where I may want to "travel" to, and I decide to pay a visit to someone I know by intentionally flying to that location. I announce to the dream where I want to be taken and I fly off toward the destination.

My dream continued to include my arrival at the desired location, my investigation of the location and my visit with the other person. Upon awakening and undergoing reflection, I felt disappointed that I did not spend my lucid minutes speaking to the baby fox and asking what it had to tell me. Instead, I quickly went about my daytime agenda. This made me realize the lack of consciousness I had even though I was aware, for the most part, that my body was asleep and that my mind was aware or dreaming lucidly. This lucidity with a simultaneous unconscious agenda left me feeling confused about where this experience could be situated within the above-described spectrum. Where such systems can be particularly helpful, however, is to offer ideas and guidance about how to engage our dreams moving forward.

In addition, dreams which are heavily influential and result in noticeable behavioral change, paradigm shift or transformation in the dreamer are also viewed as extraordinary (Bulkeley, 1995; Ebon, 1966; Knusdon & Minier, 1999; Krippner & Faith, 2001). While somewhat common across various populations, dreaming of the deceased, as well as premonition dreams, may also be considered extraordinary. Although some consider dreams of deceased people (of any nature) to be negative, even possibly predicting that something bad will happen, others do not find them disturbing and may view them as positive experiences. When it comes to "big" dreams, Hartmann (2008) found that these dreams tend to have one or two powerful central images and hold noticeable emotional power for the dreamer.

In September 2016, Daniel, a new father in his thirties, shared one of his meaningful experiences. While our conversation in a quaint Oakland café that sunny afternoon began with our ideas and histories surrounding dreaming with lucidity, it quickly moved into experiences that I refer to in this book as OBEs, which Daniel considered as astral travel. His experience was quite extraordinary on many levels, in particular because of the meaning it held for him. Since elementary school, Daniel had had many past experiences with lucid dreaming and OBEs, and he had become quite skilled in this area. When Daniel was in his late twenties, he had an experience that impacted him deeply. On one particular afternoon, he decided to utilize his ability with the purpose of understanding a long personal history of suffering and alienation. Daniel had a highly lucid experience that he described as something different from his past lucid dreams and more closely related to what has been described as an OBE.

Almost from the moment he laid down and relaxed his body, Daniel began flying high above the Midwestern Plains and noticed a depression in the earth. He decided to fly lower, moving toward that feature in the land. It was then that he saw stones and noticed that the stones "had an architecture to them, like ruins." He noticed an opening at each end, like doorways, when he saw what appeared to be "a group of Native American men on horseback and on foot." They were leading one figure through a doorway, but they did not follow. The men stopped and watched the lone figure walking away. Once Daniel returned to the physical waking state, he understood this to represent his being shown a past life, where he had been exiled from his community for transgressing a tribal law, or as a metaphorical scenario that helped him to visualize his feelings. Daniel stated, "Either that was me in a past life when I was booted out of this tribe, or that was just my subconscious's way of giving a form to the feelings I was having." Overall, this experience didn't change the way Daniel operated day-to-day, and it did not bring about a sudden transformational shift. As one of many profound and illuminating experiences in Daniel's life, he has been left with a mind open but skeptical, as well. The memory of this particular experience did not hold a privileged place in Daniel's consciousness, although the memory would return when he engaged in conversations about consciousness and his personal life history. Today, as Daniel prepares for fatherhood, the experience has been impactful in that he regards the baby girl coming into his family not as a blank slate, but instead as a being with a possible complex history—a beautiful quality, indeed.

Significant Dream Studies

Knudson and Minier (1999) acknowledge that the literature on significant dreams is expanding, yet they claim that, within this body of literature, minimal attention has been given to the strong impact these dreams have on the dreamer's life. When attention is placed on significant dreams, the spotlight seems to shine only on the dream's bizarre, rather than beautiful, qualities (Knudson, 2001). In addition, it is suggested that significant dreams should be regarded as illuminating and instructive instead of as simply representative of the dreamer's dominant concerns or emotions (Knudson, 2003). Some authors suggest that researchers look into how the dreamer's meaning-making processes are influenced by a significant dream (Knudson, Adame, & Finocan, 2006).

Kuiken and Sikora (1993) recruited 168 young adults and administered a questionnaire asking about the frequency of experienced dreams that influenced waking activities. Data analysis revealed three types of impactful dreams: anxiety dreams (nightmares), existential dreams, and transcendent dreams. The dreams were reported to carry intense effects and seemingly real imagery after the dreamers awoke. Kuiken and Sikora reported that impactful dreams seem real to the dreamer, have powerful or intense endings, are accompanied by distinctive body sensations and are not a rare occurrence.

Similarly, Kuiken, Lee, Eng, and Singh (2006) conducted a two-part study to explore the relationship between dreams and their immediate effects. Participants for the first part of the study (Study 1) included 145 undergraduates attending the University of Alberta in Canada. Participants were mostly female, and all were enrolled in an introduction to psychology course. Each received partial course credit for participating. Study 1 was a replication of previous research, which demonstrated that existential dreams facilitated self-perceptual depth. Study 1 also examined whether the effects of nightmares were comparable to their novel, emotion-guided mnemonic connections. In addition, the study explored transcendent dreams' reported spiritual effects. The 54-item Impactful Dreams Questionnaire (IDQ) and the Post Dream Questionnaire (PDQ) were used for Study 1. The researchers found that, unlike mundane dreams, transcendent dreams, or nightmares, existential dreams were linked with reports of self-perceptual depth. In addition, transcendent dreams were paired with reports of spiritual transformation, unlike mundane dreams, existential dreams, or nightmares (Kuiken, Lee, Eng, & Singh, 2006).

Participants for the second part of the study (Study 2) by Kuiken and colleagues (2006) included 52 primarily female undergraduates enrolled in an introductory psychology course from the University of Alberta in Canada who, again, received partial course credit for participation. Study 2 was designed to explore the "existential aspect of these dream-effects more fully" (Kuiken, et al., 2006, p. 267). The IDQ and the PDQ were again utilized. Study 2 findings for existential dreams replicated those of the first study. Kuiken and colleagues (2006) noted that "both existential and transcendent dreams moved the dreamer toward an unbounded sense of life in all things" (p. 258).

More recently, Carey (2010) interviewed twelve middle-aged (i.e., over fifty) female dreamworkers from the San Francisco Bay Area in California about their meaningful dreams. Carey defined dreamworkers as those who have been actively engaged in their dream lives for at least ten years. Meaningful dreams were defined as "dreams that significantly reorient a dreamer's internal life (that is, beliefs, values, perspectives), affect the dreamer's life path, and continue to be meaningful for the rest of the dreamer's life" (Carey, 2010, p. iii). Carey conducted in-depth (90- to 160-minute-long), semi-structured interviews that were thematically analyzed. Her results revealed that dreams positively influenced "psychological development, spirituality, career, female identity, interpersonal relationships, experience of synchronicity, worldview, and perception of dreams" (p. iii).

In the fall of 2015, I was strongly considering resigning from a convenient, yet unfulfilling, management position for a variety of reasons. I had not yet sought other employment, nor had I interviewed for a single future position, and I knew that resigning at that time would impact my life in a number of ways, both positively and negatively. That time was filled with hesitation and uncertainty. One night, I had a vivid dream that influenced my course of action. The dream began with me entering my apartment, which appeared as it usually does. The window blinds were open, and the space was filled with natural light. Two others were with me, but I didn't know exactly who they were, and their presences were not completely solidified. I wasn't concerned by their presence nor was I very attentive to them. As I walked through the door and took a few steps in, I noticed something shining on the floor—it was very tiny. I wondered if the object could be a piece of glass or glitter. I bent over to have a closer look, and then I realized that it wasn't an object or particle after all, but instead a small, pin-sized hole with bright white light shining through. I felt perplexed for a moment, and then I noticed there were other such holes in front of me on the hard wood floor, some of which were growing in diameter. More holes opened, all around my feet: some were only a centimeter, others were a couple of inches in diameter. As more holes manifested in various sizes, some growing larger, a soft yet bright white light shone through each hole. It seemed that this light shot straight up through the ceiling. I looked down again and could see into the apartment below me. Still feeling somewhat puzzled, I then realized that the ground could open up, and my companions and I might fall through. I calmly announced that we had to leave now and began to slowly walk backwards toward the door where I had initially entered. That was it—I woke up. About a week later, I wrote the resignation letter, and felt confident when handing it to my manager. It was after closing that metaphorical door that others opened.

Even after these waking life and dream events took place, I still felt unsettled, although to a minor degree. For the past few years, I had been attending a monthly dream group where the Ullman Method was used. The Ullman Method is used in dream groups and involves a six-step process to assist the dreamer toward greater insight and to encourage action based on the dream's message. Desiring an opportunity to gain clarity, I shared my dream with the group. Each group member's insights were personally profound, and it was then that I announced to the group that I had, in fact, resigned. I experienced increased confidence and certainty in the decision. I moved forward with a greater sense of courage and purpose. To this day, I can recall the vivid dream that assisted me in my decision.

Dreams of Practitioners of Traditional Ways

Dreaming can be thought of as a tool to generate authoritative knowledge on both individual and community levels. This is the case for shamans, priests and priestesses, and even for psychotherapists and physicians (with competence in dreamwork) who heal or help sick or injured members of their communities and who work with members of their communities to promote self-determination and solve social problems. Sidian Morning Star Jones (grandchild of Rolling Thunder) and Stanley Krippner (2012) wrote *The Voice of Rolling Thunder: A Medicine Man's Wisdom for Walking the Red Road*. This book gives voice to the incredible life of Rolling Thunder, and it includes a chapter titled Shamanic Dreamwork. It was there, in that chapter, that I came across the following ten questions used in the 1990s by Dr. Krippner and April Thompson (a student at the time) to understand early Native American models of dreaming:

1. What is the function of dreaming?
2. What motivates people to recall their dreams?
3. What is the source of dreams?
4. What is the language of dreams?

5. Are dream meanings universal?
6. How is one's life situation reflected in dreams?
7. What procedures are used to work with dreams?
8. What is the role of the dreamworker?
9. What role does dreamworking play in the culture?
10. How are visionary dreams viewed? (Jones & Krippner, 2012, p. 120)

After analyzing the information from sixteen different Native American tribes, a synthesis of the common elements of Native American dream models was created. Great similarities among the tribes' views were noted, although differences do exist. I condensed the results of Krippner and Thompson's synthesized model into several points.

According to the results, dreams function as power sources for tribal defense, healing and hunting. Because a unique form of knowledge and power can be gained, people are motivated to recall their dreams, which come from the spirit world in images and stories, therefore informing the dreamer's understanding of that reality. Dreams may be personal or universal, and context must be taken into account to understand the meaning. The past, present and future are reflected in dreams, which may help to solve problems, offer a warning or prompt action. When it comes to the important social function of working with dreams, one can share the dream, act it out or request consultation. Furthermore, it was found that "dreamworking is a valuable activity, because it provides beneficial knowledge and power to community members and especially to shamans, who often use dreams to diagnose illness or solve a society's problems" (p. 127). On one hand, while everyday mundane types of dreams might be only pertinent to the dreamer, visionary dreams, on the other hand, might be beneficial for the entire community, as these dreams contain power and knowledge related to distant or future events and former life experiences (Jones & Krippner, 2012).

With Dr. Krippner's permission, I decided to borrow these ten questions as a way to influence and inform my discussions with those practitioners of other religious or spiritual groups: a Lucumi practitioner, members of a local pagan congregation and a traditional practitioner of Native American tradition.

Lucumi

Lucumi embodies a rich spiritual tradition and is known by many names, but it is often misunderstood and underappreciated in the West. The following names for this tradition are fairly interchangeable: Santeria,

Regla de Ocha, La Regla de Lukumi or simply Lucumi/ Lukumi because its liturgical language, a Yoruban dialect, is also known as Lucumi. This religion developed as West African peoples and those of the Yoruba tradition were enslaved and forcibly transported to the Caribbean during the time of the Spanish Empire. Those enslaved took their native religious beliefs and practices with them; as time went on, the practices were blended with elements of Spanish culture, including Roman Catholicism. In essence, Lucumi mixes together influences from many ethnic peoples (African, Native Caribbean and European) with various religions (indigenous African, Catholicism and indigenous Caribbean). Some of these religions are monotheistic, while others are animistic.

During the spring, summer and fall seasons of 2016, I had the opportunity and privilege to discuss the role, purpose and meaning of dreaming with Eshu Alaiwo (the initiate name of a Lucumi practitioner currently living in Southern California). Born in New York, Eshi Alaiwo is of Puerto Rican and Cuban ethnicity. While initiated in 1969 and crowned to Elegba, she has been a spiritualist since the age of five. Elegba (also spelled Elegua, Elewa, Eleggua or Legba) is one of the Orishas, or deities. The Orishas have ownership over some human element or experience and are represented in nature. Each Orisha is represented by a number, a dance, a food and colors. Eshu Alaiwo began to really develop her skills and work as a spiritualist (*espiritista*) at the age of thirteen. Eshu Alaiwo has been served and supported by her dreams ever since she was a child. She had paid attention to her dreams and has noticed that they tended to come true most times. At the age of fifteen, she began to consistently write them down; through this process, she noticed messages, advice and warnings related to current and future events. Dreams also helped her to discover her many past lives. All of these experiences led to her decision to use dreams in the spiritual workshops she offered.

According to Eshu Alaiwo, Lucumi religious people have many dreams about Orishas, saints, ancestors and spiritual guides, who "appear in human form in a certain place that may or may not have meaning." In addition, Orishas, saints, ancestors and spiritual guides may "appear through people in our lives and have messages to share." Eshu Alaiwo gave an example—"If we dream with a person in our lives that is a Lucumi priest, the message may not be about the actual person, but the Orisha they are crowned to." For example, Eshu Alaiwo is crowned to Elegba— the Orisha that lives at the crossroads between the physical (human) and the spiritual (divine). Nothing can be done in this world without Elegba's permission—he opens doors between this world and the divine. He embodies the playfulness of children and is a child-like messenger. Since Elegba is also associated with the beginning and end of life, as well as consciousness and transformation, it seems fitting, in my opinion, that such a deep dreamer, like Eshu Alaiwo, would be crowned to this Orisha.

Eshu Alaiwo continued, "In other cases, we may dream with a specific ancestral spirit or spirit guide that have a message to share." At this point, I noticed how Eshu Alaiwo framed these experiences as dreaming "with" instead of dreaming "of" a spiritual guide. This reminded me of what has been referred to as *mutual dreaming* in some contemporary Western writings. It also prompted me to consider that people dream "with" their children-to-be, as well as the deceased, instead of dreaming "of" them. The linguistic frame of reference is significant, especially given the difference from a relational standpoint. Eshu Alaiwo commented on the reality of God and how we may be contacted through the Orishas and ancestors about how to live a better life. Eshu Alaiwo said that traditions all over the world teach something similar: that we are spirit energies, growing and learning to be better human beings. I added the idea that by dreaming "with" spirit energies that are either soon-to-enter human form or have recently left human form, the relationship evolves.

To gain additional information, dreams are analyzed and shared. Dreamers follow through with any messages and advice that is learned. Eshu Alaiwo continued, "Sometimes the dreams are just to let us know we are loved and guided, and a confirmation that God exists to us." Dreams can also be thoughts from long ago. When resting, "our subconscious mind opens up," she said. "The subconscious mind takes our thoughts from a long time ago and hides it. Then the thoughts pop up when we least expect: in our dreams, during a ceremony or in the midst of a feast for the Orishas. The subconscious lives in the opening at the back of our neck. We have a specific way of cleansing it to keep it clear."

With regard to spirit travel, I noticed a common theme among many groups when Eshu Alaiwo told me, "When we dream, our spirit can travel to past, present, or future." With regard to community ritual and ceremony, she said, "Usually before any feast or ceremony we dream about the Orishas. They usually tell us what they want or what could be missing. Ancestors also appear in our dreams for blessing or for what they want as an offering."

Dreams messages or advice are not always given in English or the first language of the dreamer. In addition to the English language, Spanish, Congo, Italian, French and other languages may be used in the dream. Since the dreamer may not understand the particular language used, Eshu

Alaiwo said that one might "have to do some research or look up some words."

As for Eshu Alaiwo's thoughts on those who report difficulty with dreaming, she believes that a problem may exist: "If a person has difficulties in dreaming or not dreaming, then there is either a physical problem or a spiritual one." If this happens, "you go to a professional priest or priestess who can help you clear the way to dreaming." I compared and contrasted this idea alongside my beliefs as a psychologist and hypnotherapist. Many people in my profession understand how dreams can mirror one's lived experience and can also be of service to one's personal growth, both mentally and emotionally; however, fewer seem to be aware of how dreaming can impact physical health and overall physical wellbeing.

Dream image and symbol interpretation can be quite the challenge and, when a dreamer's life situation is reflected in a dream, it is not always clear to them. "If you understand certain signs and symbols, and it applies to you," Eshu Alaiwo said, "then automatically you know off hand how to engage with your real life situation." To get to this place, dream recall is absolutely necessary. Logging or journaling each and every dream supports this process toward increasingly greater levels of understanding. Eshe Alaiwo provided some suggestions regarding procedures to follow when working with dreams. Thinking positively or holding a positive thought is the best way to begin, followed by prayers, she claimed. Just a couple of short, simple prayers are sufficient as long as they are to the point and "from your heart." She suggests placing a "clear glass of cool water by your bed side," as this is for clarity. "Don't go to bed angry," she states, instead, "smile and be thankful." Upon awakening, "write your dreams down, read it, and take it from there," she told me.

Many of the world's cultures have, or have had, dream workers: someone in the community responsible for assisting in dream interpretation for its members. Today, some people form groups and come together weekly or monthly to aid in the interpretation of the dreams of its members. Such groups exist here in California's Bay Area, and many other regions or cities across the United States. My experience and participation in such groups has been very positive, and I have come away with great insight and clarity around current situations or predicaments. I asked Eshu Alaiwo about the role of the dream worker among Lucumi religious people. She shared that "a Lucumi priest or priestess who sees a lot in dreams usually helps others to understand the meanings of what the dreamer is dreaming. They do this by helping to decipher, connect some dots and get a full, complete picture of the puzzle." Because dreaming is very important in Lucumi, "every Lucumi dreamer shares and talks about their dreams." She continued, "Dreams have a big influence on us and how we live our lives. It is very important for us to follow certain steps when working with our dreams, as far as in having a recipe on how to manage our life better." The power of dreams and how they can be protective and of great service to an individual, family and community was reflected in Eshu Alaiwo's words to me; she said, "Dreams prevent us from certain casualties that we may not be ready for. Dreams warn us of natural disasters. They also confirm our thoughts, decisions, and actions; as well as our doubts, insecurities and lack of faith." Here, I couldn't help but think about announcing dreams, the phenomena in which I have dedicated years toward investigation and understanding. While much of my attention has been on pleasant dreams, nightmares are no less worthy of attention. Eshu Alaiwo reminded that "there are messages in bad dreams as well." When it comes to dreaming in general, she said, "we just have to listen, pay attention, analyze, and follow through." "After all, we are just spirits on a continuous journey experiencing a human life," and dreaming can "help connect this continuous journey."

Whether one attends a dream group, seeks a professional dream worker or consults a religious person such as a priest or priestess for dream interpretation, it is really left to each person to decide "what we're going to do with the information we get from dreams." I really like how Eshu Alaiwo views dreaming as a way to weave together our (possibly endless) journey through time. If dreams have the power to connect memories of this life with all past (and possibly future) conscious experiences, there is no end to how deep we may be able to go when it comes to understanding ourselves, others and what it is to be alive. In fact, dreams and out-of-body experiences have shown some dreamers that consciousness is anything but ephemeral and instead there is no self, no other. The position of separation would be the grand illusion. Not only are we connected to past, present and future in the here and now, but we are connected to all that exists. Moving beyond a thought or idea, the lived experience of this connection has far-reaching potential for how we chose to live each day. This lived experience of connection is rare in modern times, as the chaos of an over-worked, overly plugged-in society has resulted in little depth or time for reflection. Hopefully, that will soon change.

Lastly, Eshu Alaiwo shared her thoughts on visionary dreams. No matter what is seen, gratitude is given for the insight. The dreamer is thankful, and at the same time, caution is given. As Eshu Alaiwo said, "Seeing something ahead of time is questioned depending on what one sees We also have tools to gain clarity and provide answers of what we see in our dreams. We can check in with our Orishas by throwing obi (coco) or cowrie shells. We can check in with our ancestors and spiritual guides by sitting and meditating, or praying and getting answers that way, or by throwing chamalongos (coco). Tools are active energies as a means of communication for getting answers."

The tools one uses vary from place to place, from culture to culture, yet they exist and are there to help. Runes, Tarot, coins, sticks, oil and water, obsidian mirrors, bones and even automatic writing, are just some examples of tools that have been used to assist people in understanding dreams, in addition to other aspects of life.

After a few months had passed, Eshu Alaiwo and I had additional conversations about the spiritual workshops she offers, including her reincarnation workshops. We understand that dreaming is a way of traveling and that, through this unique way of traveling, much can be discovered about the past, present and future of a person or place. From our conversations, I have come to learn Eshu Alaiwo has had hundreds of predictive dreams since she was a child. She sees many different places or locations in dreams only to find herself there weeks, months, or even years later. Similarly she has met various people in dreams before she is introduced to them in physical waking reality. On one memorable occasion, she dreamt about Barak Obama becoming the president—this dream took place about a year before he announced that he would run for presidency.

As our discussion continued, Eshu Alaiwo told me about one particular young woman she has worked with spiritually for many years. This young woman was curious about how her past may be affecting her today. Eshu Alaiwo told her about a dream that seemed to have some sort of connection. Eshu Alaiwo dreamt that she was in some country unknown to her. It was a very beautiful country with mountains, trees and a museum. As she walked through this lovely environment, she had the urge to enter a particular building. This building had been empty for years, and inside it was an extra room that was calling her attention. She felt a little fear inside her body, but decided to continue on and enter the room anyway. Once inside this abandoned space, she witnessed a woman being raped, killed, and then left there. In the dream, Eshu Alaiwo noticed that the dead woman in the dream had similar features to the young woman she was currently working with. When Eshu Alaiwo awoke, she did not completely understand the connection. Apparently, the images in the dream described a location in which the young woman had visited during a recent vacation she took in an attempt to "find herself." As the young woman and Eshu Alaiwo spoke and allowed all of this to unfold, it became much more clear that the young woman's past (life) was still affecting her today, as the dream reflected some of her present day conflicts. This is one example of how dreaming can offer assistance to another person, taking dreaming beyond an experience of the self.

PAGANISM

Having recently been introduced to Come As You Are (CAYA) Pagan Congregation, I decided to ask the group's members about their understanding of dreams and dreaming. CAYA Pagan Congregation is open to those whose spiritualties are polytheistic and earth-centered, thus, the approach to dreams and dreaming may differ from the beliefs of other groups covered so far in this book.

Three CAYA Pagan Congregation members agreed to share their ideas about dreaming with me in the fall of 2016. The following is a synthesis of their ideas. These members shared the belief that dreaming serves some purpose or role for dreamers. "Dreaming offers total freedom of the soul," said one group member. Dreams can act as a doorway to one's past, present, or future. They can be used for divination and guidance, and they can give insight to events that are currently taking place in one's life. Dreams can even warn or protect the dreamer.

Because dreams are meaningful and useful, people become motivated to recall them, noted the members. Even if few images or details from a dream are recalled upon awakening, the feelings associated with them may stick around throughout the day or longer. The members suggested that that experience alone might be motivational. For others, any bizarre imagery or subject matter recalled could be so fascinating that it prompts a quest for interpretation of dream symbols.

Dreams blossom out of imagination, emotions and a person's accumulated experiences. Unresolved issues surface in dreams, which may highlight "a need to explore more deeply into one's true feelings and what issues they need to work on in their life," according to one CAYA member. Another member suggested that sometimes outside influences bring on dreams, such as entities that have an agenda to enter a person's sleeping body and do what they will.

The interviewees agreed that dream language is symbolic and can sometimes be recurring. A dream's language includes images and symbols, scenes, colors, feelings and animal spirits. While the meaning of dreams and dream symbols is not necessarily universal, the language of dreams appears to be a universal truth going beyond human understanding: "it is in the crossroad of life and death." Similar to a deck of tarot cards, some of the meanings behind dreams can be the same for a variety of individuals; however, for the most part, the members said that dream meanings were not universal. Because of differing social contexts and other factors, the meaning of a dream may be unique: meant only for that particular person and no one else.

One's life situation may be reflected through dreams in various ways. As one CAYA Pagan Congregation member wrote, "The level of terror in the dream is directly related to the level of fear that one is holding in their life. Conversely, the level of joy is directly related to what one has in their life." Another noted, "Many people dream about what they did that day. Your mind has been on a task for eight or more hours a day and your brain can't get off it. This may be telling you to try something else, because your day and night is absorbed in one activity. Emotional upsets can provoke nightmares just as good days can invite pleasant dreams." Another continued, "I think that I process my feelings, including fears and hopes, about my life in my dreams. So although dreams are often surreal, they are dependent in some way on each person's own experience of life."

Shifting to discussing approaches to dream-work, the CAYA Pagan Congregation members were asked about procedures used to work with dreams. Depending on what one might be trying to accomplish, some rituals before going to sleep were suggested, such as spending time in prayer, using fragrant oils, or writing down an intention. Upon awakening, the members said to write the dream down in a notebook and hold a space for gratitude towards the messages received. Later, after weeks or even months, the dreamer should look back and see patterns within the dreams that have been recorded. In addition, lucid dreaming was mentioned as an effective approach to working with dreams due to the interplay and influence the dreamer can have in this state. According to the CAYA Pagan Congregation interviewees, the dream-worker holds the role of giving advice regarding techniques to support the dreamer along his/her path of personal investigation and understanding of the symbolism that arises. The dream-worker can assist with the interpretation of dreams, although this makes the most sense when the dreamer and dream-worker are both "deeply embedded in the same culture," thus, having "similar associations with particular images." The dream-worker should also be working with his or her own dreams so that nothing is projected onto the dreams of the dreamer seeking assistance. After all, "we all dream," one interviewee told me, so working with dreams is "something we can all relate to."

In general, visionary, prophetic, and premonitory dreams are not always welcomed, and working with them can be viewed as a type of magical practice. One interviewee said, "I think society has very mixed views on them.... Though, if it brings a message through, I'm sure most people would be interested in hearing about it." Another said, "In my religious community, and with most of my family, visionary dreams are considered gifts from the divine/divine self, and as such are treasured and taken seriously. I think doing dream-work the way I do might not be received in the same light in other groups...."

After having some time to reflect on the ideas and beliefs shared by the three interviewees of CAYA Pagan Congregation, I noticed similarities among these group members and other group members (as well as individuals) that I had previously interviewed. The most striking similarities included concepts like the soul's freedom during dreamtime; the dream as a doorway to past, present and future; and the divine gift of extraordinary dreams. Soon after, I had the good fortune to not only interview another practitioner, but to also learn a little from direct experience.

NATIVE AMERICAN TRADITIONAL WAYS

In late 2016, I asked a friend if her husband, Eli, would be open to being interviewed about dreaming. Eli identified himself as a practitioner of Native American tradition (contemporary Western scholars sometimes refer to such types of practitioners as shamans). Eli had taken on a leading role in healing ceremonies for the past nine to ten years. His current role began after spending over two decades as a participant and helper in Native American traditional ways. I hoped to learn about Eli's understanding of the role dreams play in one's life. So that I could understand the deeper context of the traditional way of life in relation to dreaming, Eli invited me to Arizona, where he resides with his wife and children, to attend one of the ceremonies he leads. About a month or so later, I traveled to Arizona and was taken to the Gila Bend Indian Reservation one night to sit up and pray with the group. The following morning, once the ceremony had concluded, Eli scheduled a time to talk with me about various aspects of dreaming, an experience deeply personal to him.

In December 2016 we met again to talk and share dreams. After answering a few questions about what led me to this work, I shared with Eli a recent dream—one I had dreamt just a few days after the ceremony in Arizona. It involved a tall, thin tornado, among other things. I had already gained much insight into this dream after having shared it with members of a dream group I attend each month. However, on this day, I learned of another aspect of tornados: they may be viewed as broken rings, meaning that something is out of place, out of order. This interpretation made sense given a challenging situation I was dealing with at that time, and so, that is how my interview with Eli began:

> That's the tricky part about dreams and everything, ... My personal experience is trying to decipher what they are and how they are coming. Like with my own, my basic things I look for, before I get all mystical, I look at the features of what it is, and how does it function, how does it move, what does it do, does it get bigger? For example, what is it like to be inside that tornado? What are the features of a tornado? Tornados are multiple broken rings and, taken at a big level, they are going to tear things apart and mess things up. In the Midwest, they take houses out of the ground.
>
> I've seen one time in a ceremony, where two tornados came in, little ones, about yay big. In the ceremony that was being conducted and the person that they were being prayed for, the light was like that, and all of a sudden all of nature started reacting. The Wind started pushing from the West and then.... They have stories about direction in which the lightning comes and what they represent.... One of the stories is lightning coming from the East, it's not a friendly lightning. There is male and female lightning, they have roads and paths, like freeways in the sky.... So [in the ceremony], that lightning came in, the wind's blowing, the rains starts, everything is shaking, and those two tornados are inside that ceremony and one of our elders is given cedar to pray. The minute he started praying, man, it was like, we all saw it, I was more touched, because I was thinking like, wow, my uncle is something really special. But it was like God itself said, "shhhh, I'm praying for my family, I'm praying for one of my children" and everything stopped! And that person that was going through that was going through a lot of issues, mental issues and stuff. Sickness comes in all different ways. People think, oh, he has cancer, but what about all the emotions tied to that and everything else connected to that physical being, maybe even thoughts about suicide? That's how they were addressing this thing at the time. It's like an identity. What are we talking about, what are we talking to?

At this point, we reconnected this experience to my tornado dream, and discussed it a little more.

I inquired further about the function of dreams in Native American tradition, and Eli told me about how we dream every day, or every night, but we can only remember so many things; we also talked about how some dreams involve specifics and are so detailed that they can be clearly recalled. Eli shared another dream with me, one he had eight years ago when he began to take on a leading role in ceremonies:

> I had this one dream, and in this particular dream, I was dreaming of having to conduct a ceremony with one man who was dealing with leukemia. He was doing some cancer therapy, but basically he was doing more natural things and didn't

want to go through chemotherapy or any of that kind of stuff. In that dream, there was a silhouette of these animals in jade, a really beautiful jade, and they were facing towards the east. Then they [in the dream] gave me a certain design that I was supposed to design in that ceremony, and I did it. And then they told me that I was supposed to basically feed this man a certain amount of medicine [among other instructions intentionally kept private]—they gave me all the directions to do it, and so I sat on it when I woke up. I really thought about this and all the details. I was given all the specific instructions—it was pretty intense, all the details in that dream. But anyway, the reason I'm leaving out all the details is because it is kind of personal, and I always say, a lot of these times for what we do, and once we start putting a price on it all the magic is gone, so we have to respect it and how it works. It's nature itself!

At this point in the conversation, Eli cautioned against following mystical interpretations of dreams over something more natural. He suggested that it was best to look at nature first:

With nature you can't lie, she doesn't negotiate for nobody. It is what it is. So it connects us all. It feels real, you know, because I can feel it ... water, fire. So in that dream, I did exactly what I was supposed to do, and, I even told the patient what I had to do.... I have to do this and this and this because I that was the way they instructed me. So be it. What we didn't realize is that a meteor shower hit us that night, and inside those coals there was a certain design, one I still use to this day when I have to run something intense. For that meteor to happen that night like that and for that man to get well, it really confirmed for me, you know, whatever's out there ... and that man is still alive. So that was my first experience and that was pretty intense. I was new to this. Now where am I?

Eli and I talked about the relationship between spirituality and ego, and how to remain humble. Events where incredible healing takes place can boost one's ego, but Eli preferred to view incredible events as stupid luck: "whatever I did last night was dumb luck," he said. Such an approach offers a way to protect against titles and the abuse of spiritual information. These early life-changing experiences also confirmed to Eli that natural forces are powerful and are not forces to play around with; for whatever reason, we have been given valuable information through dream, and we are not to abuse it. The teachings and lessons should be respected.

After speaking about the impact these earlier experiences had upon him, Eli then told me about his beloved mother, and proclaimed to be a "mama's boy." Eli's mother was Catholic, from Mexico, and had died eighteen years ago. During one of his travels a few years ago, he had an extraordinary dream that involved her. He recalled the dream, which he really enjoyed:

In the dream, I'm going through a village (a typical Mexican village, pueblo style, with adobe style houses and dirt roads) and there's a church in an L-shape [shaped like the letter L]. So I'm walking alongside my mother, and me and my mom decide to go inside the church. We were sitting on the first bench because there was no room, just stairs, so I got to sit on the top stair and my mom sat between my legs. There's all kinds of Bishops and an entire hierarchy, the whole enchilada. I just remember the big hats and red outfits, and the white outfits, you know. I know I'm dreaming, I know where I'm at, I realize I'm dreaming but I don't even care where I'm at because I was so happy that I was able to hug my mom, and I can smell her. I can literally smell her.

Eli had a sense of emotion in his voice when relating this dream about his mother. He continued:

I thought, you know, wow, this is great! I'm looking around, all of a sudden these people are singing, they're singing these church songs. Out of nowhere, my mom starts singing but she sang at this high pitch, this real pitch that wasn't a song. I couldn't even mimic it—it was almost like the sound that an eagle can make with that high pitch, like a really high frequency. But when that frequency came out, it spiraled. I was seeing the frequency spiral like that, then it turned like this, then it went like that.

Eli used his hands to show the direction of the spiraling movements. He added:

It was almost like a whirlwind, but it didn't have that whirlwind effect. It was just like a spiral effect that continues to keep on growing, which, basically, we call a Quiquitzli (the spiral found on a conch shell trumpet) which is my mom's name, the conception of life that is a beginning with no end. And I'm sitting there, and there's this old man, and all of a sudden everything gets quiet and the singing stops. They turn around and look at us, and I'm just sitting there. Then this old man goes, "Is that your aunt?" I go, "No, that's my mom." He asks me, "Do you know how to sing like that?" I kind of got so quiet, and I didn't answer him. This man (one of the participants inside this church) continues to tell me, "Well, I came here for all these men, all these men that are supposed to be men of prayer and all these things. And through that sound … your mom just healed me!" Then I woke up.

I commented on the power of such an experience, that it's as if the entire universe were there in that dream. Eli continued:

So that's just the dream, but now what did it mean? Okay, so later I'm conducting a ceremony again. Sometimes I conduct a ceremony for two nights—I go straight through. I'm in Colombia, it's my second night, and my voice goes out. I couldn't sing. I couldn't sing the songs that you heard me sing [referring to my time with him in Arizona], and then I was stuck. I was already getting sick, catching a cough and as I started my voice got worse and worse and worse. I sat there and thought, what is this? The man that I was running that ceremony for was someone's father who was addicted to drugs. I'm thinking, I've got to go through it, keep on going. Once I start a ceremony, I've got to keep going, there's no way I can say let's do it tomorrow. I can't stop, I've got to finish. So I'm going through it and I then I find this sound, this third sound, not an aggressive sound or a pitiful sound, but this frequency in the middle, one that everyone can respond to. That's where I found my voice at, it was a very low sound, and I was able to pull out that one sound and go through the whole ceremony. I just used that one sound. Whatever that frequency was, however that frequency worked … that old man is sober to this day. That was someone's father and that man is still sober to this very day.

I commented to Eli how his dreams appeared to be directly connected to the physical waking state in a very meaningful way, such as inducing healing, and how the traditional way of life supports that connection. Eli suggested that answers are shown in dreams by those that are there to help us. Different traditions have different names for these helpers, whether they are angels, spirits, ancestors, God or what have you. When one is dreaming, they may be shown what is needed to heal. The dreamer is given a recipe, if you will, for how to cure a sick person, or assist them in improving their condition. The medicine is truly natural, as it is an element of nature, such as a particular plant. Eli added, "You ask yourself, is there life and death? Is there really? Why do they call it 'everlasting life?' Maybe this is just a pit stop. I always tell people I'm looking forward to it because there's a lot of people crossed over I want to visit." In addition to relatives, he named particular artists, and we laughed.

In reference to the dream he related and its link with the ceremony, Eli said:

We've become tone-based people. We've lost it due to the way we are living. There are certain frequencies that we all tap into, that we all understand, that nature responds to, and that connect us all. What was I to do then [in the dream]: panic, say I can't sing, stop? No, I had to keep going through, stay, understand it and find that frequency. I already knew the outcome from my mom [in the dream]—she already knew it. I had to keep on, walk through it, keep going through it. I understood that if I could stay and understand it, I could possibly have that same outcome [referring to healing the man in the physical realm as he was healed in the dream]. I knew they were going to come in and help me, as long as I put in the effort to keep going forward. That's one thing … never surrender. Whatever it is, whatever's out there, whatever you want to call it, go forward at all means, never choose to surrender.

Our discussion reminded Eli of another experience, one he found to be funny. This particular one involved sleep paralysis, and how what takes place in one state (whether the sleep state or the physical waking state) does affect the other state. Eli recalled the following:

I came home one night, sitting at the house, and I go to bed. Do you ever have those dreams where you just cannot move? In my dream I was stuck, and it felt like it was forever, but it might have been only five minutes. I was feeling pissed off because I couldn't move. There were two little young ladies, about the age of my daughters, but they weren't my daughters, and there was this "thing," or whatever you want to call it. A "thing" I'll call it—it was not good or healthy … something that you could call evil, and I couldn't get to my box to where my instruments are at, you know, so I could not get what I needed to defend myself. At that moment, I'm stuck. I can't move, my legs won't move, my arms don't move and that thing is coming. And those little girls are like they need me. And I'm making all kinds of noise and racket in the bed, and my wife is tapping me on my shoulder telling me to calm down because she didn't know what was going on. So finally, I just said "forget it man"—I'm going to swing my legs off, and I'm going to drag myself to my instruments, and I'm going to grab my instruments that I need. So I go for it and I swing those legs and I fall off the bed, smack my head on the side of my table. I fall off my bed and hit my knee, smack myself. I'm going for it! I propelled myself off of the bed. I hit myself, I jump back up on the bed. My wife is still tapping me, consoling me. Come morning time, my wife tells me that she had a bad dream last night, that I was making all kinds of noise and everything … a nightmare and that there was some lady over here.…

As he was dealing with entities in the dream world, his wife assumed something else was going on—we got a good laugh.

One a more serious note, Eli told me about seemingly dual, or overlapping realities that support each other. For example, as an experienced traditional practitioner, Eli knows when he is currently in the dream state. He also knows what tools he needs to go get in the physical world (or dream world) to solve problems, such as dispelling negative energies. He knows what instruments he was given to defend himself and what he needs to get to do his work in either state. Whether he came out of that experience of paralysis into the dream body or into the physical body that night, the work would still continue. The result would be similar, as it is perceived to be the same space, so whether the dream instruments or the physical instruments are used, the space is cleared, or cleaned, in all realities. I asked about eyes and multi-dimensional sight. He claimed to have sight in both worlds at any given time, an ability that I have heard exists with other traditional practitioners, regardless of origin. "But it doesn't always work both ways.… Sometimes these eyes (pointing to his physical eyes) are worthless," Eli stated.

To emphasize his point, and with regard to the intermediary space between wakefulness and sleep, Eli shared another much more recent experience:

Probably the last one I had that was pretty interesting, I came home off a trip and I was just lying in bed, and right before you wake up, you know that part right before you wake up, I'm literally again inside a ceremony doing what I do, I'm using tobacco to pray for somebody. And in that part where I know that I'm in that ceremony, but I'm also waking up, I'm literally talking out loud, and some of the words that I remember were like, "and whenever they say those words to that individual, however they're going to say it, and people are having that negative thought, that in motion and before the words get to that individual that it turns into something very positive." So like, in the dream, I can see the words coming out negatively, but then they tumble in the middle, and as it's coming, that person is actually smiling.

I ask for clarification, and that he repeat this part of the process he experienced in the dream. Eli added:

So when the curse comes out, it's going to tumble, and it turns into something very positive so that it cannot have a negative effect. But, I'm waking up in the morning, and I said this out loud before my eyes opened and my wife is sitting next to me, listening to me. I have never had that happen to me! I knew that I was in the final stages of this dream, but I didn't know that I was verbally saying it out loud for someone else to hear me. I thought I was in the dream, but I heard myself saying it. Both worlds were together, they became one.

Since traditional practitioners are often asked to speak on behalf of others and pray for people, they may experience themselves behaving in ways that shed light on the sick person's ailment. In this case, Eli understood that the person he was praying for absorbed a lot of negativity, negative words (curses) and emotional abuse. Through the dream, not only did he see this, but saw the transformation that came in service of healing the sick man. When traditional practitioners speak on behalf of someone, they speak honestly, and they do not lie on one's behalf. Who are they speaking to? God, creator, the spirit, the elements? Traditional ways follow nature itself, not necessarily human beings, and practitioners can get information through the plants.

At this point in the conversation, we reflected on the ceremony that Eli ran in which I was a participant, as it related to this story. Eli spoke about learning to wait, learning to go along, and he referred to the gifts brought on by the plants used. According to Eli, the traditional medicine used during ceremonies can be helpful for this purpose. It remains in a person forever. It's basic things we use every day, and it connects us all. When one is ready for healing, it can happen, but sometimes a person is not ready, and there is no one who can prevent a "train wreck" from coming. Sometimes, one must go through it, no matter how painful. Eli said, "We can trust it, trust the plants. Everything we need is right here. The darkness, it can be sneaky, and can convince us otherwise. …When it comes to bad habits, substance abuse, negative relationships, one can easily return to it when the feeling is forgotten." Eli said. "Some will wake up [referring to living consciously] and some will stay asleep, sometimes for their entire life."

I wondered how one's experience in a dream state might bleed over into the physical senses upon waking up in the body. Dimethyltryptamine (DMT), the active ingredient found in ayahuasca, can aid in dreaming while awake, but that's not the only plant-based helper. Eli recalled a time when he came out of a ceremony and was still feeling the medicine, as it was powerful, and suddenly, a participant asked him "when does this stuff wear off?" Such a question was surprising and unexpected because the individual came to the ceremony seeking a spiritual experience. Why would one want a medicine that awakens one's spirit to "wear off?" The goal is to be consciously awake all of the time, even while one's body sleeps. Eli said, "I'm awake right now, and I'm grateful for these plants. I see things all day long. It's just that frequency. It's a matter of staying awake. Don't fall asleep [referring to going back to old habits], stay awake so you can keep on growing. This is a way of life."

That "frequency" Eli spoke of reminded me of the vibrational state some attain right before an OBE. Whether with the help of peyote (a cactus, that when ingested in ceremony, mediates the spirit world and the world of people) or the natural elements (earth, air, fire, water), the traditional way of life supports one's spiritual growth and can bring one toward increased conscious awareness each day and night. Some ceremonies last a night, and some can last an entire week. Some involve medicine while others work solely with the elements. All are done to promote growth and greater levels of consciousness.

Simply being in nature itself can assist us in our day-to-day lives. Eli spoke about nature as a space for rejuvenation: "We can thank nature by giving back—we can acknowledge it and give it anything we want." With regard to dreaming consciously and the traditional way of life, he named the sacredness of these natural ways of living. The contemporary western experiential divisions and compartmentalizations that I came to him with do not exist for many traditional peoples. Somewhere along the way, through colonization and being made to live in a very different, unnatural way, basic knowledge of the elements was lost for Native people. Eli concluded, "We lost the sense to communicate with all this: that's where our main source was." Eli shared how he felt fortunate to have been brought up with elderly people that encouraged him to move forward instead of resisting, and who helped him understand his early spiritual experiences, whether they took place in the dream state or the physical one.

After I finished writing the last few paragraphs above, I went to bed and awoke in the morning recalling a dream: I am with my father. We are picking up someone we know in a SUV or minivan ... waiting for her to return to us. She runs up, drops off a couple of her things, and then runs back into the school's campus to get the rest. Before she runs off, she hands us a couple of thick, pure tobacco "cigarettes"—hand-rolled in corn husks. I begin smoking one as I wait in the passenger seat with my dad in the driver's seat. As I continue to smoke, I say something about how I am looking forward to what the woman is returning with (which is peyote). As my father and I sit alone waiting, I begin to cry and can't hold back the tears. The tears run down my face and this gets my dad's attention. I say to him, "we are all so lost." I'm not sure if he understands me. I connect my statement to the way we are living and how no one seems to be connected to anything that matters anymore. In the dream, I'm thinking about how plants can help us reconnect to mother earth as I find myself in my bed, slowly waking up.

CHAPTER THREE

Dreams
During Pregnancy

Similarities and differences are found in the dreams of pregnant woman and expectant men. Some are quite common, while others report extraordinary dreams to include the child-to-be. These dreams will be discussed in detail.

Not all dreams of labor and birth indicate pregnancy. For example, On August 19, 2011, my dream felt as if it went on for hours and hours. I was pregnant throughout the dream and approaching the birth. Near the end of the dream labor began, as greater levels of intense sensations were felt, but no pain. In the dream, I anticipated an increase in pain and went into a preparatory mode. I wanted to go deeper into myself, to be in a relaxed hypnotic state in a dark room. There were three others present, but their identities were not clear. I don't think I was in a hospital and may have been at home. A midwife was present along with some other knowledgeable figure, so I felt safe in the dream. I awoke suddenly and desired to return to this dream, but I couldn't fall back asleep.

These types of dreams appear to be common among those "birthing" a big project. In my case, and those of my classmates, it was a dissertation. I was definitely not pregnant.

Pregnancy encompasses simultaneous changes in physiology, psychology, body image and social status (Leifer, 1980); indeed, it is a unique period of womanhood. Sleep patterns become altered (Schwiger, 1972), and dreams typically diverge from the usual pattern, becoming extremely vivid and extraordinary (Evans & Aronson, 2005). Research suggests that expectant mothers are able to recall their dreams more easily and in greater detail than prior to pregnancy (Maybruck, 1986), and that primiparae—women giving birth for the first time—may be more likely to report dreams (Sered & Abramovitch, 1992).

One Polish woman in her thirties had a series of dreams. While living in the United Kingdom, pregnant with her first child, she told me of vivid recurring dreams. These dreams took place around the fifth month of gestation, when the baby just started kicking. On February 9, 2016, she told me:

> My baby somehow came out through my stomach and I would tell it "you're too early—you need to go back," and the baby went back as if nothing happened. In the last dream, the baby felt very real, I even showed it to my partner but it was too early. My stomach swallowed it back and the hole closed afterwards as it does in films when someone is immortal…. Hehehe.

The woman continued, and told me that "the baby was so real, and almost natural size." In the past, before she was pregnant, she recalled that her frequent dreams about babies contained imagery of small, even pea-sized babies. She joked that since these dreams took place during an actual pregnancy, then the dream baby must be life size. She told me that these dreams helped her to feel more connected to the growing baby inside of her.

Theories put forward to explain why dreams during pregnancy are different mention that hormonal changes, possible lifestyle changes and irregular sleep patterns account for the particular nature of these types of dreams (Maybruck, 1989). Dagan, Lapidot and Eisenstein (2001) proposed that "the pregnant woman processes what she is undergoing, emotionally and cognitively, through different channels—one of which is dreaming" (p. 19). Well over a decade ago, Krippner and colleagues (2002) synthesized the extant pregnancy dream literature, which contained a number of studies. They revealed that when a woman is pregnant, the content of her dreams reflects striking changes from that of her dreams before pregnancy. Recent research supports this notion—pregnant women's dreams do, in fact, reflect changes of the transition toward motherhood (Coo, Milgrom, & Trinder, 2014). However, no single theory exists to explain some dreams' unusual manifest content, which typically consist of images of ripe fruit, amphibians, fish or small, furry animals (Knaan-Kostman, 2006; Maybruck, 1986, 1989). One young woman, nearly seven months pregnant with her first child, recently told me that when she dreamed about her baby girl-to-be, the baby appeared as a shark. This shark-baby dream occurred frequently and left her puzzled.

Well-known American psychologist Stanley Krippner and his colleagues conducted one of the first studies on pregnancy dreams in the early part of the 1970s. Thirty-three dreams, from eleven pregnant subjects (three dreams each) were analyzed in this study (Krippner, Posner, Pomerance, & Fischer, 1974). The findings were published in the *Journal of the*

American Society for Psychosomatic Dentistry and Medicine under the title, "An Investigation of Dream Content during Pregnancy." These investigators noted that "the dreams suggest an attempt by the subject to maintain a tranquil environment—an attempt which is not always successful" (p. 120). When compared to the normative sample, the pregnant women dreamed more about physical activity and settings. In addition, the investigators found that the content of the pregnant subjects' dreams contained more anger, again, compared with the normative sample. The researchers (1974) concluded, by stating that "the content analysis of these dreams indicates that the process of pregnancy is a healthy one for the sample studied" (p. 120).

Fetal Sex Predictions

Some pregnancy dreams contain a predictive element, notably regarding the sex of the developing fetus. A variety of beliefs as well as methods and folkloric practices surround this element of pregnancy. Folkloric practices include but are not limited to the way a woman carries the pregnancy, or using devices that are similar to a pendulum suspended over the woman's body to divine the sex of the fetus. One practice is to tie a string to the woman's wedding ring, which a friend or family member holds above the pregnant woman's abdomen, using the device as one would a pendulum. This is a way of determining the sex of the baby-to-be. My mother told me a story about when she was pregnant with me or my sister—she couldn't recall which. She said, "Well, in my day, it was commonplace for a pregnant woman to lie down on her back with another person there to hold the wedding ring from a string, in which it was tied to, above the pregnant woman. It could spin in a circle or back and forth. This would tell you whether it was a boy or girl." My mother couldn't recall what the circular spinning of the ring versus it moving in a line meant. One movement indicates a boy and the other, a girl. "It was too long ago," she told me.

Dreams are another avenue through which a pregnant woman may discover the sex of the child she is carrying, as the following study demonstrated. Perry, DiPietro and Costigan (1999) recruited 104 women from a major university hospital in Baltimore: the women were eighteen-weeks pregnant or more with singleton pregnancies, and they did not know the sex of their fetuses. Over half of the participants identified as black (57%) and the remaining participants identified as white (37%) or other (6%). The mean maternal age was 27.3 years. The researchers administered questionnaires to explore fetal sex perceptions and the basis for those perceptions. The results of this study showed that fetal sex predictions were poor in general: yet, among those with more than twelve years of education, 71% correctly predicted fetal sex, while only 43% of those with less education made correct predictions. The group with more education, especially those with four-year college degrees, tended to be older. In addition, correct predictions were found among those who made forecasts based on psychological criteria, such as a dream or feelings, as opposed to those utilizing folkloric methods. Eight highly educated participants made fetal sex forecasts from a dream, and all were correct in their prediction. Perry and colleagues (1999) stated, "We are at a loss to explain an education-based difference for a subject that is not directly related to educational attainment" (p. 176). They speculated that women in the less educated group (not beyond high school) give the issue "the same degree of evaluation" as the more highly educated group (Perry et al., 1999, p. 176), and seemed more likely to allow their child sex preference to influence their predictions. Perry and colleagues (1999) suggested that maternal perceptions of fetal sex may contribute to mother-child bonding.

Regardless of whether these predictions are accurate, women across time and place dream of the sex of the baby throughout their pregnancies, and, at times, prior to conception. These dreams leave many women with a sense of acknowledgment and conviction. One thirty-three-year-old woman, acknowledging her inner knowing, wrote that "in previous pregnancies I have always dreamt about the gender of my kids and the dreams were always correct."

Resolving Issues Related to the Pregnancy

When a woman is pregnant, her dreams may represent a variety of internal or unresolved psychological issues, such as conflict about pregnancy or becoming a mother (Winget & Kapp, 1972). During her fifth month, one thirty-eight-year-old woman from my study reported that her dream baby "was born with missing limbs, eyes, always with some type of horrific deformity caused by my personal choices ... what I ate, drank, or thought." Might such imagery be helpful in some way? Winget and Kapp's (1972) classic study was designed to investigate the relationship between dream content during pregnancy and duration of childbirth. They examined the dreams of seventy women, ages fifteen to twenty-six, in the third trimester of their first pregnancy. The participants were recruited from prenatal clinics, were healthy and were of lower-to-lower-middle class. Of the participants 75% were black and 67% were unmarried. The researchers assigned participants to one of three groups: Group 1 contained thirty-one women who delivered in less than ten hours; Group 2 also contained thirty-one women who delivered in ten to twenty hours; Group 3 contained the eight women whose labor lasted longer than twenty hours, which was considered to be prolonged. Winget and Kapp (1972) found that "pregnant women in whom anxiety and threat themes are missing from their dreams are more likely to undergo prolonged labor due to inefficient uterine action than their counterparts whose dreams contain anxiety and threat" (p. 317). Interestingly, those women with the shortest labors (Group 1–under ten hours) had dreams which contained high frequencies of anxiety and threat. Winget and Kapp (1972) interpreted their findings to mean that dreaming functions as an adaptive mechanism; in this case, as a coping mechanism of pregnancy.

In her dissertation, Knaan-Kostman (2006) analyzed the content of the dream diaries and monologues of forty-two pregnant women, aged twenty-one to forty-three, throughout their early, middle and late gestation, to explore dreams as an avenue for working through conflict, since pregnancy is thought of as a time of transition. One aspect of the study utilized the Core Conflictual Relational Theme (CCRT) method. The CCRT is a list of the most frequent, intense and pervasive patterns of a wish, a response from others and a response of self, and it is used to measure and depict patterns in one's relationships. Two judges rated the frequency of these three relational episodes and found there to be patterns indicating mildly increased aggressive themes.

Other researchers have tried to understand different psychological issues for new mothers. Kron and Brosh (2003) designed a study to investigate whether the dreams of pregnant women could help identify the early signs of postpartum depression (PPD). The researchers retrospectively examined "differences in the dreams of pregnant women who later develop PPD and those of women who do not" (p. 72). One hundred and sixty-six primiparae participated in this two-stage study during their last trimester of pregnancy (Stage 1) and again at six- to ten-weeks postpartum (Stage 2). The Edinburgh Postnatal Depression Scale (EPDS), which is used for determining risk for perinatal depression, was used during Stage 2 to affirm or deny the occurrence of PPD. Women with PPD had fewer "masochistic dreams," as well as fewer dreams with manifestations of apprehension, while women without PPD had a higher frequency of "masochistic dreams" and a higher frequency of dreams with manifestations of apprehension (Kron & Brosh, 2003, p.76). This study appears to show that PPD can be predicted based on the dreams women have during pregnancy.

The question of bonding and attachment arises when considering the conflicts around becoming a mother. Leva-Giroux (2002) conducted a phenomenological study to understand the experience of maternal attachment to the unborn child, as well as how that attachment may convey such behaviors during pregnancy. Leva-Giroux (2002) recruited ten professionally employed, college-educated primiparae from two southern California private physicians' offices and by word of mouth. Leva-Giroux (2002) conducted unstructured interviews at 14- to 16-weeks gestation and again at 26- to 28-weeks gestation. Her findings suggest that dreams are one avenue through which pregnant women attach to their unborn babies (Leva-Giroux, 2002).

Bonding to the baby during pregnancy as a result of dreaming can take place after a series of dreams or even just one dream. The dreams can be detailed, or they may be "non specific," as one pregnant dreamer told me. This woman went on to say, "I'm just holding her, taking her some place with me. The common theme to all the dreams is a great love and connection toward her...." This pregnant woman continued to express "a sense of anxiety about not being able to financially provide," and revealed that she believed this arose from her "own material related to my past as a child and also deep fears I have presently even before getting pregnant."

During her second pregnancy, Victoria, an Italian woman in her thirties who resides in the Boston area, reported three dreams that she recalled having taken place during her first pregnancy. Each dream differed in its content and resulting emotional impact. Victoria and her husband owned a home and were employed full time. They were both established in solid careers. The pregnancy was planned and the couple looked forward to starting a family. The first dream took place during the early part of her second trimester. In the dream, Victoria was living in a small room. She couldn't fulfill the needs of her dream baby, because she couldn't locate a bottle for feeding, nor could she find appropriate clothing to keep the baby warm. In this dream, Victoria felt apprehensive and inadequate about her ability to care and provide for a newborn's basic needs. Upon awakening, Victoria felt that the dream was odd. In a second dream, which took place during the end of the second trimester, the dreamer was holding her newborn in bed, sitting with her legs crossed, back against the wall, but had the sense of not actually birthing the child herself, as if someone had done it for her. She felt no pain. She sensed other females around her with a soft light filling the space. Upon awakening, Victoria felt that this meant that the birth process would not be traumatic. She felt no anxiety about the approaching labor and birth. In Victoria's third trimester, she told me about a third and final dream that took place. In this dream, the baby's foot popped out of Victoria's dream belly. Victoria recalled that she remained calm in the dream, even though she knew this was not normal. Since she was medically knowledgeable, she simply pushed the dream baby's foot back inside her. When she awoke, she found the dream to be comical, and she did not worry about future events. Victoria told me that she shared all three dreams with her husband, even though he did not appear in them.

Together, these stories, and the research findings above, indicate how attending to the dreams of pregnant women may provide beneficial information that can be used by health care providers during treatment or consultation. Professionals in obstetrics and psychotherapy are beginning to initiate discussions with pregnant women regarding their dreams. This is important because these discussions may reduce apprehension, anxiety, tension and requests for drugs (Krippner, et al., 2002). If a dream stands out because it is threatening or extraordinary, it may incite arousal as particular physiological processes become activated. Since the growing fetus experiences what the pregnant mother experiences hormonally and neurochemically, the impact of such dreams may have direct effects on the baby's physical and psychological (psychoneurobiological) development (Lipton, 2005). Although psychological and physiological processes are an interconnected system, it may be useful to separate the two for a more simplified picture. Perception of events in both waking and dream states elicit physiological responses (Erlacher & Schredl, 2008). For example, running in either the waking or dream state results in increased heart rate. Physiological reactions, such as the rise or decline of hormones and growth factors, take place in the pregnant mother and guide the growth of the fetal body (Christensen, 2000; Lesage, et al., 2004; Rossi, 2002). One's perception—thoughts and beliefs—has the power to initiate this chain reaction.

Stress During Pregnancy

Psychological stress is experienced in most pregnancies, even when the pregnancy is intentional (Raphael-Leff, 1990). There is a relationship between prenatal stress and Hypothalamic-Pituitary-Adrenal (HPA) axis programming (Glover, O'Conner, & O'Donnell, 2010). The HPA axis is a collection of structures that are involved in stress response regulation (Smith & Vale, 2006). Sandman, et al. (1994) found that "stress and HPA activation can influence behavior and brain mechanisms permanently" in the human fetus (p. 207).

In a prospective study of 170 pregnant women, Huizink, Robles de Medina, Mulder, Visser and Buitelaar (2003) found stress during pregnancy to be one of the determinants of delay in development. This is associated with lower mental and motor developmental scores in infancy. Prenatal conditions have also been linked to diseases arising in adulthood (Barker, Osmond, Kajantie, & Eriksson, 2009; Bonetta, 2008).

Near the end of the pregnancy, and especially near the due date, new information may cause stress for pregnant women, such as learning that the baby is in breech position. Many of us have seen this first hand. A long-time friend in her last trimester told me about her fear that if the baby didn't flip soon, a Caesarean section would be prescribed. Talking to the baby, telling him to turn and get his head down, I said, especially before falling asleep and when waking up, might be helpful. My friend agreed and acted on my suggestion. Soon after, she had a dream in which the baby turned with the help of some women. She told me that "there were some women [in the dream] helping with the procedure here in my room." To this mother's delight, the baby had in fact turned. This was a relief. What's more is that this dream may have also helped to prepare the mother for the birth to take place four weeks later. About a month later, during active labor, it seemed the baby needed help to reposition himself to make his way into the birth canal. As the hospital's medical staff prepared for a Caesarean section, shortly before the baby was actually born, the doula and the private midwife who had accompanied my pregnant friend helped with a particular technique. This resulted in a vaginal birth. So, it was twice (in dream and waking physical life) that some women helped with a procedure saving this pregnant woman from major abdominal surgery, in other words, a Caesarean section. I was very happy for her.

Pregnancy Dream Imagery

Pregnant women's dreams have been collected and studied in many nations, such as Australia, Israel, Italy (Margherita, Gargiulo, & Martino,

2015), Kenya (Harkness, 1987), Korea and the United States, including the experiences of Native Americans (Eggan, 1966). These research findings reveal a variety of information, from complicated obstetrical histories, to the emotional status of pregnant women, to predictions of what is to come; however, these findings feature minimal mention of announcing dreams. A fairly large body of literature exists that explores general cross-cultural comparisons of dream data (Levine, 1991; O'Nell & O'Nell, 1977), yet cross-comparisons of dreams during pregnancy are not as commonplace. Kitzinger (1978) posits, "In many societies, dreams, especially those experienced during transitional phases of life such as pregnancy, are considered especially significant" (p. 78).

As a social anthropologist, Kitzinger (1978) is one of the few researchers who made an early contribution to the field intersecting cross-cultural psychology and pregnant women. In a comparison of pregnancy dreams between Jamaican and English women in Kitzinger's case studies, it was found that the English women's dreams were more likely "to be disturbing and to involve danger" (1978, p. 79). In contrast to the pregnant Jamaican women, the pregnant English women's anxiety dreams were associated, most often, with a hospital (Kitzinger, 1978).

The meaning of pregnancy dream imagery varies from culture to culture as well. For example, among the Tikopia of Polynesia, dreams of fishing with a small scoop-net are believed to suggest that the unborn will be a daughter, whereas fishing in the sea means that the child will be a son (Carman & Carman, 1999). All the while, the age, sex and profession of the dreamer play a role in the interpretation. For instance, water dreams indicate conception for newlyweds, but indicate a fishing expedition for a tribal elder (Carman & Carman, 1999).

Research reveals that some differences exist in the manifest dream content between males and females (Brenneis & Roll, 1975; Domhoff, 2003; Rubinstein & Krippner, 1991), but that, during the time of pregnancy, expectant fathers report more dreams than nonexpectant fathers (Zayas, 1988), consistent with those of expectant mothers (Maybruck, 1989; Smith-Cerra, 2007). Changes in dream imagery also occur during pregnancy for both expecting partners (Krippner, et al., 2002; Zayas, 1988). An early example is King Phillip of Macedonia, whose dreams confirmed the pregnancy of his wife (Krippner, et al., 2002). Among certain Australian Aboriginal groups, fathers dream of the child (Akerman, 1977), and it has been noted that "every baby must be dreamed by its father before it comes into the world" (Carman & Carman, 1999, p. 11). Australian Aboriginal cosmology includes explanations for dreams, but differing ideas exist.

Some report that the soul leaves the body during sleep and travels. This may have some relationship to how a father "finds" his child in a dream.

COUVADE SYNDROME

Couvade syndrome is a condition by which "pregnancy related symptoms such as nausea, vomiting, and abdominal pain in expectant fathers" are reported (Lipkin & Lamb, 1982, p. 509). Just as Couvade syndrome has been noted among expectant fathers (Brennan, Ayers, Ahmed, & Marshall-Lucette, 2007), it seems reasonable that a father's dream content shifts due to his changing reality (Zayas, 1988). Zayas (1988) studied the dreams of twenty married men. He found that the dreams of the ten expectant fathers differed from those of the other ten men (those whose wives were not pregnant). The participants recorded their dreams during three two-week periods in their wives' pregnancies. The dreams of the men with pregnant wives contained references to the fetal environment, and feelings of loneliness and exclusion during weeks 13 through 16 of the pregnancy. Near the end of the pregnancy, the fathers reported dreams of their babies. From his research, Zayas (1988) indicated that for the expectant fathers, unconscious preoccupations were depicted symbolically in dreams and developed throughout their wives pregnancy.

In addition, Maybruck's (1989) doctoral dissertation revealed that some couples "envisioned similar themes, characters, or settings, either on the same nights or two subsequent nights" (p. 268). Some expectant couples experience spontaneous (non-incubated) dreams that turn out to have similar content. From her collection of anecdotal reports, Hallett (1995) noted, "Some couples experience shared dreams while expecting a baby" (p. 53).

Koukis' (2007) dissertation compared dream report content between English-speaking North American pregnant women and expectant men. Koukis (2007) analyzed the sixty-four dream reports gathered from twenty-four women and twenty-four men, ages eighteen to forty-two, using the Hall and Van de Castle Scale of Content Analysis. There were measurable differences in the dream content of pregnant women and expectant men. Differences in sex norms from past research were significantly distinct from the differences found in Koukis' data (2007). Koukis (2007) found a common thread in the dream content of pregnant women and expectant men: An increased amount of family members existed for both the men and the women.

Given the classic, persistent, cross-cultural understanding of dreaming as an access point to the supernatural, or as the wanderings of one's soul, what might this say about the dreams of parents-to-be, particularly, announcing dreams? Among various cultural groups, truth is produced by dreams' inherent authority. Ultimately, dream experiences marry reality, more often than not, across human societies.

CHAPTER FOUR

Dreams That Announce an Arrival

Announcing dreams are a unique type of pre-birth communication between parent (usually the mother) and unborn child that occur during pregnancy (or soon before). In an announcing dream, the child-to-be is made known to the mother or father in the dream state, either through visual or auditory channels (Hallett, 1995; Verny, 2002). More than just a mundane, fantasy-like dream about a baby, this visual, tactile, or auditory dream perception leaves the parent with the belief that genuine communication has taken place with the child-to-be. Some parents do not realize that they have conceived until an announcing dream occurs, revealing that the woman is, in fact, pregnant (Hallett, 1995; Sered & Abramovitvh, 1992).

Conception and Fertility Dreams

The concept of "conception dream" or "fertility dream" has been used as well, and usually refers to a dream announcing that conception has taken place. Often times these dreams are metaphorical, such as small animals that grow into bigger animals over the course of the pregnancy (Adams, 2014). These fascinating dream-visions date back to ancient times, such as the well-known Western example of the announcement to Joseph of Jesus's conception (by Mary). The King James Version of the Bible states, "But while he [Joseph] thought on these things, behold, the angel of the Lord appeared unto him in a dream, saying, Joseph, thou son of David, fear not to take unto thee Mary thy wife: for that which is conceived in her is of the Holy Ghost" (Matthew 1:20). In addition, an angel also announces the future birth of John the Baptist to his father: "The angel said unto him, 'Fear not, Zacharias, for thy prayer is heard, and thy

81

wife Elizabeth shall bear thee a son, and thou shalt call his name John. And thou shalt have joy and gladness, and many shall rejoice at his birth. For he shall be great in the sight of the Lord, and shall drink neither wine nor strong drink, and he shall be filled with the Holy Ghost even from his mother's womb'" (Luke 1:13–15). Soon after in the first book of Luke, it was written that Mary (the mother of Jesus) is contacted by an angel, who announces the future birth of Jesus: "And the angel said unto her, 'Fear not, Mary, for thou hast found favor with God. And behold, thou shalt conceive in thy womb and bring forth a Son, and shalt call His name Jesus. He shall be great and shall be called the Son of the Highest; and the Lord God shall give unto Him the throne of His father David, and He shall reign over the house of Jacob for ever; and of His Kingdom there shall be no end'" (Luke 1:30–33).

While pregnant women's visions and dreams have been ignored or dismissed in much of Christian history, attention was given to women's visions and dreams if they indicated that the women would bear a future saint. Merovingian, or Frankish, hagiography includes birth prophecies. Two dream annunciation threads exist: (a) the pregnant mother has a vision of the child's future; and (b) an angel, or other spiritual figure, announces the child's future.

Hagiographers "emphasized that the women did not interpret the dreams themselves, but rather relied on priests or other 'skilled' interpreters" (Moreira, 2003, pp. 641), even though dream interpretation was not institutionalized by clergy. For example, the conception of future bishop and saint Eligius of Noyon was announced in a dream to his mother. Her vision included an "eagle flying above her bed and thrice proclaiming promises to her" (Moreira, 2003, pp. 639–640). After many months had passed, it was said that a priest was brought to her bedside when her labor put her in danger's way. Naturally, the priest interpreted her "conception" dream prophetically, pronouncing the holiness of the coming male child (Moreira, 2003).

Such dreams were documented during the Anglo-Saxon conversion to Christianity in 596 AD (Davis, 2005). Davis (2005) presented reports of dreams and visions extracted from historical sources and grouped them into eight categories to emphasize the human life cycle. One category was conception. Jainism is a centuries-old religion of India highlighting non-violence. The Jaina text, *Angavijja*, has "a classification system of the beings in the dream" (Wayman, 1967, p. 6), including the unborn. In addition, conception dreams may not reveal the child-to-be, but indicate conception metaphorically (Davis, 2005). From her fieldwork, Kitzinger (1978) reported that "in Jamaica a woman expects to have a fertility dream when she becomes pregnant, and it is this rather than the obstetrician's examination which confirms pregnancy" (pp.78–79).

Korean Taemong

As is the case in some cultures, a particular type of dream must take place for a pregnancy to occur—one must first be dreamt in order to be born, some have said. Korean families have a long tradition of *taemong*, or conception dreams (Pritham & Sammons, 1993; Seligson, 1989). Korean conception dreams (*taemong*) foretell the gender, personality or career path of the child-to-be. *Taemong* are a source of pride and identity, and they are very much a part of the vibrant culture of dreaming in Korea. This is in direct opposition to what Koreans refer to as "dog" dreams, which are meaningless, scattered or simply mundane dreams. *Taemong* seem to be quite the opposite—these dreams are clear, realistic, intense, strikingly vivid and unforgettable, leaving the dreamer convinced that conception has taken place—there is no doubt that it is a birth dream. According to a study in the early 1990s, *taemong* are experienced by 57.5% of pregnant women in Korea (Pritham & Sammons, 1993), although that percentage increases when expectant men, family members or best friends have *taemong*. *Taemong* imagery often include animals. For example, cats, pigs, fish, turtles, snakes, dolphins and birds have been reported, as well as large, plump or ripe fruit. In addition, an unreal brightness, such as an incredibly bright flower, may also be interpreted as a conception dream. As for the sex of the baby-to-be, some have said that small animals in large numbers signify a female child, while one large animal points to a male child. When it comes to foretelling conception, others have noted that flowers, fruit and jewels symbolize a girl (Kang, 2013), while dreams of a particular range of animals point to a boy. Dead animals or rotten fruit may indicate misfortune, such as declining health or miscarriage. *Taemong* have also been bought and sold in instances where a couple does not have one or dislikes the one that was dreamt. If one's *taemong* is undesirable, a better one can be bought. Once *taemong* has been had, the *tae kyo* ritual for pregnancy is followed. *Tae kyo* includes "rules for safe and easy childbirth that, when closely followed, protect the infant" and family from misfortune (Pritham & Sammons, 1993, p. 148). An additional cultural belief and practice, such as *t'aegyo*, exists in rural areas of Korea. The concept of *t'aegyo* can be thought of as pre-birth education.

Conception- and fertility-related dreams occur within many diverse cultures. An example of a dream before conception is included in *Soul Trek* by Elisabeth Hallett:

> My husband John and I were planning to have a child after eight years together. I was "working on" my health, trying to overcome allergy problems and some other concerns. Somehow having a baby didn't seem imminent. Then I had a dream that I was standing in the woods, and a little ways away there was a small glade or clearing where the sun was shining on a little child. He was a blond-headed, slim boy, perhaps around three years old. He was just standing there, looking very beautiful in the sunshine. Then along came the doctor with whom I was working on my health issues. He, too, saw the little boy and said to me, "Well, I see you have a fine young son!" It occurred to me instantly that he was mistaken in assuming that the child was mine; I knew I didn't have a child. But I said nothing, letting him believe that the boy was indeed mine. And somehow that set up a feeling of wondering inside me.

This dreamer recognized the importance of the dream and claimed that it was unforgettable. She conceived two months after this dream and, when the boy grew older, looking like the slender little boy in the dream, she believed that the dream was her introduction to him, knowing that her first child would be male. Many years later, this woman had another dream, which appeared to also introduce her to her second child.

Reincarnation Investigations

In the twenty-first century, these types of dreams have surfaced in reincarnation literature. It's quite a controversial field, whose most credible sources began in the 1960s with Ian Stevenson, the father of reincarnation research, and others who subsequently followed his protocols. Stevenson's subjects (children) appeared to spontaneously recall previous lives, which he called *cases of the reincarnation type*, or "CORTs" for short. While announcing dreams were mentioned, particularly in his 2001 publication "Children Who Remember Previous Lives," they were mostly in the background of the research because the phenomena of interest were specific to evidence for reincarnation. Stevenson (2001) explains that so many of his cases include how a person "connected with the (future) subject has a dream in which a deceased person appears to the dreamer and indicates his wish or intention to reincarnate" (p. 99). While spouses, relatives and friends may have this kind of dream, it is most often a woman who is married and able to be a "mother for the next incarnation of the person who is to be born" (p. 99). Stevenson refers to these phenomena as "announcing dreams," as they occur before the birth or even conception of the subject (p. 99). These were typically case studies and were largely conducted in cultures that already believe in reincarnation. Nonetheless, Stevenson recorded announcing dreams in all the countries in which he investigated cases. The Burmese, the Aveli of Turkey, and the Tlingit (An Alaskan Native American group) and other peoples of northwestern North America commonly report announcing dreams, unlike the Igbo, the Druses of Lebanon or in Sri Lanka, where these dreams are said to be rare. For instance, the Lebanese Druse belief system does not include discarnate souls or that the soul or mind can exist outside of the body. The Druses say that reincarnation takes place upon death, therefore there is not a possibility for an announcing dream to take place—at death, the soul is reborn in an infant body. Other cultural variations exist as well. In India, for example, announcing dreams are reported only in association with same family cases, although there does exist a rare exception (Stevenson, 2001). Cultural variance has been noted with regard to timing as well. For example, announcing dreams tend to take place before conception among the Burmese, while they are reported to occur near the end of a pregnancy in the Pacific Northwest (Stevenson, 2001). How long is the interval between death and rebirth? Stevenson's research suggests that this interval can be as short as a few hours all the way to upwards of twenty years. According to Stevenson, "The median interval among 616 cases in ten cultures was 15 months" yet "the members of most cultures believe that no fixed durations exists for the interval between death and birth" (2001, p. 175). "The dreams also vary in their form," according to Stevenson (2001, p. 99), who explains that the intention to be reborn into a particular family may be conveyed in a symbolic way, such as when the dream figure is said to enter the home of the couple and lie between the husband and wife on the bed, or instead drop off a suitcase in the home of a couple. This way is more common to the Alaskan Native Tlingit, whereas among the Burmese, the discarnate personality makes a request, which can be affirmed or denied by the dreamer. Stevenson (2001) shares a funny story:

> A Burmese wife whose husband was away from home on a long journey had a dream in which a deceased friend seemed to be asking for permission to be reborn as her child; she did not like this proposal and (in the dream) told him not to come to them. When her husband returned from his journey, he told her that he had dreamed of the same old friend and had told him (in *his* dream) that the friend would be welcome to be reborn in their family. In due course a child (Maung Aung Than) was born who later made statements suggesting that his father's acceptance had prevailed over his mother's attempted veto. His mother accepted the situation with good humor characteristic of the Burmese [p. 100].

Like this example, most dreamers are able to recognize the person who makes an appeal to be reborn, however, according to Stevenson, some dreamers claim that they cannot identify the person in the dream, and then after the birth, the dreamer claims that the baby physically resembles the one who had appeared earlier in a dream.

In 2005, Tucker synthesized Stevenson's work, which consisted of thousands of case studies and interviews. The families interviewed claimed that their dreams foretold the coming of a deceased relative's return into the family. Announcing dreams were present in 22% of 1,100 cases examined. Tucker explained:

> An announcing dream can occur before the birth of a child. With this feature, a family member, usually the subject's mother, has a dream before or during the pregnancy in which the previous personality either announces that he or she is coming to the expecting mother or asks to come to her. Such dreams usually occur in *same-family* cases, ones in which the previous personality is a deceased member of the subject's family, or in cases in which the subject's mother at least knew the previous personality [2005, p. 8].

Because of their nature, the information gleaned from these cases cannot be generalized to a population of pregnant women.

While reincarnation cases are reported much more rarely in Europe, they do exist. For many years now, Hassler (2013) has been searching for CORTs in German-speaking nations. He added that he found only two cases that appeared to be worth investigating in a period spanning a decade. However, in late 2011, a priest contacted Hassler about a claim. Hassler followed up. This fairly recent case, to include an announcing dream with elements of reincarnation and precognition, or a strong coincidence, came out of Europe and was published in 2013. According to Hassler's investigation, a nurse and psychotherapist recalled assisting a young, male accident victim, who died by her side late one night, right there by the highway. Around dawn that same day, the woman had a dream about the accident victim in which he expressed that be wanted to come to her and be near her. The dreamer was opposed to the idea. The next night, the deceased accident victim reappeared to her in a dream again, asking her to become his mother. Once again, she did not approve; in fact, she strongly opposed the notion. On the third night, a third dream occurred. Again the young accident victim "declared his desire to be with her, as he had done twice before" (Hassler, 2013, p. 22). This time, the dreamer said she would accept him, although under certain conditions, one of the conditions being that he should return in eighteen months. The deceased seemed content with her response and conditions, and embraced her before the dream ended. Even with her intention to not have any more children, or get pregnant, the dreamer did in fact become pregnant, and gave birth to a boy eighteen months later. When this child was around three or four years old, he spontaneously told his mother (the dreamer mentioned earlier) that he had been alive before and had "died in a traffic accident," along with other details matching the incident from years ago. The statements left the mother feeling stunned because she had forgotten about the events of the night of the accident and the subsequent dreams as they had taken place years ago. Hassler (2013) writes, "One might wonder if the case would ever have occurred without this connection" (p. 29), in reference to the mother-dreamer being at the site of the accident, and assisting the young man who died there. See the full report for many more fascinating details of this unique case (Hassler, 2013).

American anthropologist James Matlock has been passionately committed to, and well-immersed in, reincarnation research since the 1980s. During our discussions throughout the summer months of 2016, he explained to me that announcing dreams hold a strong presence in the reincarnation literature and beyond. He introduced me to a book titled *Imagining the Course of Life: Self-Transformation in a Shan Buddhist Community*, written by Anthropologist Nancy Eberhardt (2006). In a Shan village in the north of Thailand, Eberhart conducted long-term fieldwork. In a discussion on June 7, 2017, Matlock told me that during Eberhardt's first period of fieldwork in Thailand, she was accompanied by her husband, who died before she went back [to Thailand] nine years later. When she was there, she was told that a child was her late husband reborn. The mother's husband had seen him in a dream shortly before they received news of his death.

In addition, Matlock highlighted a phenomenon I was completely unaware of, known as "departure dreams". Being quite familiar with Ian Stevenson's work, Matlock shared his notes with regard to Stevenson's cases that featured departure dreams. In short, he told me that departure dreams take place when a member of a deceased person's family has a dream telling her/him that the deceased has been, or will be reborn. Departure dreams usually include where to find the reborn (such as a specific location). On Matlock's "Signs of Reincarnation" Facebook group homepage, he writes, "Departure dreams occur when the reincarnation is into a stranger family and a spirit wants to let his former family know he has been reborn." Announcing dreams are reported much more often than departure dreams. Another distinction is that departure dreams most often take place after the birth, unlike announcing dreams. Referencing

Stevenson's work, Matlock told me that, in some departure dream reports, the reincarnated child complains (to the previous family) about his/her present circumstances. Currently Matlock teaches a course online, called "Signs of Reincarnation." For more information, I suggest taking a look at his Facebook group of the same name (Signs of Reincarnation), which provides an online interactive space for all to intellectually engage on this topic.

In early June of 2016, a reincarnation report with the inclusion of departure dreams from 2004 was shared on this group's Facebook page. This report was authored by Dr. P. V. Vartak of India. In January 2014, during his study of a reincarnation case, Vartak met the subject: a little boy who spoke of his past life. This boy, claiming to have been reborn, made an astonishing number of statements about his past life—eighty-five total! The average number of statements in these cases is typically in the mid-to-high teens, thus making this case remarkable. All eighty-five statements made by the little boy were corroborated by relatives. Firstly, by the age of two, the boy began making statements, alluding to the place of his past life, including his former name. Particular towns, incidents and previous relatives' names were included as well, as time went on, along with other specific details such as the time of death, location and how it happened (he claimed to have drowned in a river). Secondly, the boy spoke about who removed his dead body from the river. Later, during the investigation when the little boy was reunited with his previous parents, he referred to himself by the nickname they had given him. So many details were correctly specified and listed that the current and "previous" parents along with local townspeople were convinced. With regard to departure dreams, the previous mother said that she had had several dreams in which her dead son appeared to her, telling her that he would be reborn. Some of the dreams involved interactions between the two in which the deceased boy told her that he was not dead.

Announcing Dreams with Women

Patricia Maybruck (1986), psychologist and pioneer in the study of pregnant women and dreams, conducted pivotal research within this field of pregnancy dreams. In her mixed methods study, Maybruck (1986) recruited 67 pregnant women from Lamaze-type classes. Most participants were pregnant for the first time. The researcher analyzed prepartum and postpartum questionnaires asking about the participants' attitudes about dreams and pregnancy. Maybruck also collected and analyzed 1,046 dreams statistically and descriptively. Maybruck found fear to be a common emotion during pregnancy. She also found a significant association between self-assertion in nightmares and labor duration. In addition, the dreams of first-time pregnant women did not differ much from those who had been pregnant in the past. Maybruck's findings showed high levels of unexpressed anxiety in the manifest dreams of pregnant women. Maybruck acknowledged the event of announcing dreams, but she did not thoroughly explore the significance this had on mothers, thus underscoring the need for further research.

For some pregnant women, a single dream is recalled, while for others the experience is frequent. A twenty-four-year-old woman at the end of her second trimester expressed positive emotions related to the continuous stream of announcing dreams she recalled, which spanned from pre-conception into the current day. This woman wrote:

> I've had several "slice of life" dreams involving a little boy of mine, feeding him food in the kitchen, walking along the beach with him and my boyfriend, traveling in the car when he's older … like spontaneous snapshots more than video. They happen maybe once every week or so. I sometimes also dream about my boyfriend's daughter from a previous marriage, and sometimes my little boy is in it too with her.

Anecdotal reports are common among pregnant women and those individuals they deem trustworthy enough to tell, such as close friends or family; however, obstetricians, physicians and other medical staff are typically not included among those trusted when pregnant women do reveal their dreams (Maybruck, 1989). This is unfortunate and still appears to be true today. A variety of anecdotal reports indicate that announcing dreams have been known to affect women's personal belief systems, as well as their behavior and decision-making. So, wouldn't dreams be important for physicians to consider? For example, from one anecdotal report, I learned that one pregnant woman decided to give her first-born the name that was expressed in an announcing dream, completely convinced that this unexpected communication was from her unborn child. She told me that her son appeared to her in a dream and offered his name—the episode was quite literal, brief and direct. Taking this dream quite seriously, she told her husband upon awakening that she knew the child's name (and that there was no room for negotiation). Her husband immediately understood the significance for her. About five months later, "Travis" was born. Had her dream son instructed her to make other decisions, it is reasonable to believe the mother would have heeded them.

The story she shared with me really resonated, but there was more. This woman said that in the mid part of 2002, in the first trimester, she dreamt of a baby girl. This was the first dream she had ever had of this kind. The dream baby visually appeared to be about eight or nine months old. Unprompted, this female dream baby clearly stated, "I'm not your baby." That was that. The woman miscarried shorty thereafter. Not long afterwards, in late 2002 now, another dream occurred. She told me that this time it was a male dream baby who looked to be between three and four months old. This dream baby clearly said to her, "I'm your baby and my name is Travis." This dream ended as quickly as the earlier one. Upon reflection, the mother said that the dream felt "matter of fact" and that it was "comforting after having a recent miscarriage."

Isabel Allende is a featured novelist in the book *Writers Dreaming* by Naomi Epel. Allende is a well-known writer who understands the impact that her dreams have had not only her work, but also in other areas of her life. Allende shared her prophetic pregnancy dreams and how she has had a knack for knowing the sex of the baby before any knowledge of a pregnancy exists. This was the case for her children as well as her grandchildren, and, at the time of Epel's publication, her soon-to-be niece. Allende said that since the children in the dream already had names, it saved her from having to come up with one before the birth. Allende commented on how the names were unfamiliar to her or her family members and were not names she would have chosen (Epel, 1993).

As long-time elementary school teacher, Amalia loves children. She is very excited to start a family. Amalia is Puerto Rican, in her thirties and is hoping to learn the name of her baby-to-be in a dream. On February 5, 2017, Amalia told me the following story:

> My husband and I had been trying to conceive for one and a half years. After a lot of struggle and frustration, we finally decided to take a break towards the end of summer 2016. Shortly after, in September, I had a dream of an adult-size baby boy kneeling on the floor by my bed. He was leaning on my bed, watching my husband and I sleeping. When I got up to look at him, he calmly whispered, "I'm coming." This freaked me out, because it was the first time a baby had ever appeared in my dreams. Maybe that dream was supposed to reassure me, inspire hope or encourage me to keep trying. I guess those were some of my feelings, but you better believe I was angry and sad, too. I felt like that dream was a tease and maybe just a sign of my subconscious longing for a baby. Well, to our surprise, I conceived the next month."
>
> Then, in early January 2017, I was about ten weeks pregnant and really hoping for a little girl. My husband wanted a boy, but more importantly we both just wanted a healthy baby. I had gone to the doctor for a check-up and was a little upset that they didn't do a sonogram—just a heartbeat check. I wanted to see the

baby, as I was honestly still shocked that I was pregnant. I didn't believe it. As if the fifteen extra pounds, constant exhaustion, profound hunger, nausea and stiffness wasn't enough to convince me! Haha. I came home that night from the checkup and meditated a bit. I was basically wanting to connect with the baby and express how much I wanted to see it. Well, that night I had another dream.

In my dream, I was laying in my bed right next to my husband. Then my husband put his hand on my belly and his hand turned into a sonogram. Immediately, my husband and I both went into my body and into my uterus. It was so intense and real looking. When we were in there, we saw the baby hooked to the umbilical cord and everything. I saw the face and all of its body. I then looked down between the legs and saw a little pee pee.

Right then, my husband was just crawling into the bed for real [in the waking state]. He comes home from work around 1:00 am. I suddenly woke up and with eyes still closed, I casually muttered to him, "Papi, I just met the baby, it's a boy." He chuckled a little bit and held me to fall back asleep.

When we woke up, he said I was talking in my sleep, and I told him, "No, I really did meet the baby" and shared what I remembered. I explained that it seemed so real and that I even remember his face. He thinks I'm crazy. Haha. I was hoping that I was losing it too and that the dream was nothing.

Three weeks later, the genetics test came back and as much as I was hoping for a little baby girl—it was a boy. I guess the dream was everything.

Amalia told me that she and her husband cannot agree on a name and that they have only come up with a handful of possibilities. She is hopeful that the baby boy will return to her in another dream and share his name or a name he would like.

Some announcing dreams are experienced differently. A young Apache woman, residing in New Mexico, became pregnant for the first time not long after getting married. She revealed to me that she had had reservations and generalized fears about being pregnant and becoming a mother until several announcing dreams began. Her announcing dreams were recurrent and solely visual instead of auditory. On June 12, 2010, she told me that during these dreams she always saw the same black-haired male toddler. She said that he would just look at her and smile, and then a sense of calm and comfort would come over her. Even after awakening, these feelings lasted throughout the day. She believed that her newly found sense of peace and joy at becoming a mother was the direct result of the dreams. She claimed that her fears and reservations severely diminished. This experience helped her; she decided that she could be a good mother after all. Later, on September 2, 2010, she told me of her surprise when her son was born with a full head of black hair like the child she had seen in the dreams, because her husband was a blond.

Another woman reported meeting her son-to-be when she was experiencing a lucid dream. She wrote to me on March 7, 2011, to share her story:

I was early in my first trimester, still trying to decide if having a baby at this time in my life was the right thing to do. My partner and I had a very tumultuous relationship. In my dream I sat with a four-year-old boy with dark hair. I asked him if he was the baby, and he wouldn't answer me, but he did tell me he would like to be named Peter, and I said no. The dream shook me when I saw him (thus inducing the spontaneous lucidity). I realized that this was the changing point in my life. I felt like this was a person speaking to me. That was the first dream and after that one I knew the baby was sticking around. In the second trimester I had another dream where the little boy came and sat by me. No words were spoken, but he calmed me. Today, my son Jet is a very soothing and gentle person. I do believe that his little spirit got me on track to be his mom, even if I wouldn't name him Peter.

The following account can be found in Hinze's (1997) book *Coming From the Light*:

> Before I even knew I was pregnant the second time, I dreamed that I had twin girls called Jill and Sarah. Later in the pregnancy, I was looking at some pretty "babies" and kept being strongly drawn to the twins. At fourteen weeks gestation, twins were diagnosed, and I said they would be two girls. Sure enough, we now have Beth and Sarah (my husband doesn't like the name Jill) [pp. 30–31].

Similar retrospective responses have been noted following announcing dreams from other women, even when the perceived names were very unusual. Hallett (1995) provides an example. Even though Wendy didn't know she was two weeks pregnant, she reported a dream in which she held a male child on her lap as she spoke to him. She came to learn that his name was "Bridger." Neither she nor her husband had heard that name before, yet they agreed to use the name if they were to ever have a male child. Two weeks later Wendy discovered that she was pregnant and had no doubt that the baby would be a boy. After "Bridger" was born, Wendy found his eyes and face to be like the one she saw in the dream.

In 2009, I met Melissa, a young woman working as a barista at an independent café in Arizona. As a regular customer at this particular café, Melissa and I would often talk about our shared interest in psychology and consciousness. A few months later, in the summer of 2009, she revealed that she became pregnant and was planning to have an abortion. Then, suddenly, she had a vivid, impactful dream. She told me that she whole-heartedly believed that she had met the child she was carrying in that extremely vivid dream. At the time, she did not want to be pregnant and did not have the financial and personal support she desired. Yet, after the dream, she told me about how her ideas, beliefs and behaviors had shifted due to experiencing that unique dream episode. In this case, she decided not to terminate the pregnancy. Eventually she left Arizona (and years later I left as well) but we kept in touch. After her baby had grown into toddlerhood, she sent me a few photos. They looked happy as ever, and she claimed they were doing well and were quite happy together. Many pregnant women have reported connecting with their babies-to-be through a dream. Love and acceptance of the developing baby are often noted among the dream images, as well as a sense of confidence and affirmation.

According to Bowman (2001), who anecdotally collected hundreds of reports of mothers' experiences and children's memories, "The dreamer, who is usually the mother-to-be, has the distinct and unforgettable sensation of actually meeting the future child in the dream state" (p. 201). For example, one woman was told in her dream that it was highly unlikely that she would ever become pregnant because of a past medical condition. Even so, she continued to try to conceive. She reported:

> Then I dreamed the most vivid dream of my life, before or since…. He [the child that appeared to her in the dream] was blond, blue-eyed, a beautiful child, and we were calling him "Zak." When I awoke from this dream, I felt more peaceful than I had ever felt and knew, without question, not only that I would become pregnant, but who the child was and how he looked, long before he was born. Within two weeks I learned that I was indeed pregnant. Throughout my pregnancy, when people asked me whether I wanted a boy or a girl, I would tell them it wasn't a matter of what I wanted—that I already knew the little person inside me, knew it was a boy and that his name was Zak [Hallet, 2002, p. 37].

From culture to culture, there is great variety among announcing dream episodes, including timing, frequency and content. Announcing dreams may be experienced diversely from place to place and across different periods of time; therefore, one should not assume that a pregnant woman's dream content, interpretation or impact will be the same across cultures (Davis-Floyd, 2003; Davis-Floyd & Sargent, 1997; Jordan, 1993; Kane 1994). Some announcing dreams may express a private moment between mother and baby, while others include the entire family. One pregnant dreamer reported giving birth with the whole family present to include the husband and son holding "the baby on our bed." Announcing dreams are one way by which parents make meaning of their current life situation.

Announcing Dreams with Men

Fathers-to-be also are the recipients of announcing dreams and are sometimes contacted first, before the pregnant mother. One expecting father told of a dream that evolved over a period of three nights. By the third dream (after the third night), he woke up to find tears on his face and realized he had seen the spirit of the baby (Hinze, 1994). This father also reported that one of his most cherished possessions is a particular photograph of his daughter, who looks just like how she appeared in his dream. Announcing dreams can be experienced by both parents, impacting the pregnant mother and expectant father.

In 1954, in the Tiwi Islands, American anthropologist Jane C. Goodale asked a mother of four whether a man ever dreamed his child before his wife told him she was pregnant. Goodale was told the following, which she collected in her field notes:

> A man [she gave his name] dreamed of his unborn child who was crippled. The *pitapitui* told his father that although he was firstborn, he had been crippled during an aerial attack during World War II and had to go first to America to be treated for his leg. But, he told his father, when I am healed I will come back to be born. Meanwhile I'll send my youngest siblings first. When he was eventually born his father recognized him because of his crooked leg.

In the Tiwi Islands, specifically Bathurst and Melville, Goodale also found (as stated in den Boer, 2012, p. 201) that a child must be dreamed by the father, "the man to whom its mother is married, before it can be conceived by its mother." Goodale continues, "...there is no conflict between the two beliefs concerning conception. In fact, there is only one belief, while there may be two fathers." Some dream reports include an unborn child asking the father about the identity of its mother. Later, after the dream had taken place, the identified woman announced her pregnancy.

Many reports have been collected with regard to fathers' dreaming of spirit-children entering their wives. For example, Elkin (1933) states (as noted in den Boer, 2012, p. 202):

> The entry of a spirit-child into its mother's womb is always associated with a dream in which the father sees or "finds" it. Further, according to the Nyul-Nyul informants, the spirit-child tells the father what its name is to be. It also tells the man that he is to be the father, and asks him where his wife is. Having given the information to the spirit-child, he may then take it in his hand and put it down near his wife, or on her naval. It will enter the womb, though not necessarily at once. At the time of the quickening, the woman tells her husband that a child has entered her womb. He then remembers "finding" the child in the dream.

All over Australia, men "find" spirit-children in their dreams—it seems to be a necessity of a husband (Merlan, 1986), and is prevalent in Aboriginal cosmology. Still, dreams of "spirit-conception takes place in different forms in accordance to the clan" (den Boer, 2012, p. 203). Therefore, the details and timing of these experiences are not expected to be the same across the Aboriginal population as a whole.

Siegel's 1982 doctoral study on expectant fathers' dreams showed that 21% recorded dreams about babies in their journals over a two-week period. Alex, a thirty-one-year-old engineer, reported such a dream during the second trimester:

> I am standing on a street corner carrying my baby fetus under my shirt against my chest. I have my hands cupped over the fetus to protect it. It is moving, and people ask me what it is. I say, "It's my baby!" Someone tries to smash the fetus by hitting my chest. I become enraged at the person and pick him up and throw him into the street [Siegel, 2002, p. 82].

When his partner was seven months pregnant, a Brazilian man living in the United Kingdom had his first dream about the child-to-be. In the dream, he was simply holding his daughter in his arms. This dream enhanced his excitement for the approaching birth. His partner, the pregnant mother, said, "He can't wait!" The photos this couple shared with me after the birth were adorable. They have been blessed with a beautiful baby girl.

"The Lucid Dream Experience" is an electronic magazine dedicated to educating, informing and inspiring lucid dreamers everywhere. It can be freely accessed at www.dreaminglucid.com. The magazine is published in the months of March, June, September and December, and it is something I look forward to during those times. The magazine features lucid dream reports, techniques for encouraging and enhancing lucid dreams, such as how to prolong lucidity, and is a platform for discussion around the potentials and applications of lucid dream activities. The 2010 winter edition (December) included the following powerful dream submitted by Michael Stafa:,

> At that time my wife was pregnant with a beautiful belly and we expected a baby girl. Since my wife is not young, she had to undergo some blood and ultrasonic tests. My wife already has one daughter from a previous marriage (nice 18y old young lassie) and she really hoped that her second would be alright. But blood test results showed that there was a high probability of baby-girl's Down Syndrome.
>
> Our world started to collapse. Upon suggestion by my wife's doctor, she underwent amniotic fluid sampling which tests results should, according to the doctor, prove the results with 99.9% accuracy. While waiting a couple of weeks for the results, we discussed this matter a lot at home.
>
> During this time, my wife's belly was already quite big. She often rested and slept so I could sleep with her, too. Within these weeks I had a couple of lucid dreams (I didn't even know the term "lucid dream" at that time and thought that all people can have such dreams).

In the dreams I appeared in my wife's belly and saw a beautiful and perfect baby-girl. We talked and baby-girl herself told me: "Daddy, don't worry. I'm healthy and am looking forward to be born. Everything is all right." Every time I woke up, assured and with gained strength, I encouraged my wife so that her sad thinking wouldn't affect our baby, and I awaited the results with a balanced and confident mind.

When the time of the test results came, they proved my dreams to be true and after a few months we were blessed with a healthy and beautiful baby-girl. When I see her now laughing and playing around me, I'm really happy!

As a lucid dreamer, Michael could have asked the dream-baby directly about her health and current situation, yet the dream-baby offered this information on her own, as the report seems to suggest. He wrote that they "talked" but did not provide other details. I wondered if he had expressed the concerns he had, as well as the concerns of his wife. Could the dream-baby have already known this? If so, that may be why such information and assurance was offered. As a healthy child was this couple's primary wish, it is also possible that Michael's mind offered what he wanted to hear. Ultimately, the hows and whys matter less than the resulting impact. This experience gifted the father-to-be with confidence and mental balance. It also spread beyond his personal world to the wife, since her husband was then able to share his freshly gained strength and assurance in support of easing her sadness. Because the fetal body is housed within the mother, such emotional support may result in hormonal shifts that have a direct physiological impact upon the developing baby.

The relationship between dreaming and physiology is worthy of attention and future research. The possibilities swirled in my thoughts for many months and resulted in my decision to move in a specific direction during my doctoral program. The outcome was that I chose to focus on announcing dreams.

Chapter Five

The Announcing Dream Study

By the end of 2013, I had completed my doctoral dissertation on the announcing dreams that took place in the lives of pregnant women. I had been interested in this topic—announcing dreams—since the mid–2000s. By the beginning of 2011, I had submitted my dissertation proposal on the subject—I was fully committed. At first though, I was indecisive about whether to conduct in-person interviews or use an online tool. In the end, I decided to conduct the study entirely online with the help of a user-friendly research tool. This allowed me to potentially recruit people from across the globe, which was important to me. If I had chosen in-person interviewing, it would have been likely that all of the pregnant participants would have resided near me. That felt too limiting, so I decided to try to reach potential participants far and wide. In the end, I got breadth, not depth.

Those were some very challenging years, and I am grateful that I chose a phenomenon that has held my interest for over a decade. Dreams about family—in this case, a new family member coming in—often hold a special place in one's heart for so many reasons, as you will see from the participants themselves. First, though, I present some demographic information about the participant group. Then, the raw data (the dreams themselves) are presented in this chapter; chapter six reveals the results from thematic analysis.

The Quantitative Data

For the doctoral study, I analyzed the dream reports of twenty-two pregnant women. The participants were pregnant women who were over the age of twenty-one, fluent in English, and were of any education level, socio-economic status, ethnicity or religion. None of these factors have been shown to impact the capacity for dreaming. In addition, participants must have been pregnant at the time of their participation in the study and were free of psychiatric drug consumption. In addition, the pregnancy must have been medically confirmed by a physician or home pregnancy test. The dream reported must have been about the child in utero, and not about a child who was previously birthed. In order to be eligible for participation in this study, the participants must have reported having a dream during the current pregnancy in which they appeared to see, hear or converse with a being believed to be the son or daughter they were carrying in the womb. All of these parameters, in the end, led to a research project with a sample of twenty-two women, even though it appeared that nearly one hundred women had been interested in being involved.

PARTICIPANT AGE

To begin participation in the study, each participant had to fill out a demographic and screening questionnaire. Once that task was complete, participants gained access to the study's interview questions. From the answers received, I learned that the twenty-two participants ranged in age from twenty-two to thirty-eight-years-old, with a mean age of 29.36 years (see Appendix A, Table 1). I had expected some of the participants to be in their forties, but that wasn't the case.

RACE AND ETHNICITY

Race and ethnicity were included in the demographic questionnaire, and it was found that the majority of participants were Caucasian (see Appendix A, Table 2). Twenty participants were born in the United States, one in Canada, and one in Australia. All but one, who lives in or had lived in Canada, resided in the United States at the time of the study. I found this to be surprising because the research solicitation was sent to doulas and midwives in several nations outside of the United States where English was the primary language. Online groups with access to a wide audience also received my study solicitation, especially those groups that had a discussion board for such things.

RESIDENCY AND EDUCATION

When asked about length of residency in the current country, one participant did not respond. Of the remaining twenty-one, eighteen participants reported having resided in their birth nation for their entire life. While women in other parts of the world did express interest, and began the study by electronically signing the informed consent form online, they did not pass the screening process due to the parameters listed above, and so, the online electronic questionnaires automatically closed.

Among the participants, education levels varied. All participants had acquired some level of education beyond high school (see Appendix A, Table 3). Overall, the sample was moderately educated to highly educated. Most participants were employed (77%) full-time (50%) or part-time (27%) at the time this study was conducted (see Appendix A, Table 4).

RELIGION OR SPIRITUALITY

Participants' religious and spiritual affiliations ranged widely. They represented many of the world's main religious traditions, including Christianity, Judaism, Islam and Buddhism. Also listed were the following: Atheist, agnostic, Pagan/Wiccan and Taoist, among others (see Appendix A, Table 5). Two of the participants marked "other," but I do not know what that entailed because I did not include a space to elaborate.

PREGNANCY HISTORY

Following those basic demographic questions, questions about pregnancy history and gestation time were included in the screening process. The women's pregnancy history is summarized in Appendix A, Table 6. Seven participants (32%) were pregnant for the first time. Of the fifteen others, six participants (40%) had been pregnant once before, another six (40%) twice before, and three had been pregnant three or more times in the past. As you can see, the participant's pregnancy history was quite varied as well. Of these fifteen participants, twelve (80%) had birthed one or more living children and eleven (61%) had one or more miscarriages or terminations. Of those six participants who were pregnant once before, three had borne a living child, and three had had a miscarriage or termination. Of the six participants who had been pregnant twice before, six had borne one or more living children, and five had had one or more miscarriages or terminations. Of the participants who had been pregnant three or more times, all had borne one or more living children and had one or more miscarriages or terminations (see Appendix A, Table 6). Pregnancies among the twenty-two participants ranged from one- to nine-months' gestation, with a mean gestation time of 6.27 months (see Appendix A, Table 7).

When asked how they knew they were pregnant, participants were provided with the option to mark one or more responses. The choices were: missed one monthly period, missed more than one monthly period, positive home pregnancy test, pregnancy confirmed by medical personnel, body changes not confirmed by medical personnel or I "just know" I'm pregnant. All twenty-two participants had had the pregnancy confirmed by medical personnel or by a home pregnancy test, making them eligible to participate in this study.

Finally, participants were asked about their dream recall. Twenty participants (90%) said they often recall their dreams. That was good news for this study! Now we will move on to the dream narratives reported by each of the women.

Participant Descriptions and Their Dreams: The Study's Qualitative Results (Part 1)

This section describes each of the study's participants, but with limited detail to protect identity. All women, as has been the case so far, have been given fake names. Following their descriptions, are their dream narratives.

The presentation of the dream narratives is sequenced according to the age of the child appearing in the dream. Thus, they were divided into four groups: Prior-to-birth, newborns or infants, toddlers or very young children, and elementary school aged. The first four dreams involve a child in utero, or prior to being born. The second set captures dreams in which a newborn or infant is present and is, by far, the largest group. Here, fifteen narratives are listed. The third grouping includes two dreams that feature toddlers or very young children. The final dream reflects one school-aged child. Regardless of the placement, each individual dream should be considered as its own unique entity. All names and other identifying information have been changed to honor privacy and confidentiality.

PRIOR-TO-BIRTH DREAMS

Four participants recalled dreams in which their child was still in utero prior to being born. Eva, Florinda, Gabriella, and Tanya (pseudonyms) are between the ages of twenty-four and thirty-eight. They dreamed of their babies in various stages of their pregnancy. The descriptions feature various levels of detail and imagery.

Eva

The dreamer, Eva, is a white, twenty-four-year-old unemployed woman who did not identify a spiritual or religious affiliation. Eva had one previous pregnancy that resulted in a living child. She had the following announcing dream when she was nine months pregnant. The dreamer was unsure about the sex of the child in this most recent dream. Eva stated, "The dream was [of] me still being pregnant and not actually [with] the baby outside of me. I was pregnant and another girl I knew was pregnant."

Much earlier in the current pregnancy, during her second trimester, another dream took place:

> I believe if I remember right that I had a dream a long while ago, maybe when I was 3 to 6 months along, and I had a girl [in that dream]. I was overjoyed!!! As we do not know what we are having and [I] am due in 2 weeks.

Florinda

The dreamer, Florinda, is a white, Catholic, thirty-eight-year-old woman. She is an unemployed married woman who is nine months pregnant. Florinda was pregnant once before and delivered one baby. She had the following dream when she was five months pregnant. The child in the dream was female and appeared as an animal. Florinda stated, "[The] unborn child was really a Springer Spaniel puppy who eventually scratched through my belly."

Gabriella

Gabriella is a thirty-three-year-old employed married woman. She is eight months pregnant. Gabrielle identified as Latino/Hispanic and labeled herself as spiritual, but not religious. She has had multiple pregnancies, resulting in miscarriage and/or termination, and has given birth to one living child. Gabriella said she was lucid during the following dream that took place when she was two months pregnant:

> I knew I was expecting twins, and I was sent for a sleep study to check for sleep apnea, and during the night I dreamt that they were able to see the genders of the babies and told me they were both boys. I was 10 weeks at that time, and at 20 weeks it was confirmed that they were both boys.

When asked how the child looked in the dream, the dreamer wrote, "It was a photo of an ultrasound."

Tanya

The dreamer is thirty-seven-years-old and employed. Tanya is a married woman who is three months pregnant. She identified herself as white, Australian, and Mystic (Mystic included Gnosis, Sufi, Kabala on the study's demographic questionnaire). One of Tanya's earlier pregnancies ended in miscarriage or termination. Tanya reported being lucid during an episode that took place the night before she participated in the study. The child's sex in the dream was uncertain:

> Last night, Tuesday … at 15 weeks pregnant, I had a spontaneous conscious out-of-body experience while asleep. I found myself floating in my bedroom near the ceiling, facing up. I realized I was out-of-body (I have had conscious out-of-body experiences before), and immediately began purposely thinking of my baby; I wanted to see if I could interact with it while out of body. I wasn't sure how to go about doing this, so I focused on my belly and called to it, "Baby, baby, baby" (we do not know the sex yet, and have yet to determine a name). I felt myself drift in and out of my physical body and tried to stay relaxed and calm so as to prolong the experience. Then I felt the baby move inside my belly; I distinctly felt it kick and twist the lower half of its body. I instinctively felt that it was reacting to me trying to interact with it. Then I woke up in my body and could not feel anything in the physical (I am too early in my pregnancy to be able to feel the baby move). Today I was scheduled for my regular OBGYN check-up, and the doc did an ultrasound through my belly. The baby was kicking and twisting just as I felt during the out-of-body experience, it was really cool to watch and it re-affirmed to me the experience I had last night! I felt it more than I saw it, but did get an impression of its tiny legs and torso. The impression I had was exactly as I saw the baby in my ultrasound today! But I did not see any in-depth detail of what the baby looked like such as distinguishing facial features, and so forth.

From this small collection of prior-to-birth dreams, we can see that these reports vary greatly. Some reports contain great detail, while others contain minimal detail or imagery. Fetal sex prediction appears already for some of the women.

Newborn or Infant Dreams

By far, dreams of newborn or infant babies outnumbered dreams of children at other ages or developmental stages. The following reports encompass a range of sensory input. Fifteen participants experienced dreams of their newborns or infants. The dreamers were Anna, Beth, Claudia, Donna, Hanna, Irene, Joan, Krista, Maria, Noelle, Penny, Silvia, Uma, Veronica and Ximena (pseudonymns). These women range in age from twenty-two to thirty-seven years. Again, these dreams vary greatly in terms of detail and imagery.

Anna

The dreamer is a thirty-seven-year-old white, Jewish woman. Anna is employed and seven months pregnant. She is pregnant for the first time. Anna said that she was lucid during the dream that took place when she was three months pregnant:

> I don't remember the exact details of the dream... [In the dream], I knew I was having a girl, and in the dream I thought to myself how this felt just as real as a dream I had had a few weeks prior, when I was holding a baby boy. In the dream I thought I could very well be having a girl and got very excited. I don't have a clear memory of her face; it was more a feeling of her being a sweet, beautiful, perfect baby girl.

Beth

Beth, the dreamer, is nine months pregnant. She is a thirty-seven-year-old employed married woman. Beth identified herself as white and spiritual, but not religious. She has given birth three or more times in the past. Beth reported two dreams about twins that took place when she was six and eight months pregnant, respectively. The twins in both dreams were female.

> I am carrying a twin pregnancy and frequently dream about them. Many times the dreams involve not having them both with me; that we are in the hospital and they have been born, but I am not allowed to have one of them and am searching the hospital for the other. I feel devalued as a parent while this is occurring. I am wearing rugged clothes, no shoes, wild hair, and people are judging me. I get lost in a maze of hallways and elevators and never get both of the babies together. It is both frustrating and terrifying. In another recent dream, one of the babies is delivered with something of a foot defect, it looks like the heel has split into a hoof. That's all I can see in the dream. In the first dream, I can't see their faces, just a little bundle of blankets. In the second dream, all I could see was the foot.

Claudia

The dreamer is a white, Muslim 27-year-old. Claudia is an employed woman who is nine months pregnant for the first time. Claudia had a dream when she was nine months pregnant. The child in the dream was male. She wrote:

> I was sitting on the benches outside my apartment complex with the decorative water fountains behind me. I cannot recall the person I was sitting next to, but we were chatting. I gave birth to [the] child pain free right there outdoors, but was told he wasn't ready and had to put him back inside until his due date (which in reality is in a few days). He looked clean, a mix of my fiancé and I [sic], and rather large. Not your typical newborn.

Donna

Donna is a twenty-eight-year-old employed married woman who is six months pregnant for the first time. Donna identified herself as white and Agnostic. The dreamer said she was lucid during the dream, which took place during the fourth month of gestation:

> I was seeing a midwife to determine the sex of the baby. Instead of doing an ultrasound, she reached inside me, pulled the baby out, confirmed that it was a boy, he [child] smiled, and she [midwife] put him back inside. He looked like a full term baby.

Hanna

Hanna is pregnant for the first time. She is white, spiritual but not religious, and thirty-four years old. Hanna is an employed woman who is eight months pregnant. Hanna had a dream when she was five months pregnant. The child's sex in the dream was undetermined. Here the child is referred to as female, because the dreamer had the child's sex confirmed after the dream took place:

> My boyfriend was holding her and we were outside in nature and it was a sunny day, pleasantly warm. I also remember us being in a pool. I only remember seeing that my child was healthy and happy, but don't recall any of the particulars, I don't remember her face. She was probably 1- to 2-months-old.

Irene

The dreamer is a white, thirty-year-old woman. Irene is employed, married and eight months pregnant. When asked about religion or spirituality, Irene identified herself as an Atheist. She reported having two previous pregnancies, resulting in one birth and one miscarriage or termination. She had the following dream when she was six months pregnant: "I was holding and nursing him, and combing out his really long hair. [He had] dark hair, which was a surprise. I couldn't see any facial features, but that didn't bother me." Irene's dream is an example of how some announcing dreams may be tactile and active, yet brief—she was simply nursing the baby in her arms while combing his hair.

Joan

Joan is a twenty-four-year-old employed woman who is six months pregnant for the first time. She identified herself as white and Taoist. Joan has had dreams involving the child she is currently carrying on a weekly basis. The dream fragments below took place from conception to six months. The sex of the child in the dreams is male.

I have many dreams, but before I found out the sex, I used to have one dream in particular where he and I would make funny faces back and forth at each other, like a game. Sometimes we'd just stare eyes-to-eyes and just feel one another, that too was like a game. This particular dream it would just be that, just his face, and we'd just play these face games back and forth. [It was a] very positive feeling. Just a few weeks ago, we finally had a sonogram done, and it's a boy! I was overjoyed, because it meant that the little boy from my dreams was actually growing inside of me. [He looked] White, with those loose brown curls that babies sometimes get, big round eyes, no freckles, long eyelashes, and always smiling ... dark colored eyes. The lighting is never great in that dream, so that might affect it as well.

Krista

The dreamer is white and identifies as Atheist. She is twenty-five years of age. Krista is an employed, married woman who is one month pregnant. This is her first pregnancy. The dream occurred during this first month, before Krista knew she was pregnant. She learned about her pregnancy one day later, via a home pregnancy test. The child in the dream was male.

I gave birth (no details on where or how), and then I proctored some sort of exam at the high school for a teacher I work with while wearing my baby [on my body]. Then I was in the lobby of the Crown Plaza [Hotel] where the FLAVA [a professional] conference was held, and I was breastfeeding the baby and introducing him to a professor at the college I got my graduate degree from. He [the baby] had beautiful red hair and blue-grey eyes. He looked 1- to 2-months-old.

Maria

Maria is a thirty-two-year-old employed woman who is two months pregnant. She identified herself as white and Buddhist. Maria has been pregnant twice before, both times resulting in miscarriage or termination. The following detailed dream occurred when she was one month pregnant:

When I had this dream, I was considering terminating my pregnancy. I was very scared and confused the first couple of weeks after I found out I was pregnant. I believe in guidance from dreams and asked for a dream to help show me what to do. In the dream, I was holding my baby. The baby was a girl. I felt tremendous love towards her. I was also very anxious. She looked at me in the dream with such presence and love, and telepathically told me her name was Sophia. She had giant blue eyes very similar to my partner. I was in an apartment and I was worried there was something wrong with her since she was very quiet and not crying. I told my partner we needed to buy a sling for me to carry her in. In the dream, I felt that would help her feel better. We were worried we wouldn't have money to buy the sling in the dream. When I woke up the dream felt so real, especially seeing her face. The image of her eyes looking at me kept flashing through my mind for days.

It was so vivid and the name, Sophia, wasn't a name I would have considered. Sophia is Greek for great wisdom. After the dream, I felt like a wise being was speaking to me in the dreams, showing me my unborn child. I felt like she was speaking to me. She [the infant] had an oval face and giant blue eyes. She told me her name was Sophia. I do not recall a hair color. She was very tiny.

Noelle

The dreamer is a white, Protestant twenty-eight-year-old employed married woman who is three months pregnant. She had one previous pregnancy that resulted in a full-term, living child. At three months pregnant, she had the following dream; the child in the dream was male:

In my dream, I was in labor and my husband and I were at the hospital. We kept walking up and down the halls trying to get labor going. We got in the tub to see if that would help. After eight hours, they told us they needed to give the room to someone else so I had to go home. We ended up leaving the hospital and I had the baby at home instead. [The baby looked] tiny and just like my daughter did when she was born.

Penny

Penny is a white, Canadian, Catholic twenty-two-year-old unemployed woman who is seven months pregnant. Her only previous pregnancy resulted in a full-term living child. Penny had several dreams about the child she is currently carrying, beginning when she was three months pregnant up until the time she participated in the study. In those dreams, the child appeared to be male one time and female the next, although she dreamt more often about a female child.

My dreams mostly center around the birth of my child. I am usually alone and in my own home. The birth is usually painless and quite peaceful. One dream, in particular, I had a baby girl born on December 26th in my bathtub, a pretty typical newborn. I can't recall any specifics.

Silvia

Silvia, the dreamer, is an employed woman who is five months pregnant for the first time. She is white, Catholic, and thirty-three years old. The dreamer said she was lucid. The following dream took place when she was five months pregnant:

I was at my parents' house and the baby needed to be changed. I put him on the kitchen counter and he rolled off the counter onto the floor and started crying. When I picked him up, he had purple lumps and bumps all over his head. [He was] like a newborn, very small.

Uma

Uma is a white, thirty-year-old unemployed married woman. She did not identify a spiritual or religious affiliation. The dreamer is four months pregnant. Uma has had two miscarriages or terminations, and has given birth to three or more children. Uma had the following dream when she was three months pregnant:

I was in the hospital and two nurses were present aiding in the birth. I gave birth vaginally to two baby boys. The first had very light hair, almost blond hair, which I thought was odd because the three children I have now have all been born with very dark brown, almost black, hair. He weighed 8 lbs., 3 oz. He was taken away from me while I gave birth to the second boy. I was annoyed that he was taken out of my sight, I presume to the NICU [neonatal intensive care unit] for a check of his overall health. The second boy was born with light brown hair and weighed 10 lbs., 3 oz. The first baby was brought back to me and I was able to see them together. I noticed on the side of his little clear bassinette that the nurses had written the names "Dale" (this referred to the larger baby) and "Bo" (Bo being the smaller baby). I got really upset that they had named my children, especially since I hate the name Bo. The nurses explained to me that they had done this to make it easier to discuss the condition of each baby with me. They said I could rename them later. My husband then appeared for the first time (I don't know where he was, but oddly I had not been surprised or worried about him not being present up to this point). He agreed with me that we would have to rename the kids and was also upset that the nurses had named him. I was sitting in an armchair at this time, nursing the 10 lb. baby, while the smaller one lay across my lap, looking into my eyes. Baby A had either extremely light brown hair, or blond hair. He weighed 8 lbs., 3 oz. He was chubby, with a round little face and the usual steel blue eyes of a newborn. Baby B had light brown hair (and not much of it!), weighed 10 lbs., 3 oz., was chubby with a round face, but looked different enough from his brother that I could tell they were fraternal, not identical. Both babies wore pajamas, but I do not recall the color or pattern.

Veronica

Veronica is a thirty-six-year-old employed woman who is eight months pregnant. She identified herself as white and spiritual, but not religious. The dreamer has been pregnant twice before, both resulting in full-term living children. Veronica was lucid during the following dream when she was eight months pregnant: "I had just had the baby An [*sic*] was trying to get her to nurse." When asked how the child looked, the dreamer wrote, "Like a newborn little girl."

Ximena

Ximena is a Hispanic, Catholic, thirty-six-year-old, employed married woman who is seven months pregnant. She was pregnant once before:

that pregnancy ended in miscarriage or termination. Ximena believed that she had some degree of lucidity during the following dream, which took place when she was six months pregnant; the child in the dream was male:

> I was holding the baby and trying to breast feed by pouring milk out of my breast like a drink. There were other things that I cannot recall very clearly, moving from hospital to home and leaving baby with friends to go to a movie. [He looked] like a baby but [I] can't really describe features.

Dreaming with infants or newborns was reported frequently among the participants in my study. The level of detail and engagement is striking in some of the reports. The impact some of these dreams had for the dreaming mother is noticeable.

TODDLER DREAMS

A few women had dreams of their unborn children as future toddlers. Twenty-eight year-old Olivia and thirty-five-year-old Quincy both dreamed of their babies as young children. Interestingly, both of these women were already mothers, and were both pregnant with their second child.

Olivia

Olivia is a white, twenty-eight-year-old employed married woman who is five months pregnant. She identified herself as Catholic. Olivia had two previous pregnancies, only one of which resulted in a living child. The following occurred when she was two months pregnant:

> I … remember vividly being at a park with two little girls [the dreamer already has one daughter] playing on a swing set. I was just told this week that it's another girl! I remember being so happy and in love. I remember a warm breeze blowing through their hair.

When asked how the child looked, the dreamer wrote, "Not necessarily like me or my husband. I just remember seeing a fair-skinned light haired happy little girl."

Quincy

The dreamer is a thirty-five-year-old unemployed woman. Quincy is seven months pregnant. She identified herself as White and spiritual, but not religious. Quincy has been pregnant twice before, only once producing a full-term living child. The following dream occurred when she was four months pregnant:

I did not know I was pregnant when I had this dream. I was driving on a cold winter day. My mother sat beside me and I pulled in front of an old stone grade school building. I turned to my mother and said, "They are going to teach him how to swim here." I got out of the car, opened the back door and there was a toddler-aged boy in a car seat. I wrapped him in a huge red ski coat and told him to "Pick one, Tigger [name of a stuffed toy tiger from the A. A. Milne children's classic Winnie-the-Pooh books] or Tiger; you can only take one inside with you." There was an antique Tigger stuffed animal and a modern Tigger stuffed animal (my favorite Winnie the Pooh character as a child). He [the child] had dark hair and a sweet round face.

These two dream reports both featured activity. In Olivia's dream, it was swinging. Quincy reported driving in her dream while also referencing a future activity, swim lessons. These are common activities in the United States, among families with toddlers.

A School-Aged Child Dream

One participant, Wilma, dreamed of her unborn baby as a school-aged child. Notably, Wilma was the only participant to experience this phenomenon. Her dream is also significantly more detailed than many other participants' dreams.

Wilma

The dreamer is a thirty-year-old employed woman who is seven months pregnant. She identified herself as bi-racial (Native American and White), and Pagan/Wiccan. Wilma's only prior pregnancy ended in miscarriage or termination. The following dream occurred when she was two months pregnant:

My partner and I were at a wedding in the desert—at our wedding. Everything was going fantastically, when all of a sudden tanks started coming, and bombs, and chaos. There was broken glass everywhere, and it was really loud. Everyone evacuated as quickly as they could. I couldn't find my child, and I was really worried that something happened to her. I was certain that she had been killed by a tank, stolen away by someone, or that I would never see her again. Then it was like the dream happened a second time, or it reversed and happened again, or perhaps it just replayed itself. The second time I learned that everything was okay. The bombings couldn't destroy her and she was safe and hidden somewhere; in fact, no one was physically hurt by the bombings, the tanks and the violence. We all got away in time. She [the child] was probably about 9- or 10-years-old, very pretty, with green eyes like mine, and long, dark, and wavy hair. She was wearing a white dress.... I think she was the flower child [at the wedding].

This final dream report is the only one to include such unique time sequencing—the dream either repeated itself or was experienced a second time in reverse order, according to Wilma, the dreamer. In addition, we have a second unique feature, which is the age of the child.

Summary of Participants and Their Dreams

To summarize, eleven participants (50%) reported dreaming of male children, and seven (32%) reported dreaming of female children. Two participants (9%) were unsure of the sex of the child, one participant (5%) reported a sequence of dreams featuring an alternating male and female child, and one participant (5%) did not answer the question. Three participants (14%), Beth, Gabriella and Uma, reported a dream involving twins; in each of these dreams, the twins were the same sex. I found this to be exciting since, until this study, none of the women I had spoken to directly shared a dream with twins. I had only read about it in the works of other authors.

Some participants recalled more than one dream. Some reported that they had dreams featuring the child throughout their pregnancy. This was not surprising given that this was a common theme among women I had spoken with in the past. In this study, four participants (18%) reported that the dream occurred during their first month of gestation, four (18%) during the second month, six (27%) in the third month, four (18%) in the fourth month, four (18%) in the fifth month, five (23%) in the sixth month, one (5%) in the seventh month, two (9%) in the eighth month, and two (9%) in the ninth month. As we can see, the occurrence of an announcing dream appears to take place at any time! Within this sample, these kinds of dreams took place most often in the first trimester, and least often in the third trimester; however, only five participants were in the second trimester, and thirteen were in the third trimester of their pregnancies at the time of the study. I was really happy to learn of first trimester dreams taking place because so many of the women who had personally shared their stories with me, long before this study, were near the due date. Again, preconception as well as first trimester dreams have been previously published and are shown to take place for both men and women across cultures.

CHAPTER SIX

The Announcing
Dream Study Continues

It was exciting to see the completed questionnaires being submitted. After reading each of them numerous times, it was time to analyze the data for emerging themes. But first, I wondered, did the dreamers themselves view their experiences as significant? Did they bother to share their dreams with anyone? What was the experiential impact of announcing dreams?

The Experiential Impact: The Study's Qualitative Results (Part 2)

The participants were asked whether they believed that dreams of their unborn children during pregnancy were significant. All responded: sixteen participants (73%) said her dream was a significant experience, and six participants (27%) said that her dream was not significant.

Most (85%) participants had shared their dreams with someone they knew: sixteen participants (73%) shared their dreams with a husband, partner, or boyfriend; five (23%) shared with family members other than a spouse or partner; nine (41%) shared with a friend or other trusted person such as a therapist or colleague; and three (14%) did not report their dreams to anyone. Two participants (10%) did not answer the question.

The following section illuminates themes that emerged from participants' responses to having their dreams. These themes include emotions, confidence and affirmation, bonding and connection, birth, hospitals and health-care professionals, a husband/partner, settings (such as residential dwellings and natural settings) and breastfeeding. Other themes that emerged involved catastrophe, lucidity, decision-making regarding the pregnancy and prediction of the child's sex.

Emotions

Participants' dreams, or their reactions from their dream experiences, led to memorable emotions for the dreamers. Fifteen dreamers (68%) had positive emotions during the dream or as a result of having the dream. These emotions include happiness, serenity and hope, or a combination of these.

Positive emotions

Happiness was the most identified emotional theme. Dreams were coded for the happiness theme by the dreamer's use of terms such as "joy," "elated," "grateful" and "happy." Eight participants expressed such terms. Tanya's response to having her dream was feeling "happy" and "grateful." Anna felt "very good" in the dream, and she felt "joy" in response to the experience. Similarly, Donna, Hanna and Joan all felt "happy" in their respective dreams.

Serenity was the next most identified emotion, signified by the dreamer's use of terms such as "at ease," "comfort," "relaxed," "peaceful" and "calm" when describing her own experience; serenity occurred among five participants. For example, Hanna wrote, "It made me feel at ease that our baby would be happy and healthy." Penny reported that the dream left her feeling "always very peaceful and serene.... It left me with a very at-ease feeling for the rest of the day." Quincy said, "I felt at peace and calm."

Hope was identified by the dreamer's vision of the future, and this theme occurred in two records. Quincy's dream left her feeling "full of the promise of the future" for the child she was carrying. Anna said her dream was significant because "[i]t made me hopeful that I was having a girl."

Negative emotions

Four women (18%) reported dreams that contained solely negative emotions. They experienced distress during the dream and upon awakening. Negative emotions were identified by the presence of anger, fear, worry, perceived danger, lack of security, embarrassment, disappointment or distress. For example, Silvia dreamt that, while in her parent's home, her baby fell off the kitchen counter and was injured. Upon awakening, Silvia reported, "I feel terrible and very panicked," in response to her dream child's injury.

In Beth's dream, which took place in a hospital, Beth felt "devalued as a parent," judged, lost, frustrated and terrified. Her experience was "upsetting," causing "fear and anxiety" that remained with her for a month or more. Similarly, Noelle reported feeling "tired and mad at the [dream] hospital." Florinda felt "embarrassed" and "disappointed" in her dream.

Mixed emotions

Five dreamers (23%) experienced both positive and negative emotions during their dreams or as a result of having their dreams. For example, Uma reported that both she and her husband were "upset" with the actions of the nurses in her dream. In the dream, the nurses gave names to her babies and even took one baby away without her permission. Upon reflection, Uma reported that she felt "excited by the babies, upset by the nurses and slightly anxious that I seemed to be fonder of baby B than baby A." Wilma wrote, "I felt panicked until I found out she [the dream child] was safe; then I felt comforted and secure."

Two participants reported differences between how they felt in their dreams and how they felt about their dreams when awake. In her dream, Maria felt "loving joy" and "also felt very anxious and insecure about having the proper means to care for her [baby]." After Maria awoke, she reported feeling "grateful," and she did not mention negative emotions in her reflective account. Uma also reported a difference between her emotions during her dream and afterward. She felt "excited," "upset" and "slightly anxious" during her dream. When awake, Uma reported feeling "happy and a little confused."

The remaining dream reports reflect no differences between how the participants felt during their dreams and how the participants felt about their dreams when awake. Beth reported that she felt upset in the dream and upon awakening, experienced distress, "fear and anxiety." Tanya felt "happy" and "connected to the baby." Upon awakening, Tanya felt inspired to continue the connection:

> I want to keep working to have more conscious out-of-body experiences while pregnant to further develop the bond and relationship with my unborn child. Immediately after waking up, I reviewed the experience and thought about how I could approach a conscious out-of-body experience differently next time to better connect with my baby.

Some dreams helped the dreamer to resolve conflicted feelings about her pregnancy. For example, Maria reported that she "felt loving joy toward her" [the female dream child] but "very anxious and insecure about having the proper means to care for her," as she was financially unstable. The dream helped Maria resolve the conflict about whether to continue or terminate her pregnancy.

Other dreams with mixed emotions contained anticipation, or a longing for the child to be born, that was not fulfilled upon awakening because gestation was not yet complete. Two dreamers (Claudia and Krista) had identifiable levels of anticipation as a result of having their dreams. For example, Claudia expressed her "need to be patient" because she felt "disappointed that he's not here yet." She discussed needing to "stop setting myself up for disappointment by thinking 'today is the day.'" Similarly, Krista felt "disappointed when I woke up and it [the birth] wasn't real."

Interestingly, the five dreamers with mixed emotions had never previously birthed a full-term living child. Claudia and Krista were pregnant for the first time. Maria, Uma and Wilma had all experienced one or more miscarriages or terminations in the past.

CONFIDENCE AND AFFIRMATION

Related to the Emotion theme, five dreamers' (23%) experiences resulted in identifiably increased confidence and affirmation. This theme emerged from examining participants' responses in which they expressed conviction in the belief that they would make good mothers or that things would work out positively. For example, Hanna wrote, "I woke up feeling reassured that everything would be okay."

This theme, in particular, emerged from the dreams of women (Joan, Maria, Quincy and Wilma) with unplanned pregnancies. Their dreams helped alleviate their uncertainties about becoming mothers. For example, Joan believed that her dream confirmed that "I'm going to be an awesome mom." Maria said that her dream "helped me to know it was all going to be okay." Quincy's dream left her believing "that I could raise him." While her pregnancy was unplanned, Wilma feared losing the pregnancy to miscarriage, as she had in the past. She explained, "It definitely reassured me during my first trimester, and throughout my pregnancy, as I have been assured that this child is meant to be a part of my life and isn't going anywhere." Interestingly, the five dreamers who reported Confidence and Affirmation had never previously birthed a full-term living child; they were either pregnant for the first time or had already had one or more miscarriages or terminations.

BONDING AND CONNECTION

Five dreamers (23%) reported experiencing an identifiable connection between themselves and the babies they were currently carrying. The themes of Bonding and Connection were identified by the dreamer's use of the word "connect" when describing her experience of having her dream. Anna, who said she was lucid during her dream, reported simply,

"I felt connected to my baby." Gabriella's dream resulted in her bonding with the twins she was carrying: "It made me feel so connected to my babies." Joan's dream left her with a feeling of "already connecting while he is inside me." The Tanya's dream was particularly significant since she was lucid. Tanya reported feeling "happy" and "connected to baby" during the dream: "I felt the bond between me and my unborn baby significantly strengthen." Wilma wrote:

> As a result, I have been more emotionally invested than I might have otherwise been. Prior to the dream, I was having difficulty connecting to her because I feared losing her, but afterwards it felt safer to do so.... I also felt far more protective of her than beforehand, as if I wanted to shelter her from the bombs and tanks [in the dream]and keep her safe myself.

None of the five dreamers who reported bonding and connection had ever previously birthed a full-term living child.

BIRTH

Laboring or the birth of the dream child was present in eight dreams (36%). For example, Noelle dreamt she was in a hospital laboring for eight hours, only to end up leaving the hospital and birthing "the baby at home instead." Uma's dream included the vaginal birth "to two twin boys." Penny wrote, "My dreams mostly center around the birth of my child. I am usually alone and in my home. The birth is usually painless and quite peaceful. One dream in particular, I had a baby girl born … in my bathtub." Claudia also "gave birth to [sic] child pain free…" in her dream.

While two of the dreams involving birth included the terms "pain-free" or "painless," the remaining four reports did not include details regarding the actual labor or birth. Of these six dreams, not one explicitly described a negative birth experience. Two dreamers, however, described an abnormal or unusual delivery. Florinda explained that her "unborn child was really a Springer Spaniel puppy who eventually scratched through my belly." In her dream, Donna's midwife "reached inside" her and "pulled the baby out." This was done to determine the sex of the child, and, after doing so, the midwife "put him back inside."

HOSPITALS AND HEALTH-CARE PROFESSIONALS

Five dreamers (23%) reported that hospital or health-care professionals were present in their dreams. For example, Ximena reported "moving from hospital to home" as an event in her dream. Uma's dream took place in a hospital with two nurses actively involved in the delivery and postnatal care. A midwife was present in Donna's dream: she wrote, "I was seeing my midwife to determine the sex of the baby. Instead of doing an ultrasound, she reached inside me, pulled the baby out, confirmed that it was a boy, he smiled, and she put him back inside."

HUSBAND/PARTNER

The dreamer's husband or partner was at least partially present in five of the dreams (23%) reported by women representing the twenty-eight to thirty-four-year-old demographic. For example, Hanna explained, "My boyfriend was holding her [the dream baby] and we were outside in nature…. I also remember us being in a pool." Maria wrote, "I told my partner we needed to buy a sling for me to carry her in…. We worried we wouldn't have money to buy the sling in the dream." Wilma reported, "My partner and I were at a wedding in the desert—at our wedding."

DREAM SETTINGS

Residential dwellings, such as a house or apartment (not a hospital) and natural settings or landscapes, such as a park or a desert, appeared in ten dreams. Five dreamers (23%) mentioned a house, apartment or home in their dreams. Ximena and Noelle had dreams with more than one location, the nonresidential setting being a hospital. Silvia's dream was unique in that the location was her parent's house instead of her own: she wrote, "I was at my parents' house and the baby needed to be changed. I put him on the kitchen counter…."

Five dreamers (23%) reported that they were outside in their dreams. The outdoor locations and circumstances varied greatly. For example, Wilma's dream took place in a desert. Olivia's dream was at a park with a swing set. Claudia was sitting on a bench in her dream. Hanna reported simply that, "we were outside in nature and it was a sunny day." Quincy's dream was unique among this subset because she was also traveling by car in her dream.

BREASTFEEDING

Breastfeeding took place in four dreams (18%); each of these four dreams were experienced by women who had never delivered full-term, living babies. Irene wrote, "I was holding and nursing him, and combing out his really long hair." Krista said that she "was breastfeeding the baby and introducing him to a professor." Ximena reported, "I was holding the baby and trying to breast feed by pouring milk out of my breast like a drink." Uma said that she "was sitting in an arm chair at this time, nursing the ten-pound baby, while the smaller one lay across my lap, looking into my eyes."

CATASTROPHE

A catastrophe, including a disaster or injury, was present in three (14%) dreams. For example, Wilma's dream contained images of tanks and bombs; she added, "There was broken glass everywhere, and it was really loud." In Silvia's dream, the baby "rolled off the counter onto the floor and started crying." When Silvia picked him up, "he had purple lumps and bumps all over his head." Beth found herself "lost in a maze of hallways and elevators" in her dream.

LUCIDITY

Participants were asked, "Were you aware that you were dreaming during this dream?" Ten participants (45%) said that they were lucid by answering "yes," in addition to one participant (5%) who responded, "not at first," and another participant (5%) who responded, "I think so." Seven (32%) replied "no." Three (14%) participants were unsure, could not remember, or did not know. While ten participants reported they were lucid during their dreams, only two narratives (9%) showed hallmarks of lucid dreaming, including awareness that one is dreaming, control over dream activities and content, and making decisions regarding dream outcome (Hobson, et al., 2010; LaBerge & Rheingold, 1990; Neider, Pace-Schott, Forselius, Pittman, & Morgan, 2011). Tanya's report was the strongest indicator for lucidity. Tanya wrote:

> I found myself floating in my bedroom near the ceiling, facing up. I realized I was out-of-body, and immediately began purposely thinking of my baby; I wanted to see if I could interact with it while out-of-body. I wasn't sure how to go about doing this, so I focused on my belly and called to it, "baby, baby, baby." I felt myself drift in and out of my physical body and tried to stay relaxed and calm so as to prolong the experience. Then I felt the baby move inside my belly; I distinctly felt it kick and twist the lower half of its body. I instinctively felt that it was reacting to me trying to interact with it. Then I woke up.

This report shows that Tanya was aware that she was asleep and in a dream, out-of-body, or dream-like state; she formulated intentions, and imposed her will in the dream, all of which are hallmarks of purposeful lucid dreaming. It is necessary to highlight that, whether spontaneous, forced, or provoked, an out-of-body experience is differentiated from a lucid dream in the literature, although some do not concern themselves with such a distinction. Tanya viewed her two experiences as similar enough.

Anna's experience also showed hallmarks of lucidity: "In the dream I thought to myself how this felt just as real as a dream I had a few weeks prior." Similar to Tanya, Anna was self-aware during the dream. Anna's experience, however, may be regarded as pre-lucid or even sub-lucid in accordance with Kellogg's Lucidity Continuum (See Chapter Two). Both of these dreams, however, helped the participants to feel more connected to their babies.

Decision-Making Regarding the Pregnancy

Three dreamers (14%) experienced dreams that had a direct influence on decisions regarding the pregnancy. Maria and Quincy had unplanned pregnancies which they were considering terminating; however, they both changed their minds as a result of their dreams. In reference to termination, Maria stated that her dream "helped me decide what to do.... I'm keeping the baby." In regards to her dream, Quincy wrote:

> I might have considered an abortion at the time of the pregnancy because I had no job, money, or partner. The dream made the person inside me seem very real and concrete, not allowing me to consider such an option.... I might have also considered adoption more seriously than I did at the time, but because of the dream I already felt that I could raise him because I had already experienced within the dream what it was to choose a school, to bundle him in warmth and to comfort him.

Tanya's dream influenced her thoughts about upcoming prenatal care decisions, specifically whether to have a second trimester blood test for Down's syndrome and other defects. Tanya wrote:

> I feel like I am much more bonded to the baby, like I have a real connection with it now that I didn't before, like I have met the little person inside me. My decisions are very much likely to be influenced by this experience. Today my OBGYN scheduled me for my 2nd trimester blood test for Down's syndrome and other defects, due in a couple weeks' time. However should the tests come back positive, I don't think that I could bring myself to terminate the pregnancy now that I feel this bonded feeling with my baby. I almost don't want to have the test because I am not interested in knowing the result, and may not go ahead with it now.

All three of these women had a histories of miscarriages or terminated pregnancies, and they were older, ranging in age between thirty-two and thirty-seven years.

PREDICTION OF FETAL SEX

Five dreamers (23%) had dreams that foretold the sexes of the children they were carrying, which was unknown at the time the dream took place, but which was subsequently confirmed. Anna's dream left her feeling hopeful that she was going to have a girl, and a few weeks later she reported, "I found out I am having a girl." At ten weeks pregnant, Gabriella's dream indicated that the twins she carried were boys, and at twenty weeks this was confirmed. A few weeks after Joan's dream of playing with a male child, she had a sonogram that revealed she was carrying a boy. Olivia's dream included playing at a park with two girls. Olivia has one living daughter already, and during Olivia's second trimester, she learned that she was carrying "another girl." Wilma "already suspected" she was carrying a female child and believed the dream to be "a clear sign that I was having a girl." Wilma reported that her suspicion was later confirmed.

Summary of Experiential Impacts

The majority of participants had dreams containing emotions, specifically positive ones. All six birth dreams that reflected a typical delivery were positive, and the two that contained an unusual delivery were viewed as positive by one dreamer and negative by the other. The presence of a husband or partner in the dream was reported by women between the ages of twenty-eight and thirty-four years. Almost half the survey participants had dreams that involved a residence such as one's home, or a natural setting such as a park or desert. While only four dreams included breastfeeding, interestingly, none of those women had ever birthed a full-term living child. Although nearly half of the participants claimed to dream lucidly, few dreams showed the hallmarks of lucid dreaming. Tanya and Anna reported dreams with the strongest indicators of lucidity.

Those who had unplanned pregnancies (18% of the sample) all had increased confidence and affirmation as a result of their dreams. Thus dreams resulted in positive emotions for this group. Two of these four women made decisions not to terminate their pregnancies after their dreams. I found this to be the case for other pregnant women with whom I spoke prior to beginning this study. As those women recounted their announcing dreams and told me of the implications, I could see how powerful their respective experiences had been for them. Witnessing their stories and being part of a dialogue left me to consider the implication of how just one dream can influes someone at a deep level during a time of vulnerability. The other two women in the study reported bonding and connection with the children they were carrying. Of those who had never had the experience of giving birth to a living child (55%), nine (75%) said their dreams were significant experiences.

CHAPTER SEVEN

Dreams of Departure

The term "announcing dream" is often associated with conception and pregnancy, yet dreams can announce many things, such as upcoming events, health related concerns and even death. This chapter looks at various aspects of dreams and death, and it demonstrates how dreams may even announce an approaching death in the not-so-distant future.

Even after death, the living report the dead (usually dead loved ones) making their presences known in dreams. Throughout history and across the globe, this phenomenon has taken place—in ancient China, ancient Greece and Persia, and pre-modern Korea, for example—and still takes place today. Just as announcing dreams may come unexpectedly, so too do dreams that feature some element related to the dead, or the process of death or dying for those near death or those close to the dying. These kinds of dreams may be vivid, memorable and clear. On other occasions, the dream may be full of symbolism, cloudy or leaving the dreamer unsure of precise details (who, when, where). In this chapter, we will look at the dreams of those who are approaching death themselves, as well as dreams of the deceased experienced by those still living.

Precognitive Episodes

Precognitive or premonition dreams are more common than one might expect. More often than premonitions of death, such dreams reveal what is to come for mundane events. In this section, precognitive dreams related to the death of friends and family are examined, followed by those dreaming of their own deaths.

DREAMS OF LOVED ONES

When my paternal grandmother was living, I probably dreamt of her less than a dozen times. About two or three weeks before her death, I experienced my final dream with her: I haven't had one since. Around the time of the dream, I had also made a visit to her place of residence, but I didn't expect that this visit would be my last. That day, I may have told her about a planned upcoming trip and how I would pay another visit to her when I returned.

In this dream, my grandmother and I were together, as I was visiting her at some indoor location, which may have been her new apartment home. She agreed to go outside with me (something she would not do in her final years in the physical waking state). We walked arm in arm, or hand in hand, very slowly toward this big expansive field outside. The field was well groomed with green grass that appeared freshly cut. There was a sweet smell in the air. The sky was clear and the temperature was just right—not too warm, and not too crisp. Everything seemed quite pleasant. Up ahead, it looked like a group of college football athletes were practicing, and since she loved American football, we sat in chairs on the grass near the end zone. Some bleachers were to the right of us and fairly empty—there were not that many people around—but we didn't seem to mind. It was a calm and peaceful scene, even with such an aggressive sport taking place in our view. We sat quietly, enjoying the freshness of the cool air and taking in the scene along with the expansive, open field.

The following month, in the beginning of August, I was visiting a friend in Santa Marta, Colombia. We were out at dinner and for whatever reason, I took a quick look at my recent incoming emails from that day. There it was, in black and white, an email from my parents alerting me that grandma had died that morning.

While my dream with her may be purely coincidence, it also brought up thoughts about precognitive dreaming and how subtle they might actually be. There was no explicit information in the dream with regard to her approaching death, yet in the dream she agreed to do something out of character, that is, to go outside. Then, while outdoors, we went to a random expansive field and sat comfortably in the "end" zone, which brought us both a sense of peace. As indirect as this experience was, others have reported experiences that are quite explicit, as we will see in the pages ahead.

Some dreams may announce an approaching death or even the deaths of several people. In February 2017, Stanley Krippner learned of some very unfortunate news: three people he knew, all unrelated, had died around the same time. Two were long-time friends: one a shaman, and the other a parapsychology colleague. The third was the young son of a close friend. The twenty-four-year-old person was killed—his life was cut very short.

What is just as striking is that Krippner's dreams, all recorded in his dream journal from January 30th to February 6th, provided clues, or "announcements" to these three approaching deaths. The first entry in Krippner's journal is dated January 30, 2017. It contains two dreams:

> 1) I am in Denver at a program. We are in an auditorium and are told to pull a hymnal out of the pew in front of us. So I suspect we are at a funeral. (Krippner last saw his parapsychology colleague just a few months prior, at meeting near Denver.)
> 2) I am with some friends rehearsing a play. It is a nude musical. I am part of a trip with a young woman and a young man, both very attractive. I am wearing an orange mustache for my part. The musical is a great success. But the young man is drafted, goes into the army, and is killed overseas. I think this is tragic because he could have had a great career.

With regard to the second dream, Krippner told me that the funeral may have been for his close friend's son who was killed.

On February 1, 2017, Krippner recorded another dream in his journal. It reads:

> I am about to see a sneak preview of a movie. It opens with a sign saying "Mortuary Productions," so I think the movie is about death. The movie turns out to be an animated comedy and is very funny and colorful.

On February 2, 2017, another dream takes place. Krippner writes:

> I am giving an invited address to a class. I am telling them how important relaxation is to counteract stress. Someone says they do not have time to relax. I respond, "I would rather see the hours slip by than see the days disappear." I explain that if one does not relax and take it easy, one might die and there will be no days to come.

No dreams were recalled on February 3rd or 4th. Then on February 5, 2017, Krippner logs another death-related dream:

> Someone is dying. I am watching. At first I think it might be me, but then I think it must be someone else because I am watching from the side. There is a healer present trying to restore the person to life. I say, "If any part of Jesus Christ is in you, use that part to bring back life." It works and the sick person rises and is well. But the healer dies in the process. I think that this is similar to Jesus dying so that humanity could have eternal life.

Krippner's following, and final, death-related dream takes place on February 6, 2017:

> I am in church for a funeral I am chosen to lead the procession into a sanctuary. I am wearing a suit and tie, as this is a somber and serious occasion. I am in grief but pull myself together and try to walk erect. I get started and everyone else is right behind me. There is no clue as to whose funeral this is but I sense it was someone very close to me, which is why I was chosen to lead the procession.

Almost two months before the dreams and the death of Krippner's shaman friend, he had the chance to visit her at her nursing home in Oregon. Krippner told me that when she died there were two double rainbows: One above the nursing home where he had visited her and another above her former home in Arizona where she had lived for many years.

DREAMS DURING BATTLE

In certain situations and circumstances, the threat of death may come without warning. For instance, Xenophon (428–354 BCE) of Athens was born shortly after the Peloponnesian war erupted. He was an elite soldier and highly educated. He spent much of his time writing on a large variety of topics. In that era it was typical to hold the belief that the gods provided information through dreams, which foretold future events. While Xenophon did not specifically write large pieces on dreaming, he did mention them in relation to other topics such as war. He noted omens of all sorts, including premonition dreams. References to dreams are commonplace in ancient literature, yet the dreams were rarely captured by those who had them. Xenophon is an exception. Xenophon reports two noteworthy dreams in the epic narrative, Anabasis—his account of his Persian expedition (Hughes, 1987). During those feudal times between ancient Greeks and Persians, Xenophon and fellow army soldiers appeared hopelessly trapped after the slaughter of several of their army captains and generals. Those who remained alive feared they would also be killed within the coming hours. As night fell, a distressed Xenophon had a startling dream that moved him to take leadership and prompted immediate action. His dream is credited for resulting in not only in Xenophon's survival but also that of the remaining soldiers in his company (Hughes, 1987).

ONE'S OWN DEATH

Dreams about the dead are mentioned in pre-modern Korean texts dating from the last and longest-lived imperial dynasty—the Chosŏn dynasty (1392–1910). Dreams can open avenues for communication from the dead and also provide spaces for real encounters between souls, where, for example, the dead can give advice to the dreamer. According to Korean Studies Professor Marion Eggert, a dream may even announce the death of the dreamer.

As we have seen in the previous section, some death-related dreams may occur before an actual death or dangerous situation takes place. Historically, these dreams have been referred to as premonitions, bad omens or warning dreams. From the ancient Greek era, Cyrus the Great had a dream forewarning his own death. Xenophon included this dream in his study of Cyrus entitled *Cyropaedia*. In the dream, Cyrus saw a figure that told him that he would soon "depart to the gods." Taking the warning dream seriously, Cyrus made considerable preparations.

Psychologist Meredith Sabini, director of The Dream Institute in Berkeley, California, inspired me to consider just that. One of the topics upon which she writes and leads workshops is how dreams can inform people about their own deaths, whether those deaths might be by suicide or natural or accidental causes. In her 2010 article, "The Mystery of Death: Noble and Knowable," published in ReVision, she presents eight cases, all of which are curious and thought-provoking. Sabini (2010) posits that, aside from the occurrence of random accidents, "death is a field phenomenon registered in the imaginal realm whose shockwaves are perceptible far and wide, and that what we call an 'accident' may be so only from the perspective of the visible, explicate world" (p. 56). The signs and synchronicities may be all around us, yet linking those to conscious knowing and action is not so commonplace. By tapping in to the signs and attending to the synchronicities, the surprise and shock that is quite typical following tragedy may transform to become processed and understood differently. Sabini's following words are personally impactful:

> In our culture, we do not have sanctioned modes of sharing such perceptions of non-ordinary reality. They tend to be consigned to the borderlands where they alternately may be degraded as wacky, flaky, or weird; or idealized as magical, mystical, or surreal. They are neither. They are perceptions of the imaginal realm or spirit world, and, as data, need to be subjected to conscious reflection and evaluation [Sabini, 2010, p. 60].

I whole-heartedly agree with her.

Death may be postponed by attending to dreams and taking action. Countless examples exist that connect dream images and messages to future or brewing disease and illness. Without taking action, many dreamers would have likely died much sooner than later. While clear verbal messages have been received, dreams most often speak in symbols and metaphors. Could images of crabs be connected to cancer? Could a feeling of choking in a dream indicate a virus and the accompanying soon-to-be swollen throat? Could a dream flood indicate something invading or flooding the physical body? Could a strike to the head predict migraines? It is up to each dreamer to determine if his or her dream suggests normalcy or if it suggests an urgent or problematic situation worthy of medical attention. Either way, the somatic contribution of dreams should be appreciated.

Often we tell stories of past experiences with ease and comfort, believing that we will for the most part be understood. When that experience is a dream, one's comfort level may decrease because of one's culture, for example. What do you think? Have you hesitated to share a dream with someone simply because the experience took place in an imaginal realm? I know I have. In my own circle of family and friends, I also know which individuals with whom I can talk with most comfortably and confidently about my dreams. I reveal more with some than with others. In my own bi-cultural family, it was evident that the spirits of the deceased held "a place at the table" among those members of the paternal side of my family. Their Roman Catholic backgrounds surely influenced this perspective.

Visitation Dreams

Research is limited when it comes to dreaming during periods of mourning and grief, especially when it comes to paying particular attention to dreams of the deceased among those bereaved (Black, DeCicco, Seeley, Murkar, Black, & Fox, 2016). Clinicians, however, learn about such dreams because they spend significant time with those that experience grief and loss. One of my clients suffered deeply after one of her younger siblings died unexpectedly. Soon after the death, she reported vivid dreams, which happened almost nightly, in which her deceased sibling would make appearances, sometimes even spending time to talk or give her hug. These dreams meant everything to my client—it was how the relationship continued even after the death. Such nightly occurrences made an impact on my client's consideration of a possible afterlife and appeared to enhance her own spirituality.

In today's modern times, nursing home residents or those in hospice who are approaching their own deaths have reported significant dreams. In Jeanne Van Bronkhorst's second book, *Dreams at the Threshold: Guidance, Comfort, and Healing at the End of Life*, she distinguishes between visitation dreams and dreams of a dead spouse, for example. Having spent much of her career in hospice work, Van Bronkhorst (2015) writes, "A visitation dream brings the dreamer a visceral sense of the deceased loved ones actual presence. The dying person might even be awake when she sees her loved ones in the room and, smiling, reaches out to greet them" (p. 77). The dying patient may report a deceased loved one hanging out in the room or engaged in lengthy dialogue. Often times, this experience takes place spontaneously as the dying person drifts in and out of consciousness. This phenomenon can startle observers, or it can bring them hope and leave them feeling content. More often than not, the person nearing death is comforted. Like the long-term care staff, Van Bronkhorst attests to the emotional power felt in those moments. Visitations should not be confused with hallucinations due to the noted difference in perception, content and meaning.

There are four characteristics of visitation dreams, according to Van Bronkhorst (2015): a sense of realness, a comforting presence, guidance and questions about afterlife. Visitation dreams encompass a vivid experience of a true visitor that doesn't account for whether the perceiver was awake or asleep—whether awake or not, the visitor was real to the perceiver and makes a real impact. Feelings of confusion or comfort may arise depending on one's perception of the afterlife or spiritual beliefs.

A comforting, calm presence is reported when visitors are near as if they are well-known to the dying person. Strangers are not reported to appear, but if they do, the patient is assessed for medical hallucination, according to one palliative care nurse. Instead, those trusted and loved appear to people who are dying, without resentment or expectation.

Visitors seem to come with a purpose—to benefit the dying and accompany them through the transition. A plane, train, window, bridge, door or even a cruise ship may be an object shown to signify the transition, but the visitor acts as the guide or loving helper when crossing over into the next existence. Even if the dying person is not quite ready to leave, the visitor is still understood as benevolent. At any age, one may dream of taking a trip or making a journey, although these types of dreams usually take place at a time of transition, such as marriage or divorce, graduation, childbirth, job change and, of course, as death approaches. Near the end of one's life, "journey and travel dreams become more common" (Van Bronkhorst, 2015, p. 72). I recall one dream in which I got on board a train and was pleased to find several deceased family members also riding on that train. As the dream came to a close, we got off at different stops. I could only interact with them on that one train car, and it was understood that we were not to exit together. This leads me to wonder whether I will re-experience this type of dream near the end of my own life, but with one difference: I'll be getting off the train with them, at the very same stop.

As for the possibility of the existence of an afterlife, visitors usually don't mention it specifically, although there is an indirect suggestion of it. Still, such possibilities can offer relief and hope for both the dying person and the family. Regardless of one's beliefs, visitation dreams bring loving comfort for so many and help to resolve distress, according to Van Bronkhorst (2015).

In Nursing Homes

As I've discussed earlier, dreams can point out something unknown to the dreamer and assist in problem-solving. Dreams can remind us of good times and enliven memories of times when things were going well. Additionally, we may also dream about what we lack and what is not experienced in waking life. One study in Poland examined the dreams of fifty-five male and ninety-two female nursing home residents between the ages of fifty and ninety-four (Owczarski, 2014). The nursing home residents dreamed about both living and dead loved ones. Some of the dreams offered familiar contact with those who they rarely saw in their day-to-day life. Both men and women dreamt of children whom they rarely saw, and for this reason alone, they were grateful for such dreams. Others recalled dreams featuring spouses and children, reminding them of a time when their families were united. These experiences enhanced a sense of love and joy for the dreamer. Such experiences can bring about wellbeing for some nursing home residents who currently live in difficult situations, taking away a focus on the here-and-now. The residents wake up feeling better. According to Owczarski (2014), "positive emotions clearly predominate over the negative ones" (p. 273).

Dreams about deceased loved ones, whether close friends or family members, are "often highly memorable and emotionally important to the dreamer" (Domhoff, 2015, p. 236). This may be especially true for those who have lost a spouse and, for the first time, find themselves alone in their home. A dream may occur soon after the death, but may also come years later. Some may have one dream; others may have several. For those who recall more than one dream, these dreams may take place during a brief period of time or be spread out over months or years. The dreams can vary greatly. The dream content may feature the deceased returning from death (coming back to life), revealing a family secret; predicting misfortune or good fortune; recovering from illness or medical procedures; offering reassurance to those still alive; and friendly, sexual, loving, or even aggressive interactions.

Trauma and Tragedy

When a person loses a loved one traumatically, suddenly or at a young age, a dream featuring the deceased can have lasting impact. The impact may be viewed as positive or negative. Well-known English poet and artist William Blake experienced visions since he was a child. When Blake's younger brother Robert died, Blake claimed to continue to see him in visions and dreams. In one dream, Robert appeared to him and taught him a method for printing. This ongoing relationship with his brother through vision and dream would likely be considered positive by many.

In addition to dreams assisting her writing, skilled dreamer Amy Tan found great meaning in the dreams that followed the murder of her friend Pete as noted in Naomi Epel's book, *Writers Dreaming* (p. 282–283). From this experience, Tan learned about a deeper aspect of herself. In one dream, Pete appeared and wanted to show Tan where he lived. When they got there, Tan wanted to fly just like the other beings around Pete's home. Knowing that Tan was still alive, Pete suggested she rent some wings, after all, the rental fee was only twenty-five cents. Tan flew around and enjoyed herself until she recalled that the wings were cheap, resulting in her falling. Realizing that she flew just seconds ago with these same wings, and then playing with the experience of flying-falling-flying again, Tan came to understand something about herself: confidence, not material, is what enables one to develop and grow. Tan's recently deceased friend appeared in other dreams to help Tan understand how she had been giving away her power and giving in to fear. Tan understood that facing fear leads to its dissipation. Such impactful dreams continued throughout the trial for Pete's murder; once the nine-month trial concluded, Pete appeared once again to say goodbye. Tan, believing she owned her dreams, became furious at Pete's assertion. Nonetheless, Tan reported that she never got to speak to Pete directly in dream—the dreams changed, the lessons had come to an end, and it was time for her to move forward with her life. He did leave her with one gift: a friend she'd meet in the future, according to Pete. Some time later, Tan met the woman Pete told her about. She's a fiction writer with whom Tan has become good friends. Tan was encouraged by this new writer friend to also become a fiction writer (Epel, 1993).

Dreams may help to soothe painful events and bring meaning, even amidst tragedy and great loss. I found that when I spoke with friends, new and old, about my interest in meaningful and extraordinary dreams, they too were interested in the topic. Many had a dream to share. One report I will never forget was told to me in a casual manner, but there was no mistaking the profound impact the dream had on the dreamer and the dreamer's daughter. Over lunch at Rincon del Buho in Sevilla's La Macarena neighborhood, I spoke with a new friend (the dreamer's daughter, in this case), who had been living in the area for quite some time.

Learning of my research and interest in dreams, she shared with me something that shaped her view on the connection between the afterlife and this reality. Her father told her about a powerful dream he had had many years ago. The inspiration to share his dream with his daughter (my new friend) was tied to his friend's death at that time.

The daughter told me that, during the evening of her father's friend's death, her father said that he woke up in the middle of the night when he felt someone kiss his cheek while he was asleep. In the morning, only a few hours later, he learned that his friend had died, and he believed that the kiss was the way his friend had said goodbye to him.

This experience led my new friend's father to recall a dream he had much earlier, when his daughter was a young girl (This was the dream that changed my friend's view about reality). In the dream, the father and his sister were at a train station, waiting on a passenger platform when his mother, who had died long ago, came out of a big steam engine, gave the father a big hug, took his sister by the hand and brought her onto the train. When my friend's father woke up, he received news by telephone that his sister had been in a fatal automobile accident that same night.

This dream is truly unique in the ones I've come across. On a personal level, it resonates with me particularly well, as I have spent some dream time in the past with adored deceased relatives on trains. Some get on or off at different stops, but those who have already died have never used the same stop as the one I've used. The dead and the living have their own destinations, I suspect. When I awaken from dreams like these, I feel calm and so very grateful. Trains are so metaphorical and an earlier example included an airplane. Why not a car, I wonder? So far, I have not heard of a dying person make the transition by automobile. One distinction between these two vehicles is that trains can carry a lot of people, while an automobile can only carry a few.

As noted in an earlier chapter, Eli's dream of his mother, who died almost two decades ago, demonstrates the deep meaning and impact that can come as a result of dreaming with a deceased loved one. In the dream, Eli and his mother enter a church and find a place to sit, taking in the large number of people and Catholic officials present. While Eli is lucid in this dream, he stays present and remains there, pleased that he can have this time with his mother. As church songs are being sung, Eli's mother makes a sound that is similar to the high pitch an eagle can make. Her frequency is visual (spiral-like) as well as auditory. A man engages Eli as the church becomes silent. The stranger tells Eli how he has been healed—

through the sound frequency emitted by his mother. Some time after this dream, Eli needed help with his voice during a ceremony for the healing of a man he did not know. Eli trusted he would be helped and so he did not give up or stop the ceremony. As a result, he found his own special frequency for that ceremony which resulted in the healing of the ill man. This example is one where the deceased are trusted and share important information. The presence of the deceased appears to offer guidance and instruction for positive changes. They are welcomed.

DREAMING WITH THE DEAD
IS NOT ALWAYS A HAPPY AFFAIR

Alternatively, constant visitation with deceased family members may not always be welcome, especially if they have a pressing agenda. In California, a married woman shared with me her frustration because of her deceased mother-in-law frequently appearing in dreams and behaving as if she were "still alive." The deceased mother-in-law nagged the dreamer on various practical matters. The dreamer recounted, literally listed, the many times she was visited by this one deceased person with all her demands. When I asked the dreamer, "So, what happens during the dreams?" I was told that she would frequently be given unsolicited advice regarding how to parent her son and the proper method of upkeep for the deceased's former home. Not only that, but the deceased mother-in-law often reported her desires to the dreamer: common desires had to do with visiting someone or going to a particular place. Even when the dreamer reminded the deceased mother-in-law that she was, in fact, dead, this didn't seem to stop her from returning in another dream soon after with more demands, instruction or unsolicited advice.

Sometimes, deceased family members arrive by surprise, even when the dreamer intends to "visit" someone else. Over the 2010 Memorial Day weekend, I became lucid in a dream and asked a divine source to take me to see my newborn nephew, as I hadn't yet met him and was very eager to do so. I found myself in my nephew's bedroom and saw him alone in his crib, yet happily engaged with several of our deceased family members. Their spirits were clear to me, and I was very glad to see them there. After taking in the scene, lucidity faded and I woke up, feeling a mix of happiness and surprise, and desiring the experience to have gone on much longer.

Two dreams reported by a Ghzawa peasant woman featured her dead mother asking for particular objects. The object requested in the first dream was the house key; in the second dream, it was the bed mattress. Both of these objects, the house key and bed mattress, are well known symbolically among the Ghzawa tribe as family and marriage, respectively. In the end, the dreamer decided to give these objects to her dead mother in the dreams, even though she knew doing so would come at a great cost. After, in the first dream, giving her dead mother the house key, the woman's daughter died. Then, later, the woman's husband died after the dreamer gave up the bed mattress in the second dream. Actions taken in dreams "are thought to be at the origin of real events" (Gonzalez-Vazquez, 2014, p. 101). In Ghzawa villages, dreaming of deceased parents is considered dangerous by some tribal members.

For some, however, a deceased relative might reveal ulterior, darker motives. Knowing that dreaming of deceased parents or family members is fairly common among some groups (as mentioned in Chapter Two) and considered just as real as anything, anthropologist Douglas Hollan directly inquired about this experience with a Toraja community elder he knew. Although being attacked in dreams is very rarely reported, this elder shared a time when his father attacked him in an attempt to take him to the afterworld. The attempt was unsuccessful due to the struggle that took place in the dream, but the elder was still fearful and shaken because he nearly lost his life at that moment and, furthermore, this dream foretold his death. The elder sought "counsel of a person experienced in dream interpretation who could help him see that his father's spirit needed to be placated," and he also said that through a ritual (sacrificing a pig to his father's spirit), he was able to change prophecy. After all, the sacrifice satisfied "his father's hunger for food" as well as "human companionship" (Hollan, 2014, p. 184).

For communities that are unable to afford to give regular offerings, waiting for a sign that one is needed is an option, although a risky one. That sign might be an angry spirit, like the deceased father above, attacking someone in a dream, or something else, such as an ancestral spirit destroying or stealing the dreamer's property or possessions or causing their "animals or crops to become sick or die" (Hollan, 2014, p. 186).

Instead of a relative, others have reported seeing deceased community members or undesirables in a dream. One Nahuat women saw a well-known witch (*nahual*) in her dream. Although he had died many years ago, the *nahual* emerged from the land of the dead in her dream and attempted to rob her baby girl of her soul. The envious dead may do such things in an effort to avoid punishment or gain access to benefits in the otherworld.

DREAMS OF DECEASED STRANGERS

Sometimes people dream of deceased individuals who are unknown to them and who appear in pairs. In the first century (in the 560s-early 570s), two deceased "virgin martyrs" (Moreira, 2003, p. 624) appeared together in the dreams of two different men—a local inhabitant and a bishop. In the dreams, the two virgin martyrs made specific, direct requests, first to the local man, then later to the bishop. In the first dream, the martyrs told the local man to build a roof for their tombs to protect them from rain. The man ignored this dream, so in the second dream, the martyrs threatened him with death if he failed to act. Now frightened, he followed the dream instructions. Afterward, he asked a Bishop to bless the oratory he had built, yet the bishop did not follow through. After ignoring the local man's request, the bishop had a dream in which the martyrs appeared, convincing him to make the blessing after all. This series of dreams together spanned over half a year and several seasons, according to the records (Moreira, 2003).

THE DEAD MAY PROVIDE
SERVICE IN DREAMS

Before western contact, religious dreams of the Asabano of Papua New Guinea often contained the dead as well as other types of spirits, and these dreams were viewed as informative across various aspects of life. While seeing the dead was traditionally considered a bad omen, contact with other non-living entities was not. In fact, there existed a perception that something might be gained, such as information for community or individual defense, successful hunts and the afterlife (Lohmann, 2000).

After the arrival of Christianity, one Asabano report included a mother's dream of her recently deceased young son. The little boy spoke to the mother in the dream and gave her a message for his (still-living) father. The perceived reason behind the message was to diffuse a current conflict in the community, fueled by the father's feelings and suspicions surrounding the nature of his son's death.

As we have seen, dreaming can remove barriers that limit interaction, information sharing or willing assistance from the dead. Northwest Australian shaman and poet Allan Balbungu explained that shamans can have productive relationships with dead ancestors or other spirits by going to the netherworld, or the world of the dead. Dead ancestors commonly become helping spirit figures, and they may teach dances and songs.

Explorations into the netherworld are done when the shaman is asleep and his soul wanders about to various places (Lommel & Mowaljarlai, 1994).

Cross-cultural comparisons of death dreams between one hundred fifty Tibetan and three hundred twenty Han Chinese dreamers were systematically investigated (Li, Yin, & Shen, 2015; Yin, Li, & Shen, 2015). Death dreams, in general, appeared to be common among members of these groups. These researchers looked at the dreams from both a manifest and an implicit perspective. A manifest perspective means that the elements are directly seen in the text of the dream studied, while an implicit perspective explores elements that cannot be seen directly in the dream text but emerge from further analysis (Li, Yin, & Shen, 2015; Yin, Li, & Shen, 2015).

Between the two groups, differences from the manifest perspective included death role (adults, children and animals), emotion, cause of death and the appearance of a helper (Li, Yin, & Shen, 2015). When it came to the "death role," the death dreams of the Han Chinese showed the death of the dreamer more often, whereas Tibetan death dreams showed the death of another that was unknown to the dreamer. Sadness and fear were primary emotions in the death dreams for both groups. While the feeling of peace, for both groups, was acknowledged, it was less prevalent than negative emotions. In general, the Tibetan group's dream emotions were more peaceful. Unknown reasons and homicide were primary causes of death in these dreams, although many more Tibetans described unknown causes of death in the dream than did the Han Chinese dreamers. On rare occasions, a helper was present in the death dreams for both groups. At times, the helper was the dreamer him/herself—this occurred when someone else was dying and the dreamer acted as a rescuer, but the end result was still death. Other times, helpers were related to religion and represented as the Buddha, Lama or associated objects. These helper "images mainly functioned as pacifiers of the emotion or guides offering suggestions" (Li, Yin, & Shen, 2015, p. 40).

Implicit differences in death dreams between the two groups included the dreamland's color tone, death image, waking coping approach and death theme (Yin, Li, & Shen, 2015). Between the two groups, significant differences in color tone as well as death image were noted. The Tibetan dreams of the death process were much more frequent compared to Han Chinese, while, for the Han Chinese, the primary death image was a funeral. Significant differences were found again for waking coping approaches. Tibetan participants responded to the death dream by sharing the dream with others as well as chanting sutras and praying or worshipping Buddha. Han Chinese participants spent more time attempting to understand the dream's meaning. Both groups shared certain dream themes: "extinction," and "separation," were at the top of the list. Overall, Yin, Li and Shen's (2015) study shows that Tibetan and Han Chinese death dreams have both differences and similarities. This makes sense given the cultural and psychological differences between the two groups studied.

DREAMS WITH PETS

Dreams that include the appearance of pets are not always straight-forward or as clear as one might like. For example, one Californian boy dreamt that his dog had died a few hours before his mother contacted him to say, "We need to talk." Upon hearing her message and tone, he blurted out that he knew the family dog had died. His mother affirmed that a death had, in fact, occurred, but that it wasn't their dog. Instead, the boy's paternal grandmother has just died. Such premonitions may twist some important details. While this idea is only speculation, perhaps the boy's psyche blended the comfort of his beloved pet with the comfort of his grandmother. The boy's psyche may have protected him by letting him know in advance that a death had taken place, without the direct impact of knowing the exact identity of the person who had died. If the boy had indeed experienced such a direct and explicit premonition dream, there might have been other consequences that he might have been developmentally unprepared to digest, such as the meaning of this way of knowing.

In addition to people, missing or thought-to-be dead pets can make appearances in dreams. In 2014 I bought a small bird as a pet. I allowed the bird to fly freely each day, since he was cage-bound when I went to work each day. In less than a year, the bird flew out of a cracked window in my bathroom. I saw him in the neighborhood that evening, but never again after that day. While I hope he survived, I presume that he died from the elements, as it was winter and he had never before foraged for food outdoors. Two days later, I dreamt of him vividly. In the dream, he flew in to my apartment, through the window, returning on his own. He brought with him another bird, and then soon after, a few more birds arrived. My bird seemed happy with these other birds, his little community. There were five in total, including him. The others looked similar in color but were larger and had longer beaks. They all seemed content together and chirped a lot. I fed them and was relieved by their presence. His cage was still out and some of the other birds easily and freely entered the cage. I was not sure if they all were going to stay and live with me or not. I awoke at that moment, feeling happy to see him, but also sad that he was still "missing" and possibly in harm's way.

CHAPTER EIGHT

A Dual-Directional Announcing Dream Discussion

Dreaming is just one avenue through which we understand ourselves and the world. Dreams have the potential to offer glimpses of what is to come, whether that future exists in this physical waking reality, the afterworld or another dimension entirely. It is one's culture that influences judgment, placing dreams in categories of being welcomed, feared or ignored altogether. While dreams that announce conception and a baby-to-be often bring a sense of peace and acceptance, dreams that announce death are more often met with fear.

Toward Birth

The elements present in announcing dreams are fairly common and include a variety of positive and negative emotional states, residential dwellings, natural settings and various people (acquaintances, friends and family members). A quick reflection upon one's own dreams from this month alone is very likely to include some, if not all, of these elements. Just this week, my dreams have included houses, apartments, a bridge, the sky, trees, friends and strangers and a fairly wide assortment of feelings, such as happiness, confusion and despair.

The elements that commonly surface in pregnant women's dreams were also found in the data from my doctoral study, such as, giving birth, hospitals and health-care professionals, one's spouse, partner, or the baby's father, breastfeeding, catastrophe and predictions of the child's sex. What is unique to the announcing dream is the presence of the unborn and a commonly reported sense of this presence being the baby the woman is carrying at that time. During the years I dedicated to my dissertation, I had dreams that involved giving birth (usually to male babies) and caring for infants. I recall about three of them although many details are fuzzy in my mind. What dozens of women have told me about their experiences is different from my experience. I awoke fairly certain that I was not pregnant, but those who have had announcing dreams often report awakening with a heart-felt or visceral sentiment—a quality difficult to articulate. While the presence of the unborn is viewed as a common theme in pregnancy dreams (Maybruck, 1989), my results suggest that the presence of the unborn is linked to confidence and affirmation (especially in unplanned pregnancies), bonding and connection and decision-making regarding pregnancy termination. There was no such impact in my dreams during that time, and I was not pregnant either. As a side note, I should mention that many people experience dreams of birthing while in the dissertation process, so my dreams were not surprising from that standpoint. Since the dissertation process is an analytical one, I considered the likelihood that that was the reason I had birthed males, as opposed to females, in my dreams during those years.

For three of the participants in my study, their dreams were catalysts for making important decisions about their pregnancies. A reported dream said to influence an important decision is supported by the scholarly dream literature (Bowater, 2012; Carey, 2010; Edgar, 2006) as well as by anecdotal reports. A pregnant woman's perception of her baby in a dream, as my study investigated, may be one manifestation by which pregnancy decisions are influenced. This bridges the impact of decision-making dreams with pregnancy dreams. While literature exists showing a relationship between dreams and political decisions (Bowater, 2012), little has been found to show a relationship between dreams and decisions or conflicts while pregnant. This area is ripe and ready for more extensive study. Fortunately, this area does appear to be gaining more attention in the west at this time.

Some of the pregnant participants in my study were contemplating a decision in the physical waking state about whether to continue or terminate their pregnancies, and the dream state was then an extension of their cognitive processing. Pregnant women in the study used the content from the dream to inform waking life contemplations and the upcoming decision. The actions taken by some participants were informed by the dream content. For example, Maria said the dream "helped me decide what to do…. I'm keeping the baby." Krippner and colleagues (2002) referred to pregnancy dreams among those considering abortion and stated, "Dreams may contain metaphors for feeling trapped, being over-burdened, or looking frantically for a solution to a problem" (p. 63). The dreams in my study differed in that those contemplating termination had dreams that resulted in increased confidence or affirmation to continue the pregnancy. We all know that abortion still holds a stigma, so of course, it is easier to openly talk with acquaintances about "keeping a baby" as opposed to those who are no longer pregnant due to abortion. It is no surprise that many women would likely not be nearly as comfortable with saying that their dreams prompted them to schedule an appointment for an abortion. Because the study questionnaire did not specifically ask participants if the pregnancy was planned or unplanned or if termination was ever considered, data only included that information when the participants volunteered it. What's more, the wording of the recruitment materials may have selected for women with a positive bias toward pregnancy, even an unplanned one. Since the samples in both studies are relatively small, more research is warranted to further investigate the significance of dreams and decisions regarding the continuation of pregnancy.

According to the complementary (or compensatory) theory, dreams re-establish balance within the psyche and restore psychological equilibrium (Jung, 1964, 1974). Pregnant women's dreams may represent unresolved psychological issues, including conflicts about the pregnancy or becoming a mother. The themes of Confidence and Affirmation arose out of the dreams from participants with unplanned pregnancies. These dreams appeared to compensate for the dreamer's feelings of uncertainty, fear and lack of confidence to support an unplanned pregnancy; thus, the dreams restored a more harmonious state for the pregnant women.

The additional themes, Bonding and Connection, emerged from the dreams of five participants, two of whom had unplanned pregnancies, and none of whom had children. This theme was not present among participants who had prior experience with being mothers. Regardless of whether the pregnancy is intentional, most pregnant women experience psychological stress (Rafael-Leff, 1990). Conflicts about becoming a mother may resolve from just one announcing dream, as appeared to happen for some of my study's participants. Feeling safe through connection, confidence and affirmation affects maternal hormones, thus influencing fetal development (Christensen, 2000; Rossi, 2002; Schlotz & Phillips, 2009; Verny, 2002). This study's findings support Jung's (1964, 1974) complementary theory and align with Leva-Giroux's (2002) findings that dreams are in fact one avenue through which pregnant women can connect with their unborn child.

Two of the four dreams with solely negative emotions shared a central image of being in a hospital. Kitzinger's (1978) case studies of Jamaican and English pregnant women connected anxiety dreams with hospitals. These dreams may be a reflection of a variety of factors, including personally held beliefs about hospital care and procedures. The dreams also may highlight unconscious feelings about the pregnancy.

The continuity hypothesis (Adler, 1936; Hall & Nordby, 1972) posits that dreams reflect a person's life in the waking state and illuminate what one should attend to in the waking state. With this hypothesis in mind, I noticed that breastfeeding was present in the dreams of the pregnant participants who had not previously delivered a child. As a woman prepares to become a mother, her dreams may reflect waking concerns about what is expected of her, such as providing necessary nourishment for the child-to-be, or they may simply reflect the internal processing of a new behavior soon to be performed.

My doctoral study results show some support for distinguishing between ordinary and extraordinary dreams; extraordinary dream qualities such as lucidity, precognition (sex of the child) and vividness emerged from the data, although minimally. Lucidity, for example, was a common claim in response to a direct question. Of the ten participants who said they were lucid, only two reports actually demonstrated the telltale signs of lucidity, such as dream awareness, control and outcome. It is possible that the remaining eight participants reported lucidity simply because the announcing dream was unusual, vivid or extraordinary, as is the case for many dreams during pregnancy (Knaan-Kostman, 2006). Furthermore, lucidity exists along a spectrum, or continuum, as do levels of conscious awareness, so it can be challenging for researchers to precisely determine how lucid one is from a dream report, especially given that some details may have been forgotten upon logging the dream in a journal, for example.

Precognition appears to be more common in my research. Five participants claimed to know the sex of the child they were carrying before medical confirmation or birth, and, according to their records, all were correct. This was also the case for other women I spoke with before and after the study. The accuracy of these predictions, however, cannot be confirmed, and it is quite possible that a bias to recall or favor confirming over disconfirming information exists (Hergovich, Schott, & Burger, 2010).

While an announcing dream may not take place for all pregnant women or expectant men, the experience, when it does occur, does have an impact for some women and men, as demonstrated in the literature and by my study's findings on women. The effect of announcing dreams cannot be fully explained; however, consistent with the collected anecdotes, overall I found that announcing dreams were meaningful for some women.

Even though it may be powerful, the announcing dream experience is a personal one that is seldom discussed in public (Bowman, 2001). If dreams, overall, were more often included in daily conversation and considered valued aspects of modern Western culture, we might find that more reports of announcing dreams would surface. In addition, Callister, Vehvilainen-Julkunnen, and Lauri (2001) acknowledged the practical value of studies that focus solely on women:

> Pregnancy is a vital part of the transitional childbearing experience. During pregnancy, a woman may gain new knowledge about her body and mind. Her dreams may be viewed as a source of knowledge in which only she is the expert. Although not universally experienced, women do report announcing dreams, the significance they hold, and the resulting impact [p. 31].

Insight into how specific dream experiences affect decisions and behaviors facilitates understanding and appreciation of each pregnancy's multidimensional qualities. Pregnant women's, as well as expectant men's, descriptions and the resulting impact of their subjective experiences of dreaming of their unborn children are significant to those who care for and work with families. A better understanding of the announcing dream phenomenon and its consequences will assist those professionals who are eager to explore their pregnant or expectant patients' internal worlds. Enhanced understanding of a one's inner world can assist in formulating important decisions about birth plan, medical decisions and other procedures. Consequently, the more this phenomenon is acknowledged and understood, the less fear of judgment and ridicule pregnant women or expecting men may experience.

As a possible protective factor, announcing dreams may act as adaptive mechanisms—such as a coping mechanism—especially in view of findings by Krippner, et al. which discuss dreams as "metaphors for feeling trapped, being overburdened, or looking frantically for a solution to a problem" (2002, p. 63). Dreams through which a pregnant woman awakens to feel bonded to her fetus, as my study has demonstrated, may serve as a protective evolutionary factor, encouraging birth and promoting health benefits. When a pregnant woman perceives a relationship with her unborn child, she is more likely to contemplate prenatal health care choices, as Tanya did, and make a greater emotional investment, as Wilma did. These early relationships are likely to support attachment after the birth.

Near Death

Death is the ultimate unknown. In modern Western culture, it may be considered the final enemy. Just as dreams can offer guidance for parents-to-be, they also can offer guidance to those preparing for death, either their own or the death of another. In addition, death dreams may prompt the dreamer toward action in the dream or in the physical waking state, resulting in either positive or negative consequences. In the aftermath of tragedy, death dreams can provide confirmation and comfort to those grieving and experiencing deep loss. Death dreams may even confirm an afterlife or the continuation of the soul's journey. It is also possible that learning takes place when dreaming with the dead. In many cases, emotions arise as the result of a death dream, whether these dreams come as warnings or are neutral. No one knows exactly when a death-related dream will take place. Sometimes such dreams occur prior to a death, soon after the death or even years later. Furthermore, it is possible that death might be postponed by paying attention to what death-related dreams offer, such as an awareness of needed medical attention. Still, death dreams are not always welcome events!

During four of the six years I resided in Phoenix, Arizona, I came to know and befriend an elderly neighbor who the community referred to as "Chief." I believe that Chief was given this nickname due to his age, status and how he kindly looked out for his neighbors. He acted as the eyes and ears of the community. Over the years, Chief showed significant signs of aging and, near the end of his time, his family considered relocating him. Shortly after they did so, I learned that Chief had died, although I do not recall any of the details. About a week later, I had the most vivid dream, which follows:

> In the dream, it is a bright, sunny day, and so I have my bedroom windows wide open. I am sitting on my bed and looking out the window, which faces the grassy community courtyard, with its plants and water fountain. All things appear vibrant and colorful. As I peacefully gaze out, Chief walks toward me. I notice how he is without his cane and appears more youthful than usual. Chief is able to come right up to the edge of my bedroom window since the large green bush that exists in front of the window in physical waking reality is not there in the dream. So, I climb halfway out and sit on the window sill as we greet each other (this would have been very uncomfortable on the body in the physical waking state). Our interaction is not lengthy, although it is warm and pleasant. We communicate without words. He looks really good, healthy, at peace and, ironically, full of life.

When I awoke, I truly felt touched. It was a heart-warming experience, and I was very happy to "see" Chief again. There was some minor grade of lucidity in that I knew in the dream that Chief had already died. I was surprised by his youthful appearance and that he did not need his cane. These things did not increase my lucidity, unfortunately. Had that been the case (as it has happened in the past), I might have chosen to ask Chief what the post-death journey had been like for him, or I might have asked him if he would like me to pass along a message to someone special. This dream left me with a sense of peace about his existence and that of my own. This dream, and several others I recall, confirmed for me the continuation of consciousness after the physical death of the body. It had that quality of realness—the first of Van Bronkhorst's four characteristics of visitation dreams. The impact would likely have been much more profound had it been experienced by one of Chief's children, instead of me, as I was just a neighbor.... Who knows, perhaps Chief visited them, too.

Death dreams like this one may serve the living in various ways. The occurrence may have helped me to cope with his sudden loss—after all, I never had the opportunity to say goodbye. The dream may have also served as a reminder to attend more closely to the elderly loved ones in my life at that time—who knows when they might die. The dream may have also helped me to compensate for any disowned parts that deny death as the final frontier. The many death-related dreams throughout Chapter Seven can also be considered as functions for adaptation, compensation and unity.

When the Two Meet

Sometimes a baby-to-be and a deceased loved one appear in one dream, together, as in the following dream. As one pregnant woman dreamt of pushing her newborn in a baby carriage, she walked past groups of people sitting on benches. The dreamer noticed that one of the people on the bench happened to be her dead uncle. Even though he had been dead for two years, he smiled and winked at the pregnant dreamer. The dreamer reported a happy feeling, overall, but also anxiety and tension as a result (Sherwen, 1991). For some, images of the deceased are uncomfortable altogether. Other questions may arise with regard to the timing of the deceased's appearance. In the example above, the uncle appeared after he had been dead for two years. One might ask why he appeared in a dream during the short period of pregnancy. This may bring up questions related to reincarnation, protection from "the other side," or other concerns, especially if the deceased made a request for something.

Another woman lost her younger brother before she became pregnant, and she dreamt about him during the pregnancy. She reported that her brother was "learning to have fun in camp," in the dream. She "knew he was going to die—but he was having fun in the pool with his instructor and it didn't bother me" (Sherwen, 1991).

In *Coming From the Light* by Sarah Hinze, a moving experience that weaves together pre-birth and after-death communications is reported. After a couple tried to get pregnant for a decade with no success, adoption was considered. The book relates the experience of the adopting parents-to-be: "One night shortly after this [decision], I was having a nightmare. Suddenly in my dream there was a light and a peaceful feeling. In the light I saw a beautiful baby with big dark eyes. Peace came over me. He said, 'I have been waiting a long time, and I have your name on me.' He spoke these words as one adult speaks to another, but I saw a baby's face. I did not know if the baby was a boy or girl" (Hinze, 1997, p. 150). With excitement, plans to adopt a child were made. Less than a year later, the baby to be adopted was born; about three days later, *Tyler* was allowed to be picked up and moved into his new home. The birth mother requested visitation with the baby just a couple days after the birth, which was worrisome to the adoptive parents. Would the birth mother change her mind and want to keep the newborn boy after all, as is known to happen? As this experience was happening, the individual said, "I sat in my office praying. Suddenly I felt the presence of my stepfather, who had passed away many years previously. He assured me that all is well. I realized that it was the anniversary of my stepfather's death" (Hinze, 1997, p. 151). It turned out that the adoption process would proceed without any problems or setbacks. The adopting parents "were later told that when the birth mother held Tyler, she had the distinct impression come to her mind that it really was God's will that Tyler be raised by the adoptive family" (Hinze, 1997, p. 151). They felt so grateful: "Three years later my sister had an experience in which my stepfather (her father) appeared to her in a dream. He told her: 'Tyler is a great spirit and was my good friend in the spirit world. When he found out his birth mother wanted to give him up for adoption, I asked him if he would come to our family. Tyler agreed'" (Hinze, 1997, p. 151).

As I considered aspects like this dream account, I wondered how this sensitive intersection might be experienced for pregnant widows of military servicemen or pregnant women widowed as a result of other tragedies. Since dreams of the deceased often bring comfort to living loved ones, could an announcing dream to include the recently deceased father offer hope or peace to the pregnant mother?

Do dreams provide reliable intelligence about the environment, the imaginal world and physical waking reality—or are they "just dreams," as some say? Could dreams be authentic, intelligent experiences of one's soul? Or is such a notion absurd? Culture makes all the difference in how one contemplates, as well as responds to, such questions. For example, Eli's dream about his mother (who had been deceased for close to two decades) guided him in his work. The dream experience was real for Eli, and he acted upon the information he was given.

Whether we originate from a polyphasic culture or a monophasic one, a Western or a non–Western culture, the barriers between cultural groups are thinning. As we become increasingly globalized, might dreams provide venues for new incorporations? How might we negotiate such adjustments?

The next chapter changes course and was created for those desiring deeper engagement with dreams. Maybe you want to recall your dreams with greater frequently or with more consistency. Perhaps you have a long-time practice of regularly recording your dreams in a journal and want to develop the skill of dreaming with increased levels of awareness and lucidity. No matter the case, Chapter Nine contains a variety of techniques, ideas and tips for further engaging a dream practice.

CHAPTER NINE

Tips and Techniques for Extraordinary Dreaming

In this chapter, tips and techniques for dream recall will be discussed; later, strategies for increasing conscious awareness and incubating dreams are offered. Similar to Austrian psychologist Brigitte Holzinger (2009), I believe that lucid dreaming is a natural ability and that lucid dream incubation is a skill that can be learned. Anyone who wants to experience a lucid dream, or any extraordinary dream for that matter, must first be able to recall one and become acquainted with what the dream state is like. Furthermore, dream recall is necessary because becoming lucid in the first place requires that you "recognize that your dream is a dream, while it is happening" (LaBerge & Rheingold, 1990, p. 36).

Well over a decade ago, I began to put great effort into daily activities that would assist me in various areas of dreaming. I wanted to recall my dreams with greater frequency and to incubate meaningful ones. I also wanted to dream with higher levels of lucidity. Sometimes, these practices resulted in an OBE (Out of Body Experience) or WILD (Wake-Initiated Lucid Dream), depending on one's theoretical orientation. One particular standard I applied was the common practice of looking at my hands. As an adolescent I had read about this technique in a Carlos Castaneda book; however, it wasn't until 2004 that I took the technique seriously. At that time I enrolled in a free course in "astral travel and dreams" in Berkeley, California. Looking at the hands was a strategy that the teachers of the course promoted. It was considered sort of an anchor, or reminder, to question whether you were dreaming in that particular moment. In my research for this book, I learned that many lucid dreamers have relied on the "look-at-your-hands" technique for many years. A lot of people actually started out this way! By giving conscious attention to something throughout the day (my hands, in this case), along with the instruction to question whether I could be dreaming at that moment, it is likely that the same event will occur in dreamtime. Then, by seeing your hands in the dream, you might be reminded to question whether you are dreaming.

Other tips were suggested as well. Some people take a little jump into the air and see if it is possible to hover, instead of falling back to the ground. Another technique for questioning whether one is dreaming is to try and pass a hand or arm through a solid object. This only works when you are dreaming and believe that it is possible. My favorite has been, and still is, pulling my finger—usually my index or middle finger—and genuinely asking, "Am I dreaming?" If my finger stretches, for example, surely I am not in the physical waking state. The instructors with whom I studied often reminded the students that it is important to ask authentically and with a true curiosity. Questioning "Am I dreaming?" in an automatic way wouldn't be much different from the way many of us go about the day on "auto-pilot." No matter what happened, though, it was important for me to ask myself, upon awakening, whether I noticed my hands, or any hand for that matter, in the dream.

Dream Recall

It may be no surprise that what we consume can have an effect on our goals. For example, if the goal is to recall a night's dream, it would be wise to avoid cigarette smoking and alcohol (and other drugs) consumption the day before. I even suggest limiting the intake of greasy, processed and heavier foods. In addition, prioritizing sleep is a must. Some sleep-deprived individuals may have a difficult time recalling dreams completely. Those who are well nourished and rested are more likely to stick to the practices and focus on the big goal. Embark on the journey by utilizing the other strategies below.

Set an Intention

Intentions are key. How often do you set the intention to remember your dreams? Before you go to sleep, whether at night or for a short daytime nap, set an intention. It can be simple enough just to say aloud, "I will remember my dreams," or, "Recalling my dreams is easy and effortless. I remember every dream with ease." Of course, saying such phrases on autopilot is not likely to get the results we want. Take a couple deep breaths and set a clear, genuine intention.

STILL BODY, CLOSED EYES

One of the first dream recall techniques I was taught was to remain still upon awakening. Basically, when you wake up, don't move your head or a single limb, not even a muscle. Usually, people wake up and pop right out of bed. They immediately begin the tasks of the day, whether it means heading to the bathroom, grabbing their cell phones, checking on the kids or walking toward the coffee pot. This quick transition may be responsible for minimal-to-absolutely no dream recall what so ever. Instead of the habitual, try keeping your eyes closed and allowing your body to stay still in order to recall dream images with greater ease. When memories come, write them down immediately. This leads to the next suggestion.

DREAM JOURNALING

This naturally segues into the typical recommendation of leaving a notepad and pen or recording device next to your bed. Some suggest leaving these items under your pillow and using a special pen to record your dreams and nothing else (Harary & Weintraub, 1989). Each night before I fall asleep, I make sure that my dream journal is placed at the edge of my nightstand with a functioning pen on top. Personally, I enjoy spending some time browsing blank journals for sale at local bookstores and other little shops until I find one that calls to me. Some of the journals I've come across have sweet phrases and inspirational quotes, and some of them are about dreaming—how perfect! If such an item isn't your preference, a plain, basic notepad will do, and it's less expensive. At home, I also have a small light clipped to my headboard in the event that I wake up before sunrise. A lamp with a low-watt light bulb works just fine too, of course. How much easier it is to capture the dream on paper when everything needed is in close proximity and one can see without the sharpness of a strong or bright light shining! Now, after I have everything written down (without judgment), including a variety of details, such as characters, scene, time, interactions, colors and numbers, I put my dream journal in a more secure place so that it remains private. From there, I can go about my day.

A word of caution: what I've done in the past, unfortunately, is to judge certain dreams as *not interesting enough* to be included in my journal. At one time, I even ignored dream fragments and only included longer, coherent dreams in my journal. These were big mistakes, and I have learned my lesson. Everything we recall may have some level of significance. Set judgment aside and write it all down, every last detail. A small fragment may be understood much later, and it is possible that it might even have a connection to a dream that is later recalled. Besides, just by doing so gives momentum for the next time—this helps to establish a habit.

If several weeks pass and you find that you have not engaged in anything from the above list, it would be good to consider your level of motivation. Remind yourself what you want to gain from dream recollection. Motivation leads to new behaviors, which lead to results.

Increasing Awareness

Once you find that recalling your dreams is a close-to-daily event and that the tips above have become part of a regular routine, you may want to consider including additional exercises. Some embark upon daily practices to increase the likelihood of dreaming with lucidity, that is, if it doesn't already come naturally. Perhaps you have had a lucid dream before but hope to have them develop in their clarity. Maybe you just want to have lucid dreams more frequently, or perhaps you wish to incubate a dream about something of particular interest. Rest assured that the effort you put in during the day, or in all waking hours, will have positive results in the dreamtime. A few suggested techniques follow.

PRACTICE RELAXATION

When I've gone to bed tense and distracted by daily events, it has lead to mundane, distorted dreams or just low levels of recall. Doing a brief relaxation exercise upon lying down helps to calm the body and prepare for dreaming. Like Holzinger (2009), I also add relaxation techniques (and hypnosis) to my practice for induction of lucid dreams and OBEs. To do so, first notice your breathing and take about five deep, abdominal breaths. To be sure you are breathing deeply, as opposed to shallowly, place one hand flat on the chest and the other hand flat over the naval in a relaxed manner. The goal is to get the bottom hand (the one over the naval) to move much more than the one on the chest. Feel and imagine the air coming in and moving down into your abdomen, and then hold it for a few seconds before exhaling completely. Then repeat. I suggest breathing in through the nose, if possible, and exhaling through either the nose or mouth. Go ahead and release all you can—maybe even a sound, a moan or sigh, can be released as well. This process helps bring one into the present moment with a sense of relaxation.

Next, relax each muscle group, one by one. You can start at the top of your body and move your way down to your toes, or vice versa. I tend to alternate, but I do like the general idea of moving downward, deeper down into my own inner world. It may be the hypnotherapist in me that prefers this direction, but either manner can work just fine. What follows is a loose example of what I have said to myself to support the relaxation process (you can even make a recording for yourself and play it each night before going to sleep):

> Notice the face and scalp, and relax those muscles ... every one of them, completely.
> Relax the forehead and the eyelids even more now.
> Relax the eyeballs and their sockets.
> Loosen the jaw by opening the mouth a little. Then imagine relaxation flowing in there, completely relaxing the jaw.
> Relax the entire head and neck and allow that relaxation to move downward into the shoulders, biceps, triceps, chest and upper back.
> A wave of relaxing energy moves down through the entire torso now.
> The lower arms and wrists are relaxed as well by now.
> Relax every finger. Even the palms feel soft and relaxed.
> As this wave of deep relaxation continues downward and washes over the body, notice how the pelvis, hips and buttocks are relaxed too.
> Now feel the thighs and hamstrings relax as well.
> Relax the knees—front and back.
> Loosen the calf muscles more and more, and this naturally allows the ankles and feet to feel loose and limp.
> Loosen the toes—each and every one—and even the bottoms of the feet ... relaxing.
> The whole body is now relaxed and peaceful.
> Every muscle and nerve and bone, deeply, is so deeply relaxed...

When this process feels complete (you may even chose to repeat it for another round), just continue to allow your body to just feel nice and loose and limp, like a rag doll.

By this point, you will probably be feeling pretty good. This process can be fairly quick and simple, even shorter than the script above. It's fine to use a more detailed extended version that attends to smaller muscles and other tinier parts of the body, such as relaxing each finger nail, knuckle or etc. Any script can be personalized as well. Just go with what feels right. In the end, however, this relaxation practice is often quite effective.

Another possible twist might be regarding the words "wave" or "wash." For some, these words may provoke tension or discomfort, especially if one is fearful of water. Since the goal is to relax, it is fine to use a term that is suitable given your individual history, preferences and tastes. Another option could include soft golden light—*Just imagine a soft golden light shining over your body. This light shines over you and through you, relaxing every muscle, every nerve....* You get the point!

TRAIN THE MIND TO FOCUS

I have found that practicing concentration during the day supports the concentration I want to have right before sleep and even during the dream state. For those new to meditation and concentration exercises, start out with a short five-minute practice—that's really just fine. Each week increase it by another two to five minutes until you have worked your way up in duration. A solid daily practice of between twenty and thirty minutes will surely have positive results. The take home point, though, is that a five- or six-minute practice is better than nothing at all.

For concentration exercises, I like to change the point of focus every week or so just for freshness. For example, one week might be simply sitting in a comfortable chair and focusing on an object placed in front of me such as a glass of water, a flower or leaf, a candle flame, a mandala image or even an image of nature like a sandy beach. The next week I might want to sit on the floor with my eyes gazing downward as I concentrate solely on my breath, paying attention to each inhalation and each exhalation. Some have suggested counting each breath. When you have found that the mind has wandered off enough to lose your place, start at the number one again. Sometimes I have gotten up there in numbers, while other times I don't even make it to fifteen. It's not a competition after all, so no judging, please. During these exercises, place all of your attention on the object or breathe (whatever method you have chosen), but do not strain yourself. If you have chosen to focus on an object, like a flower for example, gently sharpen your attention on various aspects of the flower. For example, notice the shape of the petals, but do not identify with them. If you notice the mind making associations ("oh, those petals remind me of when..."), gently bring your attention back to noticing the flower petals just as they appear.

By dedicating a half hour, more or less, each day to a concentration exercise, I have learned that it becomes easier to concentrate while lying down. One can then hold a fair level of concentration as the body relaxes and the breathing slows. Sometimes I can maintain awareness as I drift off to sleep. While relaxed in a comfortable position, focusing and concentrating upon my intention during the process of falling asleep has lead to what I believe is an OBE, what is for others a WILD (defined below). This has worked for me many times over the years. If this is a new experience for you, know that the unusual sounds and sensations are to be expected and that you are completely safe.

LaBerge's Wake-Initiated
Lucid Dream

WILD stands for Wake-Initiated Lucid Dream. I had heard of Stephen LaBerge's WILD technique for lucid dreaming, but I didn't know what it actually entailed until recently. This technique can be helpful because, for some people, achieving a lucid state can be easier this way. However, according to experts in the field, entering a dream in this manner is rare. As LaBerge and Levitan (1995) state, "A minority of lucid dreams occurs when the sleeper enters REM sleep with unbroken self-awareness directly from the waking state" (p. 159). The WILD technique involves consciously perceiving the external environment before re-entering into the dream state (LaBerge, 1990). This technique can be used even before entering into the night's initial dream state, and it can be used again after waking up in the middle of the night. As noted above, some say this type of dream state is rare, but the technique has worked for me on a number of occasions. The advantage of entering such a state directly from a waking state is that the resulting experiences are quite vivid and memorable, and once mastered you can do so every day or night. Furthermore, the unusual sensations and often-feared "sleep paralysis" become expected and, for me, intriguing instead of bothersome. The sensations of paralysis have been so mentally troublesome for some dreamers with whom I've spoken that those sensations become very real barriers to progress. In extreme cases, some people intend to block all dream-related experiences and any dream recollections for that matter. By intentionally playing and experimenting in this arena, I have found that the awareness of the sensations of paralysis will pass by either falling asleep or realizing that I am halfway to my goal. That realization encourages me to continue to focus until I am able to move about in my other "vehicle." That "vehicle," whether a dream body, astral body, soul, etc., will depend on one's orientation. If you find that fear is your main obstacle, I suggest joining a lucid dream group (many exist online) to offer assistance and encouragement and to normalize an experience had by many other dreamers. A group supports a platform for discussion where families, friends and coworkers may not.

Here are two examples of what might be considered OBEs, or WILDs. Both were taken from my 2009 dream journal:

> After weeks of doing consistent reality checks (pulling my index or middle fingers, or taking small hops into the air), I had another lucid experience on January 10, 2009. It was just about 10:00 a.m. As I fell asleep, I could feel my body vibrate, so I kept concentrating, questioning the state I was in and pulling my finger in my mind. My body continued to vibrate, and, as soon as I perceived myself to be somewhat detached, I rolled onto my left side—I wasn't sure if my physical body was with me because, if it was, I'd be crashing onto the floor in a second. But I did not fall to the ground and immediately pulled my finger to confirm the "reality" I was in; I then asked a divine source to take me to the Giza Plateau in Egypt. I was pulled through space and saw only blackness and some starry-like details. Soon I was hovering down to earth over Egypt. I landed on a pile of rocks and ran, jumped around and hovered in the air for a few seconds. I couldn't see the pyramids clearly because of other structures and debris. There were wooden walkways above so I jumped up about one story high into the air and landed on the walkway. There were many people around—it looked as if they were tourist groups. To do another "reality check" I decided to test things out by hovering on my back, watching my foot and calf pass through a woman's chest. She didn't pay much notice or even react; however, a tall white male that appeared to be in his thirties did. This person made strong eye contact with me. I wasn't sure of his motives or if he was safe, so I sang a short tune that I was taught for dispelling negativity. I had difficulty speaking, but I persisted. I was thrown off when a group of American-looking students or tourists began to sing along with me—how did they know this song? Was this a trick? I continued singing and suddenly woke up.

Here is the second example:

> I woke up in the late morning hours of April 11, 2009, and after a few minutes I decided to return to sleep and try to stay conscious. I focused on my breath and my goal, as I allowed my body to relax more and more. Believing that I may have transitioned into another state of consciousness, I asked a divine source to take to me see _____ [a particular person I knew well]. I must have been out-of-body [aka, having a WILD] because I found myself flying over the earth—I was pretty high up. I enjoyed looking at the attractive landscapes below. When I arrived at my destination, it was dark, like at night, but I knew it was really several hours past sunrise in the physical waking reality, so this was surprising. There, in front of me, was a gravesite and a little girl sitting over it. We were not in a cemetery but in some open area that was not very well kept. I was confused at what I was seeing. I left with the little girl, who seemed frightened, or sad, or alone. At this point, as we were leaving the scene together, all lucidity appeared to be lost. I did not wake up right at that moment, it seemed, but when I did, all I could recall ended there.

In both cases, sleeping paralysis-like sensations are perceived as a moment along the path to such states, if they are even perceived at all. By sticking with it and going along with the sensations, they come to pass. Again, one may label these occurrences as an OBE, a WILD or simply an experience, depending on one's culture.

ENHANCE VISUALIZATION

One who has obtained a fair level of concentration ability will find that visualization comes easily. Have you ever purposefully tried to visualize, or imagine, a relaxing setting—maybe a place you enjoyed in the past? Well, without a disciplined mind and an ability to concentrate, visualizations can be difficult or frustrating because fantasies of the mind can quickly take over. Once you have some consistent concentration practices under your belt, add a visualization practice. To start, pick a place you have visited in the past that is associated with pleasant feelings. A backyard garden, a park or another natural, familiar setting will do. Allow yourself to have ten minutes of uninterrupted time, find a comfortable place to sit and close your eyes. See the scene in your mind's eye. Notice all details, sizes, shapes, colors and textures. Even notice the ground and the sky. Practice concentrating on the details that really bring this scene to life. What do you smell? What do you feel under your feet? Visualization becomes easier the more experience one has with concentration; after all, this exercise and the one above go hand-in-hand. The bonus is that this practice can bring about relaxation and a sense of peace to the busy day.

Visualizing a scene in detail as one falls asleep may result in dreaming of that place or even lucidly projecting there. With that said, imagine safe, comforting scenes. Avoid imagery that is brutal or frightening as the body may tense up leading to anything but a relaxing experience.

QUESTIONING AND BELIEVING

Am I dreaming? The more we question during the day whether we are in the dreaming or waking state or somewhere in between, the likelihood increases of doing the same in an actual dream. In a dream, we can hover, fly and move from one place to another in a flash. This is not so in the waking state. How do you know you are not dreaming now? Seriously, how do you really know? As mentioned near the beginning of this chapter, one way to know is to test it out. Take a little jump in the air with the intention of flying or hovering. Do you stay afloat or do you find your feet back on the ground immediately? Additionally, what happens when you walk through a wall in a dream? What happens when you try that while awake? Ouch! You get the point.

While we play around with the law of gravity, among other things, realize that intention is something not to be overlooked. Those who believe flying in a dream is possible are usually able to fly. Those who don't, stay on the ground. Similarly, when I firmly intend to walk through a wall or fly through the ceiling in my dream, it will likely take place. Basically, what you believe you can do in the dream state happens. Remember that "automatic" reality checks that are detached from attention and meaning won't give the expected or desired results. I know this one from experience. When questioning whether or not we are dreaming, we must mean it.

I was taught that some of the best times to question yourself are when you notice something odd, unexpected or out of place. Let curiosity fuel the question. For example, aside from wearing shoes, a nude adult male stands on the corner. Even though I am standing on a street in San Francisco, I will still be sure to ask myself, "Am I dreaming?" Conduct a comfortable reality check and see what happens. In this case, I pulled on my left index finger, and nope, nothing. Turns out I am in San Francisco and the naked man in shoes is often seen on that same corner, so I am told. I am awake, in the physical waking state. Another time, I find myself in Egypt. Hmm, I don't recall taking a plane there, let alone time off from work for a far-away trip. Am I dreaming? I take a little hop and hovered about a foot or two above the ground: that's impossible in the waking state. Turns out I am asleep and dreaming. The reality check helps me confirm my suspicions.

From Ordinary to Extraordinary

Having become accustomed to recalling and tracking dreams on a daily basis, along with practicing relaxation, concentration and visualization exercises, extraordinary dream experiences may have manifested for you. Perhaps, by now, your dreams have become more vivid, lucid, precognitive or have even offered up a solution to a problem or difficult situation. Maybe you have been introduced you to your child-to-be, or maybe you have been brought closer to a deceased loved one. My hope is that the attention and time spent practicing has likely paid off. While these developments can be exciting, it is wise to consider that slowing down or ceasing practices (losing the momentum that was built up) will likely correlate to decreased clarity, memory, awareness or vividness in the dream state. We are rewarded by our efforts. I've been taught this lesson many times! When I stop for too long, I notice how challenging it can be to get back on track. For that reason, I have found that practicing for just five minutes a day is better than nothing.

DREAM INCUBATION

Thinking about intentions once more, it is a good idea to know what you want to gain or understand from extraordinary dream experiences. This understanding can be the guiding light, or sign post, toward incubating meaningful dreams. On several occasions, I have intended to seek help in dreams with several tasks. One such situation took place the night before my sister's wedding. I knew I was going to give a speech during the reception the next evening, but until that day, nothing inspirational had come to me in the waking state. Everything I had written up to that point felt flat. I was not interested in presenting anything that I had previously considered or noted. Fortunately, I had enough trust in my dreams at that time to assist me when needed, so I didn't worry too much. I asked to be helped in a dream (dream incubation) by finding just the right words for the speech. I woke up in the middle of that night to use the bathroom and recalled nothing at all—no dream inspiration just yet. I soon fell back asleep and stayed asleep for a few hours. As I began to wake up that morning, drifting in and out of a lovely hypnopompic state, I saw and heard myself giving the wedding reception speech. As the dream state came to a conclusion, I hurled myself out of bed to grab a paper and pen. I frantically scribbled the words down on the little pad of paper, obviously not wanting to forget a single detail. Then, I read what I had written back to myself and was quite satisfied, as well as relieved. That evening, the speech I gave was well received, and I was pleased to have offered something that was not only appropriate but that felt good as well. This is one example of how intention and experience with the practices listed above came together to bring forward a dream that assisted me in creative problem solving, not to mention offered a vividness filled with personal meaning.

Contemporary dream incubation can be as spontaneous as described above, or it can be made into a more complex, ritualized process. Classic examples of dream rituals and rites have been associated with particular locations such as the secret chambers of Egyptian temples (Carey, 2010) or Greek sanctuaries in honor of the god Asclepius (Meier, 1967). To incubate dreams, some people have spent days or weeks in preparation. Historically, one would partake in purification rituals and go to sleep at a sacred site; however, in the current era, preparations may be different.

Today we will likely go to sleep in our own home or in our family's home. Still, preparations can be just as important. Today, such preparations might include attention to the environment in order to create a soothing, pleasant sleep space. De-cluttering the bedroom, removing electronic devices and instead placing items associated with relaxation, such as beautiful art or flowers, in the bedroom might be included. Others may practice intense meditation or complete other types of rituals as preparation for dream incubation. I have used crystals known for dream support, such as amethyst, and quartz (Herkimer Diamond and clear quartz). Some suggest placing mugwort near your place of rest and smelling it before falling asleep. Other medicinal plants can support dreamwork as well.

With continued practice, you learn what is most comfortable to you, personally. These factors associated with dream incubation can be tailored to suit personal preferences. Some preparations may lead to better results than others. Of course, be sure to have your paper and pen handy so that you may immediately record the experience upon awakening. As with anything new, come into this experience with an open mind and experiment upon yourself. Know that you are involved in a practice that has likely taken place since the beginning of time. You are not alone. Retreats, online groups and workshops exist for those who desire the extra support. There are numerous opportunities in California.

APPLYING SELF-HYPNOSIS TO MEET YOUR GOALS

This section has been adapted from my blog, which contains two short articles (www.consciouschimera.com). Slightly different versions were originally released on May 1, 2016, and June 1, 2016, respectively, as articles are posted once a month.

Before I provide an exercise in self-hypnosis, I'll offer a little general explanation about hypnosis, a process that is sometimes misunderstood. Hypnosis is a tool used to induce a non-ordinary state of consciousness (also known as an altered state of consciousness). It involves deep relaxation coupled with focused concentration. Brain waves, breathing and heart rate slow down. The body may feel light or heavy. The eyelids may flutter and the eyes may become teary. Hypnotic states vary—they can be light or very deep, but being asleep is not being in hypnosis. The hypnotist (that's you, in the case of self-hypnosis) may include the use of mental/ visual imagery, sound (music, chimes), counting down numbers and, with permission, light touch. While the application of hypnosis and hypnotherapy can be utilized for a variety of needs and desires, in general, this tool is often used to explore the deep inner mind, or subconscious, and to support positive changes in one's life. Some possibilities are that we can use this tool to support dream recall and even increase lucidity, if desired.

Self-hypnosis is a very valuable tool. As the name implies, you do it yourself—no need to make an appointment, buy a CD or download an app! I often utilize self-hypnosis before any event or experience that provokes some nervousness, such as an interview, teaching a large class, public speaking or giving a presentation at a conference with unfamiliar faces. Self-hypnosis has also assisted me at home, when I am not sleeping well or when I want to encourage a particular mood, attitude or inspiration. I've also sought assistance with this tool in order to increase dream recall and lucidity. There are many ways to use self-hypnosis—there is not just one right way. It is important to do what feels safe and comforting.

To prepare, I may set an intention, then spritz the room and my body with a lavender water concoction (other essential oils such as wild orange, clary sage, grapefruit, rosemary or a combination of these are fine, of course). Other times I might light a candle of a particular color (orange for grounding and focus; blue, purple or violet for the higher realms), play chimes or use my voice (vowel mantras are a personal favorite) to clear the space. Sometimes I place a special crystal in my hand, pocket or under my pillow, or I may even burn a little sage or juniper on a warm day when I can leave the windows at least partially open. Before beginning, I like to say words of gratitude for what is happening, such as, "Thank you for such deep, restful sleep," or "I'm grateful for the lucidity I am about to experience when I dream," or "I remember my dreams with ease, thank you."

Next, since I am working with myself here, I find a comfortable position on my bed in which to fall asleep, and I then pay attention to how my body feels against the respective surface (body supported by the mattress, head supported by the pillows, light pressure and warmth from the blanket on top of me). However, if I am doing this as an exercise in the middle of my day, I would likely be sitting in a chair, so I would alter some things listed above.

Once situated, in a chair or in bed, I begin an induction by counting down from twenty to one. I say, "20, 19, 18, 17, 16…" and so on. In between some numbers, I add phrases, such as saying, "13, 12, 11, doubling my relaxation with 10, 9, 8, going deeper now with 7, 6, 5, 4, feeling so relaxed and peaceful, 3, 2, 1." After counting down, I speak aloud some phrases that are meant to assist me in what I would like to do. For example I say,

"This relaxed and peaceful state remains with me as I drift off to sleep. My mind remains aware so that I dream with lucidity." Another example is saying, "Even though I sleep deeply, I recall my dreams vividly and record them immediately." Statements of gratitude can correlate with the phrases of intention.

After a few target sentences or phrases are spoken, I either allow myself to drift off to sleep, or, if I need to continue my day, I tell myself that I will count from one up to five, and when I reach five I will open my eyes and feel energized, relaxed, peaceful or whatever state that matches my intention. If I want to begin writing productively, for example, I may use "energized." If I want to fall asleep, I may use "relaxed" or "at peace." Once this process is complete, I always say a word of thanks. I think it's nice to begin with gratitude and conclude with gratitude.

Self-hypnosis methods can, of course, become very creative and elaborate, but I suggest keeping your intentions straightforward and simple. At all times, use affirmative statements. Remember, the mind/psyche moves toward the dominant thought. For example, when we hear the words, "don't run," we first process the word "run." Avoid such phrasing, in general. Instead, say aloud what you want! In this example, it would be "walk." We can create what we want in affirmative language, so plan out the statements to be used in a self-hypnosis session. For someone desiring a better night's sleep, for instance, I suggest the following: instead of saying, "you won't wake up in the middle of the night," try something like, "sleeping through the night happens easily," and/or "any noise or movement during the night helps me sleep even more deeply." Another example would be instead of saying, "I won't forget my dreams this time," say, "This time, I remember my dreams easily." Keeping your intentions clear and your language affirmative will improve the experience all around. As always, make the experience enjoyable and have fun with it!

The tips and techniques contained in this chapter have helped me to be successful. Some may be more suitable for you than others; after all, everyone is different. I hope you find some of them useful and beneficial.

CHAPTER TEN

Coming Full Circle

Birth and death are at the forefront of the circle of life. In my quest to understand dreams, death dreams appear to be less taboo than initially expected. They are commonly reported among those who are not near death themselves, and these types of dreams also appear to be a more accepted part of the dialogue centered in extraordinary dreaming. On one hand, this could be because death dreams are experienced by the young and old, and by men, women and children alike. Announcing dreams, on the other hand, take place primarily in the lives of women and most often at the time right before or during the nine months of pregnancy. While the time span during which announcing dreams are reported is narrow, it still surprises me that these dreams are not at the forefront of conversation because they are experienced at a time that has much joy and celebration. Baby showers, where pregnant women and babies-to-be are celebrated, are common practice in the West. While the physical subjective, inner experience is often shared, the narrower slice of nocturnal subjectivity is ignored. For example, we might ask the pregnant mother, "Are you sleeping alright these days?" However, we do not also ask what extraordinary experience might have taken place during those hours. The same is true for those approaching death. We often ask the dying if they are comfortable (physically), but we ask about their emotional and spiritual life much less often. Might such questions bring about a greater sense of closeness and authenticity during these grand life transformations?

For hundreds of years before the common era and across the globe, dreaming has been considered many things: a method of communication, a way to know divinity, a method for obtaining knowledge, a natural aspect of the human experience and much more. Whether one looks to dreams for guidance, comfort, solutions to pragmatic concerns or something more, they can be considered gifts, and dreaming can be considered as one's birthright.

Stanley Krippner writes:

When Western science claims to be speaking about what is real, it implies that other people's realities are merely myths, legends, superstitions and fairy tales. This is the way in which a dominant society denies the authenticity of other people's systems of knowledge and strikes at the very heart of their cultures. As a result, what is deemed the acceptable world becomes smaller for the minority society and its members [Jones & Krippner, 2012, p. 29].

New Thinking Allowed is hosted by Jeffrey Mishlove. In one of the programs entitled "Working with Extraordinary Dreams with Stanley Krippner," Mishlove interviewed Krippner on the topic of extraordinary dreaming. Mishlove made a statement that I feel is worthy of inclusion when considering all that dreams are and all that dreaming is. In this program, Mishlove said, "I've always felt that when it comes to dreams, that it's as if, when a person wants to become the best person they can be, there are invisible powers that are just waiting to reach out and help." We may not be able to say exactly what these powers are or where the invisible resides, but across time and place the acknowledgment of assistance and guidance is not a new story. This thread appears to be long standing and timeless. No matter how one feels about dreaming, it cannot be denied that some dreams leave a life-long mark upon the lives of many dreamers. In the final analysis, it is up to the individual to determine whether the dream state will be accessed and utilized for personal benefit, growth and transformation, or if it will instead be given little attention. I'm shooting for the former.

Glossary

Aborigine Australia's indigenous people, who are comprised of many diverse language groups and clans.

Activation-synthesis hypothesis A biological explanation for dreaming that claims that dreams are the by-products of the brain's electrical impulses.

Analytic psychology Also known as Jungian psychology, developed by Carl Jung, a Swiss psychologist and psychiatrist.

Asabano A small ethnolinguistic group found in the highlands of Papua New Guinea.

Asclepius Greco-Roman god of medicine and healing.

Baha'i One of the youngest of the world's major monotheistic religions, with roots in Persia and the Middle East, that emphasizes humankind's spiritual unity.

Barzakh A space where dead souls reside before joining God, according to Sufism. The soul of a sleeping person can visit this space.

Clairvoyance The ability to receive information beyond the five senses.

Continuity hypothesis The idea that dreams reflect a person's life in the waking state.

Couvade syndrome A condition in which expectant fathers experience pregnancy-related symptoms, such as nausea.

Daesh Also known as the Islamic State or ISIS.

Diné A Native American group sometimes referred to as the Navaho.

DMT An abbreviation for Dimethyltryptamine, the active ingredient in Ayahuasca.

Dream incubation The process of cultivating dreams, often for guidance or problem solving.

Dream interpretation An approach (and there are many) by which someone attempts to understand the meaning of a dream.

Ghzawa A tribal group of Morocco's Western Rif mountain villages.

Hamadsha A religious brotherhood in Meknes, a city located in northern central Morocco.

Hypnagogia The condition or state experienced immediately before sleep.

Hypnopompia   The condition or state experienced immediately after awakening.

Iamblichus   A Syrian philosopher born in 245 CE.

Imaginal world   A realm said to exist beyond the ordinary cosmos and conventional world.

Inuit   An indigenous group also referred to as Alaskan Eskimo.

Istikhara   The Muslim form dream incubation, which is still practiced today.

Kabbalah   A mystical branch of Judaism.

Lucid dreaming   A state experienced when a dreamer has the awareness that he/she is dreaming while dreaming occurs.

Lucumi   Developed by the people of West Africa's Yoruban tradition. Also known as Santeria, Regla de Ocha, La Regla de Lukumi, or simply Lucumi or Lukumi.

Mapuche   A large South American indigenous group and the original inhabitants of vast areas now known as Chile and Argentina.

Mehinaku   An indigenous group of Central Brazil.

Oneiromancy   Divination by means of dreams; the practice of interpreting dreams to foretell the future.

Precognition   Foreknowledge of an event, which is sometimes referred to as a premonition.

Psyche   The essence of life, the mind in its totality (conscious and unconscious) or the human soul. Also the name of the ancient Greek goddess of the soul.

Quechua   An indigenous group found in the South American Andes Mountains.

Salem   A U.S. town in the state of Massachusetts, commonly known for the infamous Salem Witch Trails.

Shaman   Originating in Siberia, this academic construct sometimes refers to those whose community has granted them special status to attend to their group's psychological and spiritual needs.

Sufism   A mystical branch of Islam.

Talmud   A body of literature containing various aspects of Jewish tradition, such as law, ethics, history and more.

Toraja   A community in Indonesia's highlands of South Sulawesi.

Telepathy   The ability to transmit thoughts to another or to know the thoughts of another. Telepathic abilities also include the exchange of information between two minds.

Xenophon   A Greek historian, philosopher, soldier and prolific writer (428–354 BCE).

Demographics
of Study Participants

Table 1: Participant Age

Age	Participants (n = 22)	
	n	%
21–25	4	18%
26–30	7	32%
31–35	5	23%
36–38	6	27%

Table 2: Participant Race

Race	Participants (n = 22)	
	n	%
Latino/Hispanic	2	9%
White / not Latino/Hispanic	19	86%
Biracial: Native American and white	1	5%

Table 3: Participants' Highest Level of Education Completed

Education Completed	Participants (n = 22)	
	n	%
Trade school	1	5%
Some college	7	32%
Bachelor's degree	8	36%
Master's degree	5	23%
Doctorate degree	1	5%

Table 4: Participant Employment Status

Employment	Participants (n = 22)	
	n	%
Full-time	11	50%
Part-time	6	27%
Not employed	5	23%

Table 5: Participants' Religious/Spiritual Affiliations

Affiliation	Participants (n = 22)	
	n	%
Atheist	2	9%
Agnostic	1	5%
Buddhist	1	5%
Catholic	5	23%
Jewish	1	5%
Muslim	1	5%
Gnostic, Sufi, Kabala Mystic	1	5%
Pagan/Wiccan	1	5%
Protestant	1	5%
Taoist	1	5%
Spiritual, not religious	5	23%
Other	2	9%

Table 6: Participants' Pregnancy History

History	Participants (n = 22)	
	n	%
First pregnancy	7	32%
Pregnant once before	6	27%
Bore one or more living children	3	14%
Had miscarriage or termination	3	14%
Pregnant twice before	6	27%
Bore one or more living children	6	27%
Had one or more miscarriages or terminations	5	23%
Pregnant three or more times	3	14%
Bore one or more living children	3	14%
Had one or more miscarriages or terminations	3	14%

Table 7: Months of Gestation
at Time of Participation

Gestation	Participants (n = 22)	
	n	*%*
One month	1	5%
Two months	1	5%
Three months	2	9%
Four months	1	5%
Five months	2	9%
Six months	2	9%
Seven months	5	23%
Eight months	4	18%
Nine months	4	18%

Appendix B

For Further Reading

Additional information and further reading can be found here, where I share some of what has guided me along the way.

Scholarly Journals

American Psychologist
Dreaming
International Journal of Dream Research
Ethos
Anthropology of Consciousness
American Ethnologist
Journal of Prenatal and Perinatal Psychology and Health

Electronic Magazines and Blogs

Lucid Dreaming Experience: http://www.dreaminglucid.com
Mark and Angela Pritchard's Blog: https://belsebuub.com/blog

Associations and Institutes

International Association for the Study of Dreams
    Berkeley, California
    www.asdreams.org
The Dream Institute of Northern California
    Berkeley, California
    www.dream-institute.org
The Lucidity Institute
    Palo Alto, California
    www.lucidity.com
The International Academy of Consciousness
    www.iacworld.org

Bibliography

Achterberg, J. (1991). *Woman as healer: A panoramic survey of the healing activities of women from prehistoric times to the present.* Boston, MA: Shambhala Publications.

Adams, K. (2003). Children's dreams: An exploration of Jung's concept of big dreams. *International Journal of Children's Spirituality, 8*(2), 105–114.

Adams, K., & Hyde, B. (2008). Children's grief dreams and the theory of spiritual intelligence. *Dreaming, 18*(1), 58–67.

Adams, R. (2014, October 14). 7 bizarre (but common) pregnancy dreams, and what they really mean. *The Huffington Post.* Retrieved from www.huffingtonpost.com

Adler, A. (1936). On the interpretation of dreams. *International Journal of Individual Psychology, 2,* 3–16.

Akerman, K. (1977). Notes on "conception" among Aboriginal women in the Kimberleys, West Australia. *Oceania, 48*(1), 59–63.

Aristotle (1952). The works of Aristotle. On dreams. Great books of the Western world. Vol. 8. Pp. 702–706. Encyclopedia Britannica.

Athanassiadi, P. (1993). Dreams, theurgy and freelance divination: The testimony of Iamblichus. *The Journal of Roman Studies, 83,* 115–130.

Bacigalupo, A. M. (1999). Studying Mapuche shaman/healers in Chile from an experiential perspective: Ethical and methodological problems. Anthropology of Consciousness, 10 (2–3), 35–40.

Barker, D. J. P., Osmond C., Kajantie, E., & Eriksson, J. G. (2009). Growth and chronic disease: Findings in the Helsinki birth cohort. *Annals of Human Biology, 36*(5), 445–458.

Barrett, D. (1993). The "committee of sleep": A study of dream incubation for problem solving. *Dreaming, 3*(2), 115–122.

Barrett, D. (2001). *The committee of sleep: How artists, scientists, and athletes use dreams for creative problem-solving.* New York, NY: Crown.

Black, J., DeCicco, T., Seeley, C., Murkar, A., Black, J., & Fox, P. (2016). Dreams of the deceased: Can themes be reliably coded? *International Journal of Dream Research, 9*(2), 110–114.

Bonetta, L. (2008). Epigenomics: Tackling the epigenome. *Nature, 454*(7205), 795.

Bonime, W. (1962). *The clinical use of dreams.* New York, NY: Basic Books.

Botz-Bornstein, T. (2007). Dreams in Buddhism and Western aesthetics: Some thoughts on play, style and space. *Asian Philosophy, 17*(1), 65–81.

Bowater, M. (2012). Dreams and politics: How dreams may influence political decisions. *Psychotherapy and Politics International, 10*(1), 45–54.

Bowman, C. (2001). *Return from heaven: Beloved relatives reincarnated within your family.* New York, NY: HarperTorch.

Breger, L. (1967). Function of dreams. *Journal of Abnormal Psychology Monograph, 72*(5), 1–28.

Brennan, A., Ayers, S., Ahmed, H., & Marshall-Lucette, S. (2007). A critical review of the Couvade syndrome: The pregnant male. *Journal of Reproductive and Infant Psychology, 25*(3), 173–189.

Brenneis, C. B., & Roll, S. (1975). Ego modalities in the manifest dreams of male and female Chicanos. *Psychiatry, 38*(2), 172–185.

Breslaw, E. G. (1997). Tituba's confession: The multicultural dimensions of the 1692 Salem witch-hunt. *Ethnohistory, 44*(3), 535–556.

Breslaw, E. G. (2003, July). Witches in the Atlantic world. *OAH Magazine of History,* 42–47.

Broch, H. B. (2000). Yellow crocodiles and bush spirits: Timpaus islanders' conceptualization of ethereal phenomena. *Ethos, 28*(1), 3–19.

Bulkeley, K. (1994). *The wilderness of dreams: Exploring the religious meanings of dreams in modern western culture.* Albany, NY: State University of New York Press.

Bulkeley, K. (1995). *Spiritual dreaming: A cross-cultural and historical journey.* Mahwah, NJ: Paulist Press.

Bulkeley, K. (2006). Revision of the good fortune scale: A new tool for the study of "big dreams." *Dreaming, 16*(1), 11–21.

Bulkeley, K. (2008). *Dreaming in the world's religions: A comparative history.* New York, NY: New York University Press.

Bulkeley, K. (2009). Mystical dreaming: Patterns in form, content, and meaning. *Dreaming, 19*(1), 30–41.

Bulkeley, K., & Hartmann, E. (2011). Big dreams: An analysis using central image intensity, content analysis, and word searches. *Dreaming, 21*(3), 157–167.

Callister, L. C., Vehvilainen-Julkunen, K., & Lauri, S. (2001). Giving birth: Perceptions of Finnish childbearing women. *American Journal of Maternal-Child Nursing, 26*(1), 28–32.

Carey, M. A. (2010). *Women's meaningful dreams: The treasure within the feminine psyche.* (Doctoral dissertation). Retrieved from ProQuest Dissertations and Theses Database. (AAT 3408066).

Carman, E. M., & Carman, N. J. (1999). *Cosmic cradle: Souls waiting in the wings for birth.* Fairfield, IA: Sunstar Publishing.

Charsley, S. R. (1973). Dreams in an independent African church. *Africa, 43*(3), 244–257.

Christensen, D. (2000). Weight matters, even in the womb: Status at birth can foreshadow illnesses decades later. *Science News, 158*(24), 382–383.

Ciccarelli, S. K., & White, J. N. (2009). *Psychology* (2nd ed.). Upper Saddle River, NJ: Pearson Education.

Coo, S., Milgrom, J., & Trinder, J. (2014). Pregnancy and postnatal dreams reflect changes inherent in the transition to motherhood. *Dreaming, 24*(2), 125–137.

Corbin, H. (1966). The visionary dream in Islamic spirituality. In G. E. Von Grunebaum, & R. Caillois (Eds.), The dream and human societies (pp. 381–408). Los Angeles, CA: University of California Press.

Corsi-Cabrera, M., Velasco, F., Del Rio-Portilla, Y., Armony, J. L., Trejo-Martinez, D., Guevara, M. A., Velasco, A. L. (2016). Human amygdala activation during rapid eye movements of rapid eye movement sleep: An intracranial study. *Journal of Sleep Research, 25*(5), 576–582. doi: 10.111/jsr.12415

Covitz, J. (1990). *Visions of the night: A study of Jewish dream interpretation.* Boston, MA: Shambhala.

Crapanzano, V. (1975). Saints, jnun, and dreams: An essay in Moroccan ethnospychology. *Psychiatry, 38*, 145–159.

Csordas, T. J. (1994). *The sacred self: A cultural phenomenology of charismatic healing.* Berkeley, CA: University of California Press.

Dadosky, J. (1999). Three Diné women on the Navajo approach to dreams. *Anthropology of Consciousness, 10*(1), 16–27.

Dagan, Y., Lapidot, A., & Eisensyein, M. (2001). Women's dreams reported during first pregnancy. *Psychiatry and Clinical Neurosciences, 55*, 13–20.

Davis, P. M. (2005). Dreams and visions in the Anglo-Saxon conversion to Christianity. *Dreaming, 15*(2), 75–88. doi: 10.1037//1053–0797.15.2.75

Davis-Floyd, R. E. (2003). *Birth as an American rite of passage* (nd ed.). Berkeley, CA: University of California Press.

Davis-Floyd, R. E., & Sargent, C. F. (Eds.). (1997). *Childbirth and authoritative knowledge: Cross-cultural perspectives.* Berkeley, CA: University of California Press.

Den Boer, E. (2012). Spirit conception: Dreams in Aboriginal Australia. *Dreaming, 22*(3), 192–211.

Domhoff, G. W. (2003). *The scientific study of dreams: Neural networks, cognitive development, and content analysis.* Washington, D.C.: American Psychological Association.

Domhoff, G. W. (2015). Dreaming as embodied simulation: A widower's dreams of his deceased wife. *Dreaming, 25*(3), 232–256.

Eberhardt, N. (2006). *Imagining the course of life: Self-transformation in a Shan Buddhist community.* Honolulu, HI: University of Hawaii Press.

Ebon, M. (1966). *Parapsychological dream studies.* In G. E. Von Grunebaum, & R. Caillois (Eds.), The dream and human societies (pp. 163–177). Los Angeles, CA: University of California Press.

Edelstein, E. J., & Edelstein, L. (1945). *Asclepius: A collection and interpretation of the testimonies*. Baltimore, MD: The John Hopkins Press.

Edgar, I. R. (1995). *Dreamwork, anthropology and the caring professions*. Brookfield, VT: Avebury.

Edgar, I. R. (2006). The 'true dream' in contemporary Islamic/Jihadist dreamwork: A case study of the dreams of Taliban leader Mullah Omar. *Contemporary South Asia, 15*(3), 263–272.

Edgar, I. R. (2007). The inspirational night dream in the motivation and justification of jihad. *Nova Religio: The Journal of Emergent and Alternative Religions. 11*(2). 59–76.

Edgar, I. R. (2011). *The dream in Islam: From Qur'anic tradition to jihadist inspiration*. New York, NY: Berghahn Books.

Edgar, I. R. (2015). The dreams of Islamic State. *Perspectives on Terrorism, 9*(4), 72–84.

Eggan, D. (1966). *Hopi dreams in cultural perspective*. In G. E. Von Grunebaum, & R. Caillois (Eds.), The dream and human societies (pp. 237–265). Los Angeles, CA: University of California Press.

Ehrenreich, B., & English, D. (1993). *Witches, midwives and nurses: A history of women healers*. New York, NY: The Feminist Press at The City University of New York.

Eliade, M. (1966). Initiation dreams and visions among the Siberian shamans. In G. E. Von Grunebaum, & R. Caillois (Eds.), *The dream and human societies* (pp. 331–340). Los Angeles, CA: University of California Press.

Erlacher, D., & Schredl, M. (2008). Cardiovascular responses to dreamed physical exercise during REM lucid dreaming. *Dreaming, 18*(2), 112–121.

Evans, J. E., & Aronson, R. (2005). *The whole pregnancy handbook: An obstetrician's guide to integrating conventional and alternative medicine before, during, and after pregnancy*. New York, NY: Gotham Books.

Ewing, K. P. (1990). The dream of spiritual initiation and the organization of self representations among Pakistani Sufis. *American Ethnologist, 17*(1), 56–74.

Ewing, K. P. (1994). Dreams from a saint: Anthropological atheism and the temptation to believe. *American Anthropologist, 96*(3), 571–583.

Fahd, T. (1966). The dream in medieval Islamic society. In G. E. Von Grunebaum, & R. Caillois (Eds.), *The dream and human societies* (pp. 351–364). Los Angeles, CA: University of California Press.

Freeman, A., & White, B. (2002). Dreams and the dream image: Using dreams in cognitive therapy. *Journal of Cognitive Psychotherapy, 16*(1), 39–53.

Glover, V., O'Conner, T. G., & O'Donnell, K. (2010). Prenatal stress and the programming of the HPA axis. *Neuroscience and Biobehavioral Reviews, 35*, 17–22.

Gonzalez-Vazquez, A. (2014). Dreaming, dream-sharing and dream-interpretation as feminine powers in northern Morrocco. *Anthropology of the Contemporary Middle East and Central Eurasia, 2*(1), 97–108.

Gracie, C. (2012, October 10). The Duke of Zhou: The man who was Confucius's hero. *BBC News Magazine*. Retrieved from www.bbc.com/news/magazine

Gregor, T. (1981). "Far, far away my shadow wandered...": The dream symbolism and dream theories of the Mehinaku Indians of Brazil. *American Ethnologist, 8*(4), 709–720.

Guggenheim, B., & Guggenheim, J. (1995). *Hello from heaven: A new field of research—after-death communication—confirms that life and love are eternal*. New York, NY: Bantam Books.

Hall, J. A. (1983). *Jungian dream interpretation: A handbook of theory and practice*. Toronto, Canada: Inner City Books.

Hall, J. A. (1989). *Hypnosis: A Jungian perspective*. New York, NY: Guilford Press.

Hall, C. S., & Nordby, V. J. (1972). *The individual and his dreams*. New York, NY: Signet.

Hall, C. S., & Van de Castle, R. L. (1966). *The content analysis of dreams*. New York, NY: Appleton-Century-Crofts.

Hallett, E. (1995). *Soul trek: Meeting our children on the way to birth*. Hamilton, MT: Light Hearts Publishing.

Hallett, E. (2002). *Stories of the unborn soul: The mystery and delight of pre-birth communication*. Lincoln, NE: Writers Club Press.

Hallowell, A. I (1996). *The role of dreams in Ojibwa culture*. In G. E. Von Grunebaum, & R. Caillois (Eds.), The dream and human societies (pp. 267–293). Los Angeles, CA: University of California Press.

Hamilton, E. (1940). Mythology: Timeless tales of Gods and Heroes. Boston, MA: Little, Brown & Company.

Harary, K., & Weintraub, P. (1989). *Lucid dreaming in 30 days: The creative sleep program*. New York, NY: St. Martin's Griffin.

Harkness, S. (1987). The cultural mediation of postpartum depression. *Medical Anthropology Quarterly, 1*(2), 194–209.

Harris, C. (2016, December 26). Texas double murder suspect dreamed of cutting off wife's head, police allege. *People Magazine.* Retrieved from http://people.com/crime/texas-man-craig-vandewege-murder-wife-son-voices/

Hartmann, E. (2008). The central image makes "big" dreams big: The central image as the emotional heart of the dream. *Dreaming, 18*(1), 44–57.

Hassler, D. (2013). A new European case of the reincarnation type. *Journal of the Society for Psychical Research, 77*(910), 19–31.

Hergovich, A., Schott, R., & Burger, C. (2010). Biased evaluation of abstracts depending on topic and conclusion: Further evidence of a confirmation bias within scientific psychology. *Current Psychology, 29*, 188–209. doi: 10.1007/s12144–010–9087–5

Hermansen, M. K. (1997). Introduction to the study of dreams and visions in Islam. *Religion, 27*, 1–5.

Henningsen, G. (2009). The witches' flying and the Spanish inquisitors, or how to explain (away) the impossible. *Folklore, 120*, 57–74. doi: 10.1080/00155870802647833

Hinze, S. (1997). *Coming from the light: Spiritual accounts of life before life.* New York, NY: Pocket Books.

Hobson, J. A., Pace-Schott, E. F., & Stickgold, R. (2010). Dreaming and the brain: Toward a cognitive neuroscience of conscious states. *Behavioral and Brain Sciences, 23*(6), 793–1121.

Hoffman, V. J. (1997). The role of visions in contemporary Egyptian religious life. *Religion, 27*, 45–64.

Hollan, D. (2014). From ghosts to ancestors (and back again): On cultural and psychodynamic mediation of selfscapes. *Ethos, 42*(2), 175–197.

Holzinger, B. (2009). Lucid dreaming: Dreams of clarity. *Contemporary Hypnosis, 26*(4), 216–224.

Hughes, J. D. (1987). The dreams of Xenophon the Athenian. *Journal of Psychohistory, 14*(3), 271–282.

Huizink, A. C., Robles de Medina, P. G., Mulder, E. J. H., Visser, G. H. A., & Buitelaar, J. K. (2003). Stress during pregnancy is associated with developmental outcomes in infancy. *Journal of Child Psychology and Psychiatry, 44*(6), 810–818.

Hume, L. (1999). On the unsafe side of the white divide: New perspectives on the dreaming of Australian Aborigines. *Anthropology of Consciousness 10*(1), 1–15.

Ibn Khaldun (1967:81). *The Muqaddimah: An introduction to history.* Princeton, NJ: Princeton University press.

Irwin, L. (1994). *The dream seekers: Native American visionary traditions of the great plains.* Norman, OK: University of Oklahoma Press.

Johnson, C. R. (2016). *Surfing the rainbow: Fearlessness and creativity in the out of body experience.* In A. de Foe (Ed.), Consciousness beyond the body: Evidence and reflections (pp. 130–142). Melbourne, Australia: Melbourne Centre for Exceptional Human Potential.

Jones, S. M. S., & Krippner, S. (2012). *The voice of Rolling Thunder: A medicine man's wisdom for walking the red road.* Rochester, VT: Bear & Company.

Jordan, B. (1993). *Birth in four cultures: A crosscultural investigation of childbirth in Yucatan, Holland, Sweden, and the United States.* (4th ed.). Prospect Heights, IL: Waveland Press.

Jung, C. G. (1943/1966). The relations between the ego and the unconscious. In G. Adler & R.F.C. Hull, Trans.), *Two essays on analytical psychology (Collected Works of C.G. Jung Vol. 7).* Princeton, NJ: Princeton University Press.

Jung, C. G. (1948/1969). One the nature of dreams. In G. Adler & R.F.C. Hull, Trans.), *The structure and dynamics of the Psyche (Collected Works of C.G. Jung Vol. 8).* Princeton, NJ: Princeton University Press.

Jung, C. G. (1964). *Man and his symbols.* New York, NY: Laurel.

Jung, C. G. (1965). *Memories, dreams, reflections.* New York, NY: Vintage Books.

Jung, C. G. (1974). *Dreams.* Princeton: Princeton University Press.

Kakar, S. (1982). *Shamans, mystics and doctors: A psychological inquiry into India and it's healing traditions.* New York, NY: Alfred A. Knopf.

Kane, C. M. (1994). Differences in the manifest dream content of Anglo-American, Mexican-American, and African-American college women. *Journal of Multicultural Counseling and Development, 22*(4), 203–209.

Kang, M. (2013, June 24). Dreams can have many meanings. *Korea Joongang Daily.* Retrieved from www.koreajoongangdaily.joins.com/

Bibliography

Katz, J. G. (1997). An Egyptian Sufi interprets his dreams: 'Abd al-Wahhâb al-Sha'rânî 1493–1565. *Religion, 27*, 7–24.

King, D. B., & DeCicco, T. L. (2007). The relationships between dream content and physical health, mood, and self-construal. *Dreaming, 17*(3), 127–139. doi:10.1037/1053-0797.17.3.127

Kitzinger, S. (1978). *Women as mothers.* New York, NY: Random House.

Knaan-Kostman, I. (2006). *Maturation, referential activity, and aggression during first pregnancy: An empirical study of pregnant women's dreams and reveries* (Doctoral dissertation). Retrieved from ProQuest Dissertations and Theses Database. (AAT 3200293).

Knudson, R. M. (2001). Significant dreams: Bizarre or beautiful? *Dreaming, 11*(4), 167–177.

Knudson, R. M. (2003). The significant dream as emblem of uniqueness: The fertilizer does not explain the flower. *Dreaming, 13*(3), 121–134.

Knudson, R. M., Adame, A. L., & Finocan, G. M. (2006). Significant dreams: Repositioning the self narrative. *Dreaming, 16*(3), 215–222.

Knudson, R. M., & Minier, S. (1999). The ongoing significance of significant dreams: The case of the bodiless head. *Dreaming, 9*(4), 235–245.

Koet, B. J. (2012). *Dreams as divine communication in Christianity: From Hermas to Aquinas.* Leuven, Belgium: Peeters.

Koukis, M. (2007). *Pregnancy dreams: Gender differences in dream content during pregnancy.* (Doctoral dissertation). Retrieved from ProQuest Dissertations and Theses Database. (AAT 3274815).

Koukis, M. (2009). Pregnancy dreams. In S. Krippner, & D. J. Ellis (Eds.), *Perchance to dream: The frontiers of dream psychology* (pp. 167–180). New York, NY: Nova Science Publishers.

Kremer, J. W. (2006). Dreams and visitations in initiations and healing. *ReVision, 29* (1), 34–45.

Kreinath, J. (2014). Virtual encounters with Hizir and other Muslim saints: Dreaming and healing at local pilgrimage sites in Hatay, Turkey. *Anthropology of the Contemporary Middle East and Central Eurasia, 2*(1), 25–66.

Krippner, S. C. (2002). Conflicting perspectives on shamans and shamanism: Points and counterpoints. *American Psychologist, 57*(11), 962–978.

Krippner, S., & Faith, L. (2001). Exotic dreams: A cross-cultural survey. *Dreaming, 11*, 73–82.

Krippner, S., Posner, N., Pomerance, W., & Fischer, S. (1974). An investigation of dream content during pregnancy. *Journal of the American Society for Psychosomatic Dentistry and Medicine, 21*, 111–123.

Krippner, S., Bogzaran, F., & de Carvalho, A. P. (2002). *Extraordinary dreams and how to work with them.* Albany, NY: State University of New York Press.

Kron, T., & Brosh, A. (2003). Can dreams during pregnancy predict postpartum depression? *Dreaming, 13*(2), 67–81. doi: 1053-0797/03/0600-0067/1

Kuiken, D., & Sikora, S. (1993). The impact of dreams on waking thoughts and feelings. In A. Moffitt, M. Kramer, & R. Hoffmann (Eds.), *The functions of dreaming* (pp. 419–476). Albany, NY: State University of New York Press.

Kuiken, D., Lee, M., Eng, T., & Singh, T. (2006). The influence of impactful dreams on self-perceptual depth and spiritual transformation. *Dreaming, 16*(4), 258–279.

Kuper, S. (2002, May 24). The world's game is not just a game. The New York Times.

LaBerge, S. (2009). *Lucid dreaming: A concise guide to awakening in your dreams and in your life.* Boulder, CO: Sounds True.

LaBerge, S., & Gackenbach, J. (2000). Lucid dreaming. In E. Cardeña, S. J. Lynn, & S. Krippner (Eds.), *Varieties of anomalous experience: Examining the scientific evidence* (pp. 151–182). Washington, D.C.: American Psychological Association.

LaBerge, S., & Levitan, L. (1995). Validity established of DreamLight cues for eliciting lucid dreaming. *Dreaming, 5*(3), p. 159–168.

LaBerge, S. (1990). Lucid Dreaming: Psychophysiological Studies of Consciousness during REM Sleep. In R. R. Bootzen, J. F. Kihlstrom, & D. L. Schacter (Eds.), *Sleep and Cognition* (pp. 109–126). Washington, D.C.: American Psychological Association.

LaBerge, S., & Rheingold, H. (1990). *Exploring the world of lucid dreaming.* New York, NY: Ballantine Books.

Lackman, F. M., Lapkin, B., & Handelman, N. S. (1962). The recall of dreams: Its relation to repression and cognitive control. *Journal of Abnormal and Social Psychology, 64*(2), 160–162.

Laughlin, C. D., & Rock, A. J. (2014). What we can learn from Shamans' dreaming? A cross-cultural exploration. *Dreaming, 24*(4), 233–252.

Leadbetter, R. (1997). Asclepius. *Encyclopedia Mythica.* Retrieved from http://www.pantheon.org/articles/a/asclepius.html

Lee, J. H. (2007). What is it like to be a butterfly? A philosophical interpretation of Zhuangzi's butterfly dream. *Asian Philosophy, 17*(2), 185–202. doi: 10.1080/095523607 01445141

Leifer, M. (1980). Pregnancy. In C. R. Stimpson & E.S. Person (Eds.), *Women: Sex and sexuality* (pp. 212–223). Chicago, IL: University of Chicago Press.

Lesage, J., Del-Favero, F., Leonhardt, M., Louvart, H., Maccari, S., Vieau, D., & Darnaudery, M. (2004). Prenatal stress induces intrauterine growth restriction and programmes glucose intolerance and feeding behaviour disturbances in the aged rat. *Journal of Endocrinology, 181,* 291–296.

Leva-Giroux, R. A. (2002). *Prenatal maternal attachment: The lived experience* (Doctoral Dissertation). Retrieved from ProQuest Dissertations and Theses Database. (AAT 3062593).

Levine, J. B. (1991). The role of culture in the representation of conflict in dreams: A comparison of Bedouin, Irish, and Israeli children. *Journal of Cross-Cultural Psychology, 22*(4), 472–490. doi: 10.1177/002202219 1224003

Li, Q., Yin, F., & Shen, H. (2015). Death dreams from a manifest perspective: A cross-cultural comparison between Tibetan and Han Chinese dreamers. *Dreaming, 25*(1), 32–43.

Lipkin, M., & Lamb, G. (1982). The Couvade syndrome: An epidemiologic study. *Annals of Internal Medicine, 96*(4), 509–511.

Lipton, B. H. (2005). *The biology of belief: Unleashing the power of consciousness, matter and miracles.* Santa Rosa, CA: Mountain of Love/Elite Books.

Llewellyn, S. (2013). Such stuff as dreams are made on? Elaborative encoding, the ancient art of memory, and the hippocampus. *Behavioral and Brain Sciences, 36,* 589–659. doi: 10.1017/S0140525X12003135

Lohmann, R. I. (2000). The role of dreams in religious enculturation among the Asabano of Papua New Guinea. *Ethos, 28*(1), 75–102.

Lohmann, R. I. (2003). *Dream travelers: Sleep experiences and culture in the West Pacific.* New York, NY: Palgrave Macmillan.

Lommel, A., & Mowaljarlai, D. (1994). Shamanism in Northwest Australia. *Oceana, 64*(4), 277–287.

Luke, D., Zychowicz, K., Richterova, O., Tjurina, I., & Polonnikova, J. (2012). A sideways look at the neurobiology of psi: Precognition and circadian rhythms. *NeuroQuantology, 10*(3), 580–590.

Margherita, G., Gargiulo, A., & Martino, M. L. (2015). Dream narration in healthy and at-risk pregnancy. Dreaming, 25(2), 88–102.

Matsumoto, D., & Juang, L. (2008). *Culture and psychology* (4th ed.). Belmont, CA: Wadsworth.

Maybruck, P. (1986). *An exploratory study of the dreams of pregnant women* (Doctoral Dissertation). Retrieved from ProQuest Dissertations and Theses Database. (AAT 8605318).

Maybruck, P. (1989). *Pregnancy and dreams: How to have a peaceful pregnancy by understanding your dreams, fantasies, daydreams and nightmares.* Los Angeles, CA: Jeremy P. Tarcher.

McClenon, J., & Nooney, J. (2002). Anomalous experiences reported by field anthropologists: Evaluating theories regarding religion. *Anthropology of Consciousness, 13*(2), 46–60.

McGee, A. M. (2012). Dreaming in Haitian Voudou: Vouchsafe, guide, and source of liturgical novelty. *Dreaming, 22*(2), 83–100.

McNamara, P., Johnson, P., McLaren, D., Harris, E., Beauharnais, C., & Auerbach, S. (2010). REM and NREM sleep mentation. *International Review of Neurobiology, 92,* 69–86. doi: 10.1016/S0074-7742(10)92004-7

McNamara, P., Pace-Schott, E. F., Johnson, P., Harris, E., & Auerbach, S. (2011). Sleep architecture and sleep-related mentation in securely and insecurely attached people. *Attachment and Human Development, 13*(2), 141–154.

Merlan, F. (1986). Australian Aboriginal conception beliefs revisited. *Man, 21*(3), 474–493.

Meier, C. A. (1967). *Ancient incubation and modern psychotherapy.* (M. Curtis, Trans.) Evanston, IL: Northwestern University Press. (Original work published 1949)

Mischel, W., & Mischel, F. (1958). Psychological aspects of spirit possession. *American Anthropologist, 60*(2), 249–260.

Moreira, I. (2003). Dreams and divination in early medieval canonical and narrative sources: The question of clerical control.

The Catholic Historic Review, 89(4), 621–642.

Morewedge, C. K., & Norton, M. I. (2009). When dreaming is believing: The (motivated) interpretation of dreams. *Journal of Personality and Social Psychology, 96*(2), 249–264. doi: 10.1037/a0013264

Neider, M., Pace-Schott, E. F., Forselius, E., Pittman, B., & Morgan, P. T. (2011). Lucid dreaming and ventromedial versus dorsolateral prefrontal task performance. *Consciousness and Cognition, 20*(2), 234–244.

O'Nell, C. W., & O'Nell, N. D. (1977). A cross-cultural comparison of aggression in dreams: Zapotecs and Americans. *International Journal of Social Psychiatry, 23*, 35–41.

Owczarski, W. (2014). Therapeutic effects of the dreams of bursing home residents in Poland. *Dreaming, 24*(4), 270–278.

Pansters, K. (2009). Dreams in medieval saint's lives: Saint Francis of Assisi. *Dreaming, 19*(1), 55–63.

Patterson, C. (1998). Seeking power at Willow Creek cave, Northern California. *Anthropology of Consciousness, 9*(1), 38–49.

Perry, D., DiPietro, J., and Costigan, K. (1999). Are women carrying "basketballs" really carrying boys? Testing pregnancy folklore. *Birth, 26*(3), 172–177.

Petchkovsky, L., & Cawte, J. (1986). The dreams of the Yolngu Aborigines of Australia. *Journal of Analytic Psychology, 31*(4), 357–375.

Pettis, J. B. (2006). Earth, dream, and healing: The integration of material and psyche in the ancient world. *Journal of Religion and Health, 45*(1), 113–129. doi: 10.1007/s10943-005-9010-9

Pritchard, M. H. (2004). *A course in astral travel and dreams: By Belzebuub.* Emeryville, CA: Absolute Publishing Group.

Pritham, U. A., & Sammons, L. N. (1993). Korean women's attitudes toward pregnancy and prenatal care. *Health Care for Women International, 14*(2), 145–153.

Punamäki, R. L., & Joustie, M. (1998). The role of culture, violence, and personal factors affecting dream content. *Journal of Cross-Cultural Psychology, 29*(2), 320–342. doi: 10.1177/0022022198292004

Qureshi, K. (2010). Sickness, dreams, and moral selfhood among Pakistani Muslims. *Anthropology and Medicine, 17*(3), 277–288.

Radin, D (1997). *The conscious universe: The scientific truth of psychic phenomena.* San Francisco, CA: Harper.

Rafael-Leff, J. (1990). Psychotherapy and pregnancy. *Journal of Reproductive and Infant Psychology, 8*, 119–135.

Rathus, S. A. (2009). *Psych.* Belmont, CA: Wadsworth Cengage Learning.

Rossi, E. L. (2002). *The psychobiology of gene expression: Neuroscience and neurogenesis in hypnosis and the healing arts.* New York, NY: Norton.

Rozehnal, R. (2014). Flashes of ultimate reality: Dreams of saints and shrines in a contemporary Pakistani Sufi community. *Anthropology of the Contemporary Middle East and Central Eurasia, 2*(1), 67–80.

Rubinstein, K., & Krippner, S. (1991). Gender differences and geographical differences in content of dreams elicited by a television announcement. *International Journal of Psychosomatics, 38*(1–4), 40–44.

Sabini, M. (2010). The mystery of death: Noble and knowable. *ReVision, 31*(1), 56–62.

Sandman, C. A., Wadhwa, P. D., Dunkel-Schetter, C., Chicz-Demet, A., Belman, J., Porto, M., Murata, Y., Garite, T. J., & Crinella, F. M. (1994). Psychobiological influences of stress and HPA regulation on the human fetus and infant birth outcomes. *Annals of the New York Academy of Sciences, 739*, 198–210.

Schlotz, W., & Phillips, D. I. W. (2009). Fetal origins of mental health: Evidence and mechanisms. *Brain, Behavior, and Immunity, 23*, 905–916.

Schmidt, S. C. E., Stumbrys, T., & Erlacher, D. (2014). Dream characters and the dream ego: An exploratory online study in lucid dreams. *Dreaming, 24*(2), 138–151.

Schönhammer, R. (2005). Typical dreams: Reflections of arousal. *Journal of Consciousness Studies, 12*(4–5), 18–37.

Schwiger, M. S. (1972). Sleep disturbance in pregnancy: A subjective survey. *American Journal of Obstetrics and Gynecology, 114*, 879–882.

Seligson, F. J. (1989). *Oriental birth dreams.* Elizabeth, NJ: Hollym.

Sered, S., & Abramovitch, H. (1992). Pregnant dreaming: Search for a typology of a proposed dream genre. *Social Science and Medicine, 34*(12), 1405–1411.

Sherwen, L. N. (1991). Fantasy state during pregnancy. *Journal of Prenatal and Perinatal Psychology and Health, 6*(1), 55–71.

Sidky, H. (2011). The state oracle of Tibet, spirit possession, and shamanism. *Numen, 58*, 71–99. doi: 10.1163/156852711X540096

Siegel, A. B. (2002). *Dream wisdom: Uncovering life's answers in your dreams*. Berkeley, CA: Celestial Arts.

Smith, S. M., & Vale, W. W. (2006). The role of the hypothalamic-pituitary-adrenal axis in neuroendocrine responses to stress. *Dialogues in Clinical Neuroscience, 8*(4), 383–395.

Smith-Cerra, K. E. (2007). *The dreams of primagravidae women: Preparation for motherhood* (Doctoral dissertation). Retrieved from ProQuest Dissertations and Theses Database. (AAT 3306494).

Solomonova, E., Stenstrom, P., Paquette, T., & Nielsen, T. (2015). Different temporal patterns of memory incorporations into dreams for laboratory and virtual reality experiences: Relation to dreamed locus of control. *International Journal of Dream Research, 8*(1), 10–26.

Stafa, Michael. (2010, December). Everything is all right. *Lucid Dream Experience, 57*, 18.

Stevenson, I. (2001). *Children who remember previous lives: A question of reincarnation.* Jefferson, NC: McFarland.

Struve, L. A. (2007). Dreaming and self-search during the Ming collapse: The Xue Xiemeng Biji, 1642–1646. *T'oung Pao, 93*, 159–192. doi: 10.1163/008254307X211124

Stumbrys, T., & Erlacher, D. (2016). Applications of lucid dreams and their effects on mood upon awakening. *International Journal of Dream Research, 9*(2), 142–145.

Taggart, J. M. (2012). Interpreting the Nahuat dialogue on the envious dead with Jerome Bruner's theory of narrative. *Ethos, 40*(4), 411–430. doi: 10.1111/j.1548-1352.2012.01268.x

Tedlock, B. (2005). *The woman in the shaman's body: Reclaiming the feminine in religion and medicine*. New York, NY: Bantam Dell.

Tucker, J. (2005). *Life before life: A scientific investigation of children's memories of previous lives*. New York, NY: St. Martin's Press.

Ullman, M., Krippner, S., & Vaughan, A. (2002). *Dream telepathy: Experiments in nocturnal extrasensory perception*. Charlottesville, VA: Hampton Roads.

Van Bronkhorst, J. (2013). *Premonitions in daily life: Working with spontaneous information when rational understanding fails you*. Woodbury, MN: Llewellyn.

Van Bronkhorst, J. (2015). *Dreams at the threshold: Guidance, comfort, and healing at the end of life*. Woodbury, MN: Llewellyn.

Van de Castle, R. (1975). The Cuna Indians of Panama. *Journal of Communication, 25*(1), 183–190.

van Eeden, W. F. (1913). A study of dreams. *Proceedings of the Society for Psychical Research, 26*, 431–461.

Verny, T. R. (2002). *Tomorrow's baby: The art and science of parenting from conception through infancy*. New York, NY: Simon & Schuster.

Waggoner, R., & McCready, C. (2015). *Lucid dreaming: Plain and simple*. San Francisco, CA: Conari Press.

Wayman, A. (1967). Significance of dreams in India and Tibet. *History of Religions, 7*(1), 1–12.

Weinstock, M. (2007). Gender differences in the effects of prenatal stress on brain development and behavior. *Neurochemical Research, 32*, 1730–1740.

Weiss, J. (1993). *How psychotherapy works: Process and technique*. New York, NY: The Guilford Press.

White, G. L., & Taytroe, L. (2003). Personal problem-solving using dream incubation: Dreaming, relaxation, or waking cognition? *Dreaming, 13*(4), 193–209.

Winget, C., & Kapp, F. T. (1972). The relationship of the manifest content of dreams to duration of childbirth in primiparae. *Psychosomatic Medicine, 34*(4), 313–320.

Yin, F., Li, Q., & Shen, H. (2015). Death dreams from an implicit perspective: A cross-cultural comparison between Tibetan and Han Chinese dreamers. *Dreaming, 25*(2), 103–117.

Yu, C. K-C. (2012). The effect of sleep position on dream experiences. *Dreaming, 22*(3), 212–221.

Zayas, L. H. (1988). Thematic features in the manifest dreams of expectant fathers. *Clinical Social Work Journal, 16*(3), 282–296.

Index